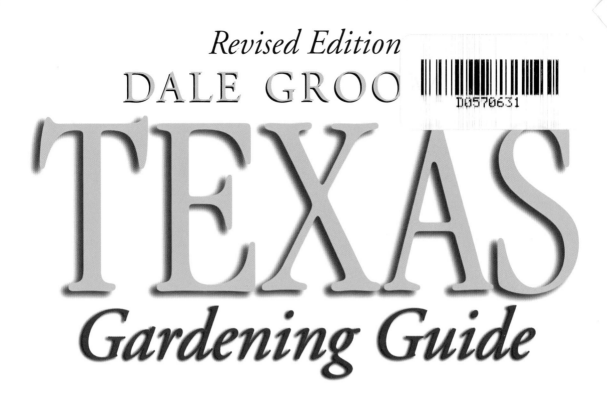

Revised Edition

DALE GROO

TEXAS
Gardening Guide

Revised Edition

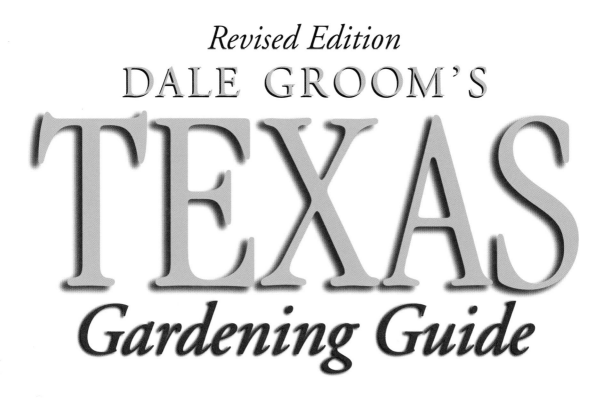

DALE GROOM'S

TEXAS
Gardening Guide

COOL
SPRINGS
PRESS

Franklin, Tennessee
www.coolspringspress.net

Published by Cool Springs Press,
101 Forrest Crossing Boulevard, Suite 100, Franklin, Tennessee, 37064.

Groom, Dale.
    Dale Groom's Texas gardening guide / Dale Groom.--Rev. ed.
        p. cm.
    Includes bibliographical references and index.
    ISBN 1-930604-39-4 (pbk. : alk. paper)
    1. Landscape plants--Texas. 2. Landscape gardening--Texas.
    3. Gardening--Texas. I. Title.
SB407.G7498 2003
635.9'09764--dc21

                    200215210

First printing 2002
Printed in the United States of America
10 9 8 7

Horticulture Editor: Dwight Hall
Copyeditor: Kathleen A. Ervin
Editorial Assistance: Mary Morgan
Designer: Sheri Ferguson Kimbrough
Production Artist: S.E. Anderson

On the cover: Black-Eyed Susan (*Rudbeckia hirta*), photographed by Mark Turner

Visit the Cool Springs Press website at **www.coolspringspress.net**

Foreword

For years, Dale Groom, known as The Plant Groom™, has shared his special knowledge and expertise of Texas landscapes and gardens with college students and gardeners alike. The author uses a multimedia approach including television, radio, and newspapers—along with public demonstrations to reach Texans in every area of the state. Through many years of study, research, and practical application, Dale has compiled an impressive amount of knowledge on gardening in the diverse and challenging regions of Texas.

This valuable material has been gathered and compiled into one complete source of information— the book you now hold in your hands. *Dale Groom's Texas Gardening Guide* is for everyone, regardless of experience level—no matter if you garden as a hobby or design landscapes as a professional.

Space does not permit me to magnify each aspect of the *Texas Gardening Guide*. I can, however, assure you that every type of plant material suitable for Texas gardening is carefully discussed—from native plants to roses, annuals to perennials, bulbs to grasses, as well as the best shrubs and trees that are in concert with Texas conditions. This book outlines in great detail the best plants to select, how to plant them and how to maintain them to ensure that your piece of Texas is as magnificent as Texas itself.

It has been a privilege to have a special friendship with Dale for twenty years—he's like a little brother to me. I am certain that the love he has for Texas gardening, for Texas and for Texans will shine through and make this a treasured volume in good gardeners' libraries all across the state.

Enjoy the wonderful world of gardening. Bon appétit.

—David Wade, The Gourmet™

Dedication

This book is lovingly dedicated to Judy Claire Lewis Groom, my wife of more than thirty-three years and my partner in life. She has made my walk wonderful and is a true blessing. How fortunate I am to have her, a dedicated wife to me and mother to our three children—Aaron, Angela, and Ashley. Judy is truly the best person I've ever known. I hope you get to meet her someday.

Acknowledgements

I've often said that no one individual knows all there is to know about gardening or horticulture. I'd like to gratefully acknowledge the following friends and associates in "the wonderful world of green" we have in Texas. I appreciate these knowledgeable and experienced individuals who reviewed my manuscript and offered their suggestions. My associates greatly helped me in my attempt to bring you usable and reliable information about landscape gardening in Texas. Thank you all, very much.

—Dale Groom, The Plant Groom™

My bill of friends and associates:

Dale Andrew Bunting, Scott Arboretum, Swarthmore College, Swarthmore, Pennsylvania

David Creech, Director, SFA Mast Arboretum, SFA State University, Nacogdoches, Texas

Calvin Finch, San Antonio Water System Horticulturist, San Antonio, Texas

Greg Grant, Mercer Arboretum and Botanical Garden Horticulturist, Humble, Texas

Dwight Hall, Horticulturist, Whitehouse, Texas

Starley Hand, President, Hand Rose Farm, Tyler, Texas

Keith Hanson, Smith County Horticulturist, Tyler, Texas

Keith Mills, Caldwell Zoo Horticulturist, Tyler, Texas

Debbie Rothermel, Landscape Designer, Carrollton, Texas

Doug Welsh, Horticulturist, Texas A & M University, College Station, Texas

Doug Williams, Humble, Texas

Grasshopper resistant plant information was compiled with the help of John Cooéper, Stan Lovelace, and Barbara Diltz.

A super thank you to Roger Waynick, Publisher, Cool Springs Press, for initially coming to Texas to meet and recruit me for this project, for "making things happen," and for being a friend.

A special thanks to Hank McBride of Cool Springs Press for contacting me about this revision, and to Ramona Wilkes for being my editor.

The Foreword in this edition was provided by my good friend and "big brother" of many years, David Wade, who passed away last year. He will be missed.

Table of Contents

Featured Plants *for Texas*

Welcome to Gardening

in Texas

We Texans have excellent opportunities for establishing all kinds of gardens in our great state. Soils and climatic zones are quite diverse, and there are wonderful plants available to all of us. This book will provide an introduction to the many plants you can select for enjoyment in your Texas home landscape. Most of the plants are readily available. Some will be a bit difficult to locate, but all are worth seeking out. Remember that the hunt for those interesting and hard-to-find plants is part of the fun too! Follow the suggestions in this book for assistance in enjoying your Texas gardening experience.

Our Diverse State

Texas has four different hardiness zones, as shown on the United States Department of Agriculture (USDA) Cold Hardiness Zone map (page 27). The state reaches from Zone 6 in the Panhandle, where minus 10 degrees Fahrenheit is common, all the way down to Zone 9 in the valley, where freezes are the exception. Few states in the country have this diversity.

The colder zones are in the northwest areas of Texas, including Wheeler, Randall, and Bailey counties in the Panhandle. The warmer zones are in the south and include Cameron, Hidalgo, and Starr counties of our Rio Grande Valley. Keep in mind that the USDA Cold Hardiness Zone map doesn't tell the whole story of temperatures in our state. Temperatures in urban areas may be 10 degrees warmer than those in rural areas due to asphalt, concrete, masonry, and a denser population—all of which create what are called microclimates.

Microclimates can also be created in our own home landscapes by fencing, shrubbery, and by our homes and structures. You may discover that your yard has a location where particular plants will survive due to a microclimate that has been created, while your neighbor may not be able to grow the same plants.

Temperature range and rate of change greatly affect gardening in Texas. If, for example, one area were to drop to a sub-freezing temperature for a short period of time and climb right back up, plants in that area would most likely receive little harm. But if the temperature dropped suddenly and remained there for several days, great damage could occur. When an unusual freezing spell struck North Texas, some of its live oak trees, which would normally be considered quite hardy in that area, were severely damaged.

Field of Bluebonnets

The USDA Cold Hardiness Zone map provides general temperature guidelines for the state and each of its zones. Plant hardiness refers to each plant's ability to withstand the freezing temperatures that historically occur in the various zones. A plant that is barely able to withstand the temperatures in Zone 8 should not be planted in the colder Zone 7. Plants that will grow in Zone 6 will often grow in Zone 9. As you can see, Texas is a climatically diverse state, and it is important to pay attention to zone hardiness.

In Texas, one problem gardeners encounter is the challenge of raising plants that have been grown and acclimated in other parts of the country. While some plants will withstand all of our freezing temperatures, they may not be able to handle the blast furnace heat that we have. So, if you are ordering plants or buying them from another part of the country, make sure they will be able to handle Texas summertime heat. For best growing results, plants need to be placed where they will receive the proper amount of light. This book contains light requirements for the plants I have featured. This information can also be found at your local gardening retailer. Even the temperatures in our shade can be too hot for some northern plants, and they may not receive the sunlight needed to grow properly. Texas sun in July and August, for example, will fry some plants that can be grown in full sun in other parts of the country. I noticed an example of this when I was in Winnipeg, Canada, taping a television show in July, and I saw impatiens being grown in full sun. Impatiens grown in the full Texas sun of July would be cooked very quickly. When you read that particular plants can be grown in full sun, make sure the writer is referring to full sun locations in Texas and not New England, the Pacific Northwest, or other relatively cool locations.

Facing the Wind

There is nothing like a Texas wind to affect your gardening activities. Make sure the plants that you select at your local garden center will be able to withstand the wind that is common in your area. Many Texans experience prevailing southwestern breezes, and in some locations they can be quite strong. I have seen significant landscape plants growing at an almost 45-degree angle due to these prevailing breezes. Make sure that trees or other tall shrubs are staked properly until they are large enough to withstand the strong breezes and begin growing in a vertical position. Trees that are properly selected and placed can serve beautifully as breaks to block out strong winds.

The Importance of Mulching

Mulching can be a confusing topic for Texas gardeners. Whether it is compost, ground-bark mulch, or another type of material, mulch simply means a blanket of these materials on top of your soil. Whether we are planting vegetables, perennials, trees, or any other plant, mulch is a blanket we put on top of the ground that aids in moisture retention, weed control, and soil improvement.

The amount of mulch that you use is determined by the type. When using high-density mulch, three to four inches is quite sufficient. Lightweight materials such as pine needles or clean hay require a bit more coverage, but six inches placed between plants is usually adequate. In fact, all the roses in the City of Tyler Rose Garden are mulched with pine needles.

Perhaps the most important benefit of mulching for Texas gardeners is conserving water. Plants that are properly mulched require less frequent watering, maintain even soil moisture content, and respond with better overall growth. If you take a walk through the woods, you will notice that our native vegetation is mulched by woodland floor debris or natural mulch. Mulching your finished plantings helps to approximate that natural environment.

Mulching is something that I encourage every gardener to do yearly, and I prefer the organic varieties. There are plenty of mulching materials from which to choose—pine, hardwood, peanut, cocoa, pecan hulls, or shredded sugar cane. Select the one that works best for you and your plants.

Garden Nutrition

Simply put, fertilization supplies nutrients to the soil for the plant to pick up. This process is sometimes misunderstood. While many gardeners think they are feeding the plant, they are actually adding nutrients to the soil for the plant to absorb. If the soil lacks sufficient amounts of naturally occurring plant nutrients, then your plants will not thrive.

Plants can be fertilized with various products including water-soluble, liquid, encapsulated, and premium-quality, slow-release fertilizers. Many

Wildflowers with Coreopsis

different forms and types are available. Make sure that you read and understand the directions before you apply any type of fertilizer. When a container of fertilizer specifies an amount, we Texas gardeners may say, "Well, if that works well, then doubling that amount ought to be really great!" It doesn't work that way with fertilizers. Make sure you apply only the amount specified on the label.

White Oak

My Granny Miller said that Granddad was known to burn up crops in the vegetable garden by putting on too much cottonseed meal. Cottonseed meal is a 100 percent natural organic fertilizer, but just because something is all organic does not mean that you can't have problems by using too much. Soil nutrients are sometimes categorized as major or minor. Plants need more of the major nutrients than they do of the minor. Nitrogen (N), phosphorus (P), and potassium (K) are considered the three major nutrients. Some horticulturists classify sulfur and calcium as secondary nutrients. The remaining nutrients are called micronutrients because they are used by plants in extremely small amounts. This doesn't mean that major nutrients are more important, just that plants use more of them. Plants do not have the ability to determine where nutrients come from. As far as they are concerned, nutrients come from the soil reservoir. With the proper application of fertilizers, you can make sure that the soil has the nutrients necessary for good plant growth.

Nutrients occur naturally in our soil, originating from various materials including stone and organic matter in the soil itself. Perhaps you have heard someone say, "The soil is just worn out." Soil doesn't really wear out, but we can deplete it of nutrients and damage soil structure. By re-supplying nutrients to soil that has been depleted and keeping soil structure in good shape, we can continue to grow in the same soils for generation after generation. If soils are deficient in naturally occurring nutrients, then we can apply those nutrients in the form of fertilizers. I always recommend that you water thoroughly after applying any type of fertilizer.

When fertilizing your lawn, apply when the grass blades are dry. Follow label directions and then water thoroughly. You should be rewarded with a nice, thick vigorous lawn if you also mow properly and water as necessary. Don't forget that your lawn may also need to be aerated if your soils are compacted or are the heavy clay types. Aeration allows oxygen, water, and nutrients to penetrate the soil and reach the root zones. In heavy clay soils or high traffic areas, aeration every two years is usually sufficient.

When to Water

When droughts occur in Texas they remind us just how important water is to us. There are many demands on our water supply and water is not available in unlimited quantities. Described as "the essence of life," water is as necessary to plants as to humans in order to survive.

Water your plants deeply and thoroughly. Lawns, for example, need to be watered to a soil depth of six inches, and they prefer to be watered to eight inches. Don't set any of your plants, including your lawn, on a watering schedule. I have seen folks who want to turn on their lawn sprinklers, for example, every morning at 6:38 A.M. for ten minutes. That is not desirable for individual plants, grass, shrubbery, or any other plant.

After watering, don't go back and re-water until your plants tell you they need it. Grass will tell you when it needs to be watered by changing from a nice pleasant green color to a kind of bluish gray. Or perhaps its sides will roll up, or it will lie flat when you walk across it, not springing back. When you see these signs, water the lawn thoroughly. You can tell when shrubs need to be watered by simply sticking your finger in the soil. If the soil is dry, then irrigate or apply water thoroughly . . . did I mention to water thoroughly? Be sure that you soak the entire root zone of your plants when watering. If you water your plants frequently and very lightly, they will develop undesirable shallow root systems. When watering containers, water until there are no more air bubbles coming out of them. You will then know that all the pores have been saturated with moisture. The excess water will drain out. Be sure that all your containers drain properly.

Certain methods of irrigation can be good for water conservation; others can be quite wasteful. Sprinklers that throw a lot of water high in the air before the water strikes lawns or shrubs are not as efficient as other methods.

Austin Xeriscape

Drip irrigation is the most efficient method of delivering water to landscape plants, including trees, shrubs, vines, groundcovers, annuals, and perennials. Drip irrigation can conserve as much as 50 percent of overall water usage. This water conservation

translates into cost savings, plus it helps provide a beneficial environment for overall healthy plant growth. I have seen side-by-side comparisons of landscape beds that were planted and irrigated by drip irrigation and sprinkler irrigation. Drip irrigation is by far superior. Many hardware stores, sprinkler supermarkets, and nurseries carry drip irrigation systems, and they can help you select the best one for your home application.

Timing is as important to watering as length. If watered at midday—especially with sprinklers that disperse the water high into the air before it falls to the soil—lawns can lose a significant amount of moisture through evaporation. Early morning watering helps to prevent some of the evaporation.

The Scoop on Soil

Soil is the foundation for all of our successful gardening experiences. It is very important that we take care of our soil so it can perform at its best to meet your personal gardening goals. Some Texas gardeners dream of running barefoot through the most luxurious lawn possible in the months of July and August. Others want the most gorgeous rose garden, azaleas, or beds of irises. I understand these desires. Soil testing is the tool that will help us obtain our gardening dreams.

It is worth performing soil tests every two years. If you are sampling several areas, the samples will need to be segregated. Each soil test stands alone. For example, your lawn soil needs to be separated from

Red Maple

your landscape shrub bed, and from your perennial garden and annual plantings.

Make sure that the soil grade in the area you wish to landscape is correct. If grading is necessary on new landscapes, complete the activity before installing grass, landscape beds, or any other plants. Grading can be done with small tractors, hand tools, or other methods.

If you don't feel comfortable performing the grading, contact a landscape contractor. In most communities, there are one or more members of the Texas Association of Landscape Contractors (TALC). When a contractor supplies an estimate, be sure you understand exactly what work is to be done and that you have the estimate and work plan in writing.

Bearded Iris

Drainage is very important and is one of the reasons we do grading in our landscape. Drainage can be improved with the addition of raised beds, which may necessitate additional soil and lots of organic matter. Soils that drain poorly tend to be oxygen-starved. This particular soil will not allow plants to grow healthy roots, and plants in this type of soil will suffer. Certainly there are plants that grow in damp-to-wet soils—including bald cypress, water-loving plants, bog plants, and weeping willows—but these are the exceptions. The general rule is that the majority of our landscape plants (including trees) need a well-drained soil in order to stay healthy.

Soil Preparation

Before planting anything in your home landscape—annuals, shrubs, perennials, vines, or groundcovers— it is important to know exactly what kind of soil you have and the soil's pH. You may have your soil tested through our agricultural extension service. Most of us call the local representative of the Texas Agricultural Extension Service, "The County Agent." The number is found in the phone directory where all the county office numbers are listed. Instructions, information sheets, and soil sample bags can be mailed to you, or you can pick them up. Offices are usually located in the county courthouse or county annex. The county agents' offices in Texas are always worth visiting for the opportunity to meet some good people who can be very helpful to you and your gardening goals. The Stephen F. Austin State University Soil Testing Laboratory is also available to you for complete soil testing. Contact the lab

Live Oaks in Landscape

directly at (409) 468-4500. There are also some private soil-testing labs throughout Texas, but be prepared to pay higher fees. After determining the soil's pH, you will need to prepare your soil for planting.

Preparing the soil includes breaking it up in some way. If planting in a small area, a shovel or digging fork may be all you need. Those planting in larger areas traditionally use various types of tillers. The incorporation of organic matter into these areas will greatly improve the soil's drainage and moisture/nutrient holding capacity.

The positive benefits of organic matter cannot be overstated. Brown Canadian sphagnum peat moss, ground bark, compost that you have made or purchased, and other types of organic matter will greatly improve the soil. Annuals and perennials usually require more extensive preparation than do shrubs and trees. When preparing for bedding plants, I recommend three inches or more of quality organic matter be blended with native Texas soil.

Trees require a simple loosening of the soil. In most cases, it is impossible to amend the soil in an area wide enough or deep enough for a tree's root system. Still, it is helpful to loosen the soil thoroughly before planting your tree, and be sure that you have selected the right tree for your soil type. The oak family is the number one shade tree grown in Texas, but some oaks do well in all areas, while others are very selective. For example, a water oak will grow in all areas of East Texas, but if you put it in the highly alkaline soils of Central or North Texas, results will be less than desirable.

Pest Control

Pest control has several meanings. Weeds, insects, and diseases are all considered pests by most Texas gardeners. Weeds in our landscape beds can be controlled by the use of mulches. Mulching beds heavily with a three-to-four-inch layer makes it difficult for weed seeds to germinate and grow. In addition, there are also various weed prevention aids available for lawns as well as landscape beds.

Making sure our lawns are well-fertilized, mowed, and watered can also control weeds. A healthy, actively growing, thick lawn will normally have fewer weed problems. A well-selected and well-maintained landscape will have fewer insect and disease problems.

The crape myrtle is a good example of the benefits of carefully choosing your plant's environment. When properly selected and planted in an ideal landscape location, crape myrtle has few or no problems with powdery mildew. When placed in areas where there is poor air circulation and frequent watering, crape myrtle is in a better environment for growth of this fungus.

Before you buy plants at your local nursery, always ask about potential disease and insect problems. If it sounds as if a plant may be too high maintenance for your taste, make another selection. Remember, plants that tend to have problems in certain landscape locations may have fewer problems when placed in other locations within a different environment.

Proper Plant Selection

Proper plant selection is extremely important for long-term success in Texas gardening. Many plants in magazines, catalogs, and on television will excite the gardener in you. They may look wonderful, but before you spend any money, be sure that these plants will grow and thrive in your area.

Pond with Hostas

Annuals with Arbor

Through the years, I have found that the best place to shop for plant material is at local garden centers. These retailers tend to handle plants that do well in their particular area. For a list of trees, shrubs, vines, groundcovers, annuals, and perennials that are well adapted to your home area, visit your local county agent's office. Additional information on some of the newer varieties and those well-tested is also available.

For long-term success with minimal maintenance make sure that you select the proper plant. There are some wonderful selections of Texas-friendly plants from which to choose, but—if they are shade grown—how much sun they receive can determine whether they thrive or die. The aucuba shrub, for example, is wonderful in shaded areas in Texas but will not tolerate our sun. It will burn like my redheaded, fair-skinned wife, Judy.

Here are some questions to ask retailers before purchasing any type of plant:

- How tall and wide does this plant usually grow in my area?
- How much sun or shade is required?
- Does this plant have special soil requirements, and if so what are they?
- Does this plant require well-drained soils, or will it grow in poorly drained or damp soils?
- Does it bloom? If so, when, for how long, and in what color(s)? In spring, summer, fall, or winter? For two weeks, six months, or longer?
- Does it have fall color? If so, what are the colors?
- Is it resistant to insect and disease pests that usually occur in my area?
- What are the watering/soil moisture requirements? Moist at all times? Tolerant of relatively dry soils?
- How often should it be fertilized, with what, and when?
- Are there any special pruning requirements? (Roses and certain other landscape plants usually require special pruning and/or training to realize maximum benefits).
- Is it deer resistant (where applicable)?

Sizing Up Your Options

Most reputable garden centers will guarantee that the plants they sell will perform true to the variety, and that is important. Plants purchased from temporary retailers or other sources may not perform as promised. For the best overall value, buy plant material from the retailer in your area.

Buying from retailers who are members of the Texas Association of Nurserymen (TAN) will put you in touch with qualified help from Texas Certified Nursery Professionals (TCNP) and Texas Master Certified Nursery Professionals (TMCNP). These professionals are available to answer your questions and help you achieve your desired gardening goals.

Fall is for planting and is a wonderful time to landscape throughout our entire state. There is usually sufficient rain after the hot, dry Texas summer. The soil has adequate moisture, and the temperatures are cooler. Often you will find nurseries that put plant material on sale. The root systems of plants that are planted in the fall will continue to grow through the season, and you jumpstart their growth by almost a year.

With so many different sizes of landscape plants available, choices can sometimes get confusing. We use size measurements in the gardening industry that are relatively close to the actual gallon size. You will find plants in 2-, 3-, 5-, 7-, 10-, 15-, 20-gallon containers and larger. Certainly the sizes will be quite large for tree-type shrubs or trees. Sizes larger than 20 gallons are most likely trees.

Tall-growing shrubs such as crape myrtles and trees are sometimes sold according to height or caliper measurement (the diameter of the trunk). According to the American Association of Nurserymen (AAN), the caliper measurement of trees should be made approximately twelve inches above the soil line. This measurement provides the thickness, thus the diameter, of the trunk. If you see advertisements offering an oak tree of three inches, this is the thickness measurement of the trunk twelve inches above the soil line. You may also find plants sold in six to eight feet, eight to ten feet, and ten to twelve feet height ranges. Certainly the tall crape myrtles, tall hollies, and some of the smaller-growing trees are classified in these ways.

Pruning with Purpose

From time to time our landscape plantings may require some pruning. But we want to prune for a purpose; we don't want to prune haphazardly. There are quite a few reasons for pruning. You may be pruning to shape a plant. You may want more light coming down through trees. You may be pruning to do some specialized training. Perhaps you want to train a tree into an espalier or prune a rose for a particular type of growth to enhance selected blooms for shows. We often prune the tips out of garden mums to induce branching and therefore thicken the overall planting so we have loads of buds that bloom in the fall.

The timing of pruning can be important. If you have a spring-blooming plant such as azalea, you certainly don't want to do any pruning until after the blooming season is completed in the spring. If you happen to have a group of overgrown azaleas that you wish to rework, do it after the major spring bloom is complete, just as you see the flush of spring growth beginning.

When pruning shrubs, select buds that are pointed outward and upward and then remove the branch just above the buds. That will give direction to the plant's branches. You can do similar types of pruning fairly often with certain types of roses. Pruning can be kept to a minimum if plants are selected and placed properly in your home landscape. Shrubs usually look best when allowed to grow into their natural form.

Great Gardening

This book is an introduction to the plants that thrive in our great gardening state. We begin with a look at annuals—different varieties that offer fine possibilities. All can be tried in the home landscape, and don't forget to let little gardeners try their hand with annuals.

Carolina Jessamine

Texas gardeners grow a lot of bulbs. We need to be on the lookout for those lesser-used bulbs that have been around for generations and incorporate these varieties into our landscapes.

Nearly all Texas gardeners like to grow grasses in the home landscape. I've included grasses for every area of Texas. Try some of the ornamental grasses that are on the market, such as blue fescue or fountain grass.

Gardeners may not pay much attention to groundcovers, but if you need an alternative for lawn grass in a heavily shaded area, groundcovers are the answer. I've included some of the best available in Texas for your consideration.

Texans love to talk about our native plants. With a well-earned reputation for being the wildflower state, we also have shrubs, trees, and vines that are all native to Texas, and this book offers a good selection. I have separated the natives into two chapters for easy reference.

Perennials are the plants that re-grow each year and bloom for three years or more. Some

Autumn Fern

of them grow for generations in our home landscapes. Some plants, such as the achillea or yarrow, are very tough and durable and can stand up to our Texas environment.

We have the world's headquarters for roses in Tyler, Texas, but we can grow roses in all areas of Texas. The American Rose Society (ARS) lists over fifty different classifications. I have grouped them together into some of the most popular and fun groups.

There are many different types of shrubs available. I have listed several for your consideration, from abelia to winter jasmine.

Trees are near and dear to my heart. I like to climb trees, build tree houses for my children, and rest in their shade. You will find a good selection of trees in this book. These are generally what we call shade trees, including some that have been used in our landscapes for generations.

We will also take a look at vines and different ways to use them. If you enjoy flowering vines, you will find some interesting selections in these pages.

To contact me for information or with questions, see my contact information provided on page 252. *Dale Groom's Texas Gardening Guide* has something for everyone. Great gardening . . . to YOU!

—*Dale Groom*, The Plant Groom™

How to Use *Dale Groom's* Texas Gardening Guide

Each entry in this guide provides information about a plant's characteristics, habits and requirements for growth, as well as my personal experience and knowledge of the plant. Use this information to realize each plant's potential. You will find such pertinent information as mature height and spread, bloom period and seasonal colors, sun and soil preferences, water requirements, fertilizing needs, pruning and care tips, hardiness zone and pest information. Each section is clearly marked for easy reference.

Sun Preferences

Symbols represent the range of sunlight suitable for each plant. The symbol representing "Full Sun" means the plant needs 6 or more hours of full sun daily. A ranking of "Mostly Sun/ Part Shade" means the plant can thrive in 4 to 6 hours of sun a day. "Part Shade" designates plants for sites with fewer than 4 hours of sun a day, including dappled or high shade. "Full Shade" means the plant needs protection from direct sunlight. Some plants can be grown successfully in more than one exposure, so you will sometimes see more than one light symbol with an entry.

Full Sun   **Part Sun**   **Part Shade**   **Full Shade**

Additional Benefits

Many plants offer benefits that further enhance their appeal. These symbols indicate some of these benefits:

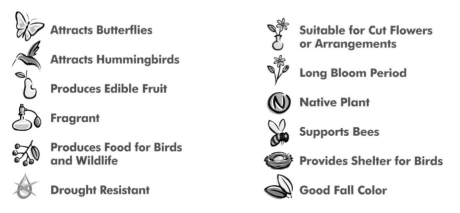

Attracts Butterflies

Attracts Hummingbirds

Produces Edible Fruit

Fragrant

Produces Food for Birds and Wildlife

Drought Resistant

Suitable for Cut Flowers or Arrangements

Long Bloom Period

Native Plant

Supports Bees

Provides Shelter for Birds

Good Fall Color

Companion Planting and Design

For most of the entries, I provide landscape design ideas as well as suggestions for companion plants to help you achieve striking and personal results from your garden.

I Suggest

This section includes my suggestions that may help you with gardening decisions and offer advice for getting the most enjoyment from your plant selections.

USDA Cold Hardiness Zone Map

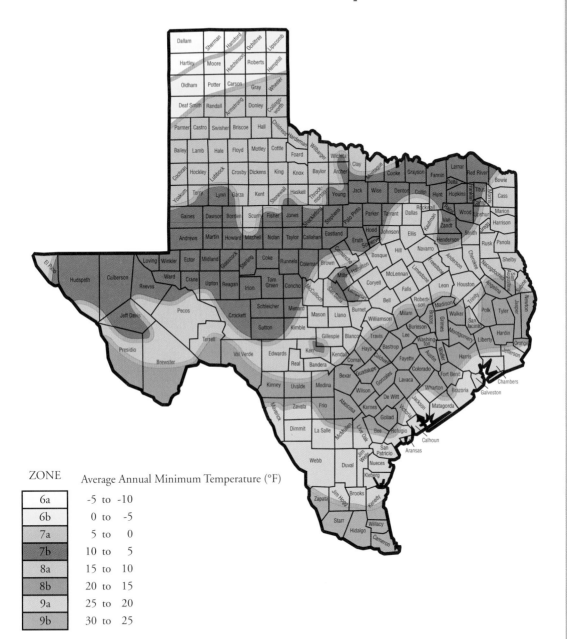

ZONE	Average Annual Minimum Temperature (°F)
6a	-5 to -10
6b	0 to -5
7a	5 to 0
7b	10 to 5
8a	15 to 10
8b	20 to 15
9a	25 to 20
9b	30 to 25

Hardiness Zones

Cold-hardiness zone designations were developed by the United States Department of Agriculture (USDA) to indicate the minimum average temperature for that region. A zone assigned to a plant indicates the lowest temperature at which the plant can normally be expected to survive. Texas has zones ranging from 6a (the coldest) to 9b. Though a plant may grow in zones outside its recommended zone range, the zone ratings are a good indication of which plants to consider for your landscape. Check the map to see which zone your Texas garden is in.

Annuals *for Texas*

To frame beds and accent key locations in the landscape, annuals provide the most spectacular color—and there is nothing that grabs our attention like color.

From seeds to cell packs, most annuals are planted in springtime, and we hope that they stay with us all summer long. Some will. Some will not. It all depends on selection and care. One of the better annuals to plant in springtime is gomphrena, or globe amaranth, *Gomphrena globosa*. It will remain through the entire spring and summer season up until the first fall frost. My Granny Miller used to call these plants bachelor buttons. For low-growing color, you can't beat periwinkle, *Catharanthus roseus*. Today there are several periwinkle colors on the market, from solid white and white with pink or red "eyes" (centers) to pinks and purples.

Annuals in Planter

Zinnia, *Zinnia elegans*, is the most popular flower to be grown from seed in the United States. As easy to grow today as it has been for generations, there are new varieties on the market, making the zinnia an even more versatile annual choice.

Sunflowers, *Helianthus annuus*, particularly the traffic-stopping, tall-growing varieties, have long been favored with gardeners. While these tall, yellow favorites are still available, there are many other different sizes and colors of sunflowers on the market today. It's even possible to create a complete outdoor room for your children by selecting and planting varieties of sunflowers. Work on this project together—it's a fun thing for kids to do!

Categories of Annuals

Annuals may be broken down into various categories—spring/summer, fall/winter or sun/shade. Spring and summer annuals are traditionally planted in the springtime after all danger of frost is past. Some varieties of annuals will cease to bloom when our July-August furnace heat blast arrives. Others will continue to bloom all season long.

There are also fall and winter annuals. The most prominent family is the pansy, *Viola × wittrockiana*, planted in Texas strictly for cool-season growth. Two members of the Brassica family—ornamental flowering kale and cabbage—thrive in the cool season as well as spring. Dianthus, *Dianthus barbatus*, with its intoxicating fragrance, is an absolutely beautiful specimen during the fall and early spring.

Annuals may also be grouped into sun or shade categories with some plants growing in both. Wax leaf begonias, *Begonia* × semperflorens-cultorum, particularly those with bronze leaves and red flowers, will grow in full sun and shade if they are set out early in the springtime. Some varieties of the colorful coleus, *Solenostemon scutellarioides*, will also grow in full sun. Traditionally, coleus is grown by Texas gardeners in shaded areas.

Soil preparation is important for successful, long-term growth of annuals. Be sure to prepare your beds properly before planting your first seed or transplant. Planting beds should be weed-free and well cultivated, with generous helpings of organic additives such as sphagnum peat moss and/or compost to ensure good drainage and aeration and to prevent soil compaction from routine seasonal watering and rain. When buying fresh seed, check the expiration date and variety and be sure to purchase those packaged for the current season. All of this information, as well as planting instructions, are found on the seed package itself. Be certain the seed you choose is adapted to Texas gardens and to the planting season. It is not uncommon to find pansies, poppies, larkspur and hollyhock, all planted in the fall, on the spring seed rack. It is equally important to choose only variety transplants well adapted to Texas. Annuals inappropriate for Texas summer heat are featured in some garden centers. For example, Chinese asters, pocketbook plant, canterbury bells, foxglove, fuchsia, and bells of Ireland, are seldom successful in the average Texas garden.

Real Winners

Not all annuals are grown for their flowers. There are some colorful foliage annuals, including flowering kale, flowering cabbage, the aforementioned coleus, and copper plant.

New annual varieties are introduced each year. "All-America" varieties are selected each year as the best out of hundreds. "All-America Selections" on the seed pack will ensure, quality, novelty, and hopefully success. The winning annuals are displayed in trail gardens across the nation. The "All-America Selections" winners are displayed in Texas each year at Texas A&M University in College Station, Texas, as well as other locations.

Because of space limitations, I have included only twenty annuals in this book, but you will find outstanding varieties and colors among those listed. Don't forget to visit your local garden centers to see the many other annuals that are available.

Coleus

Bachelor Buttons
Gomphrena globosa

The most important flower grown by my Granny Miller in her old-fashioned, non-irrigated garden at Indian Creek, Texas, was bachelor buttons. Granny Miller had one of those old-fashioned country gardens that many rural landscape gardeners had before the turn of the century and that are continually enjoyed by succeeding generations. If any of Granny's plants received water, it was hauled one bucket at a time. Needless to say, her plants had to be tough and quite drought tolerant to make it through our blazing summers. Gomphrena is one tough annual that all Texans should have in their gardens. It continues to bloom all summer until the first fall frost.

Other Common Name
Globe Amaranth

Bloom Period and Seasonal Color
Summer to fall in purple to magenta, red to reddish orange, pink, white, and yellow.

Mature Height × Spread
9 in. to 2 ft. × 6 to 8 in.

When, Where, and How to Plant
When planting from transplants, make sure all frost danger is past and wait until nighttime temperatures have been at, or above, 70 degrees Fahrenheit for two weeks. Plant seed indoors approximately six weeks before transplanting outside. I prefer to purchase fresh packs of bachelor buttons transplants at my local nursery. Place in well-drained locations taking care not to plant in shady or poorly drained spots. While bachelor buttons usually do well under adverse conditions, for best results, plant in improved soils. Add approximately 3 in. of high-quality organic matter and blend with the top 3 in. of soil. Install transplants no deeper than the top of the rootball, firm the soil, water thoroughly, and apply a root stimulator. Special formulated, slow-release bedding plant fertilizers may be applied at planting time. Mulch the planting area with 3 in. of a material such as pine bark mulch.

Growing Tips
To ensure good results, water enough to prevent soil dryness. Do not overwater. Maintaining a season-long, thick mulch layer will greatly aid in soil moisture conservation, prevent soils from becoming compacted from watering, and reduce weed populations.

Care
This plant has no serious pests. Deadhead if desired. Liquid, water-soluble, and specialty granular fertilizers may be applied as needed throughout the season.

Companion Planting and Design
Try these beauties for summer-long color in areas where you have tried annuals that can't tolerate the Texas heat. Use the shorter dwarf varieties such as the purple flowering 'Buddy' or the Gnome series in pink, white, and shades of purple, in border plantings. For background color, use taller, standard types such as *G. haageana* in pale red to orange, or 'Lavender Lady' in pale purple. Bachelor buttons also make wonderful pots of color. A dark-purple gomphrena in the center of a large terra-cotta container with a solid white periwinkle or annual vinca planted around the pot's edge is most pleasing.

I Suggest
This tough, pretty, annual is an easy plant for children to grow and enjoy.

Cockscomb
Celosia argentea var. *cristata*

When, Where, and How to Plant

Plant in early spring after all danger of frost is past from your particular zone. Celosia or cockscomb does best when planted in improved soil—do not plant in heavy clay soil or in areas of poor drainage unless improved with organic matter. Incorporate 3 in. of high-quality organic matter into the top 3 in. of your existing native soil. I prefer planting celosia from transplants. This gives me control over which varieties, colors, and sizes of containers I desire to select and plant. Install transplants in your improved planting bed no deeper than the plant's soilball top. Firm the soil, water thoroughly, and apply root stimulator. After the entire planting is complete, mulch the bed well with approximately 3 in. of bark mulch.

Growing Tips

Remember always to plant celosia in well-drained locations. Maintain a moist, not wet, soil throughout the entire growing season. Mulch will aid in soil moisture conservation. If a season-long, granulated, bedding-plant fertilizer is applied at planting time, no additional fertilization should be necessary.

Care

This low maintenance plant requires little but to be planted in well-drained soil and full sun. This plant usually has no serious pests, and very little pruning, if any, is required. Remove any damaged or spent blooms or leaves as needed.

Companion Planting and Design

Cockscomb works well when used in color gardens to outline other varieties and colors. I believe the most spectacular use of cockscomb is in large numbers of single colors. It also works very well as a container plant to provide color in outdoor areas such as porches, decks, gazebos, or swimming pools. For a spectacular look, plant an apricot-colored plume in the center of a large container, with solid white annual vinca or periwinkle drooping down the sides. Celosia, with its fiery colors, can be over-powering visually. Do not overplant. The colorful blooms make excellent dried flowers.

I Suggest

This is a popular plant with new gardeners and children because it is easy to grow. In fact, it's one of my daughter Ashley's favorite warm-season color plants.

There are basically two types of cockscomb or celosia. One is considered the plume type and includes 'plumosa', and 'Apricot Brandy'. They look much like feathery flowers. The older of the two is the cockscomb type, and includes 'Floradale', and 'Jewel Box'. These are crested with very tight flowers that resemble the comb of a rooster. They both work well in mass plantings or borders. The tall, three-foot standard types are stunning as background plants, while the very low-growing six- to twelve-inch dwarf types are wonderful by themselves. Some additional popular cultivars include 'Corona', Century Mixed, 'Apricot Brandy', 'Red Fox', 'Forest Fire', 'Flamingo Feather', 'Dwarf Fairy Fountain', 'Prestige Scarlet', and Kimono Mixed.

Other Common Names
Celosia , Amaranth

Bloom Period and Seasonal Color
Spring, summer, and fall blooms in vivid, fiery colors of wine, yellow, red, pink, and purple.

Mature Height × Spread
6 to 36 in. × 6 to 12 in.

Coleus
Solenostemon scutellarioides

In my hometown of Brownwood, Texas, our yard was blessed with many shade trees. When I was in the Navy, I mentioned to a sailor from New Jersey that my family had seventy-three oak trees in our yard. He thought this was a Texas tale, but it was absolutely true. Because of all this shade, Mom had to look for plants that would grow in shady conditions, and coleus was one of those. She once grew a particular variety of the old-fashioned coleus that was nearly six feet. high. Hybrids are not as tall, but we do enjoy a vast array of colors, textures, and forms because of hybridization. Some cutting-propagated varieties will also grow in full-sun locations.

Bloom Period and Seasonal Color
Foliage in many vivid colors of green, chartreuse, red, pink-white, maroon, bronze, and yellow.

Mature Height × Spread
6 to 36 in. × 12 to 48 in.

When, Where, and How to Plant
The best time for installing coleus in your home landscape is early spring when all danger of frost is past. Coleus is a standard in Texas shade landscapes since we are rather limited as far as good color is concerned. Some varieties will grow in full sun, but they require more care because coleus has a high moisture requirement. Plant in well-prepared beds. To thoroughly improve beds, blend 3 in. of top-quality organic material including compost, brown sphagnum peat moss, and ground bark into the top 3 in. of the existing soil. Install transplants no deeper than their soilball, firm the soil, water thoroughly, apply root stimulator, and, after the planting is complete, mulch the entire area with approximately 3 in. of bark mulch.

Growing Tips
Keep blooms pinched, and do not let plants dry out. Maintain a moist soil throughout the entire growing season by continuing to maintain a 3 in. layer of mulch. For proper plant nutrition, add an encapsulated, season-long fertilizer at planting time, or apply water-soluble fertilizers as needed. Pinch back terminals, along with blooms, to induce branching and more colorful foliage. It is usually best not to allow coleus plantings to bloom.

Care
Sucking insects may visit coleus throughout the growing season. Your local garden center can offer several control possibilities.

Companion Planting and Design
Coleus works well in front of evergreen shrubbery in shaded areas. It works equally well in beds among shade trees. Try hanging baskets, tubs, and planters of coleus. I've done this for years and they look marvelous. Coleus is an excellent companion to other shade-loving summer annuals.

I Suggest
There is no other group of old-fashioned plants that have been "modernized" as much as the coleus. The Sun varieties are varied, colorful, and will grow in the Texas sun. Colors range from deep burgundy to bright lime green and multicolors of various shades of rust, green, purple, and burgundy.

Copper Plant
Acalypha wilkesiana

When, Where, and How to Plant

Copper plants love warmth, so do not set them out until the air temperature is consistently above 65 degrees Fahrenheit—70 degrees Fahrenheit is even better—both day and night. I usually set mine out after Easter. Use copper plant virtually anywhere in your home landscape where there is full sun. Do not plant in heavily shaded areas. It will not grow properly, nor will you see the great coppery color. In containers, use a lightweight potting soil. To plant in improved soil, add 3 in. of high-quality organic matter and blend with the top 3 in. of native soil. Install plants no deeper than the soilball. Firm the soil well around newly transplanted selections, water thoroughly, and apply a root stimulator. After the planting is complete, apply 3 in. of high-quality mulch. (I usually use pine bark mulch.)

Growing Tips

Water sufficiently to prevent soil dryness. Do not over water or keep wet. Maintain a season-long layer of mulch to conserve soil moisture, and be sure to use fertilizer for optimum growth. Pinch back growing tips or terminals to induce fast growth and branching.

Care

In my years of growing copper plants, I have experienced no serious pest problems. Shape or prune to specific forms throughout the growing season. You may take cuttings from your copper plant to be rooted for additional plant materials.

Companion Planting and Design

Use as a background, and place salvia, periwinkle, lantana, or other Texas heat-tolerant, color plants in front. It may be used as a natural divider or as a specimen plant. I have even seen these plants trained into small annual trees. For a sunny area where space is limited, consider a tree-form copper plant. Copper plant is excellent in pottery containers and does not mind hot spots in the garden. Copper plant grows well in a Xeriscape.

I Suggest

Almost foolproof, copper plant is a super plant for anyone to try. Grow these colorful sun-lovers anywhere tall color foliage is desired.

The sun-loving copper plant is one of my favorite summertime annuals. A wonderful background plant, it will take all the heat the sun can dish out. I often place copper plant as the center planting in large, black, 15-gallon nursery containers in our driveway. I plant some solid white periwinkle around the outside edges, allowing them to cascade down. Even on black asphalt, it continues to grow and provides outstanding color all season long. A color plant for Texas gardeners doesn't get much tougher than that! The 'Louisiana Red' variety looks like its parent but has much larger leaves in red, bronze, and pink.

Bloom Period and Seasonal Color

Foliage in copper, red, bronze, and pink, and green.

Mature Height × Spread

2 to 4 ft. × 8 to 12 in.

Dianthus
Dianthus chinensis

Pinks is the common name for dianthus in Texas—a staple of cool-season color in our gardens. While it is true that many are pink, they are also available in white, red, and blends. Why then is the common name pinks? It could be that the first species used was pink and subsequent species retained the name. Another possibility is that the petal edges look as if they have been "pinked" by a pair of pinking shears. But no matter how this family received its name, they are a wonderful addition to any Texas color garden. Some are classified as biennial or short-lived perennials, but pink often behave and are used as annuals in our landscapes. Pinks do best in cool weather.

Other Common Names
Pinks, Sweet William

Bloom Period and Seasonal Color
Spring, summer, fall, and winter blooms in white, pink, red, and blends.

Mature Height × Spread
4 to 18 in. × 6 to 12 in.

When, Where, and How to Plant
For seasonal color during fall and mild winters, plant in late summer after high temperatures are gone. For spring to early summer color, set out transplants in late winter/early spring after hard freezes and killing frosts are over. Start seeds for transplants approximately six weeks before planting in the landscape. For best results, plant in areas with good soil drainage and morning sun and afternoon shade. Dianthus may be grown in day-long full sun, but their blooming season will be shortened. Improve the soil by blending 3 in. of high-quality organic matter with the top 3 in. of the native soil. Do not plant in poorly drained, wet or difficult-to-water soils. Set transplants into well-amended beds at the same depth as their soilball, firm the soil, water thoroughly, and apply root stimulator. After the entire planting is complete, mulch with 3 in. of bark mulch.

Growing Tips
Maintain a moist, but not wet soil. Mulch with a season-long 3 in. layer of bark mulch. This helps to conserve soil moisture, control weeds, and moderate soil temperatures. When transplanting, fertilize with a season-long encapsulated fertilizer, or as needed with water-soluble fertilizers. Remove spent blooms and stems to encourage additional flowering.

Care
Aphids may visit tender growth, but they usually aren't a serious problem. If needed, visit nurseries that offer a wide range of control possibilities.

Companion Planting and Design
Dianthus is an excellent addition as a border plant, while the taller standard varieties make for great background plants and cut flowers. Dianthus may be grown solo in large containers or with additional flowering plants such as lobelia and verbena. The fragrance of some varieties, such as *D. barbatus*, is most pleasing, and we Texas gardeners like to use them near our entryways. Dianthus is adaptable to rock gardens and detail designs, often forming low mats and drifts of color.

I Suggest
If you have limited space but would like some color, try these relatives of the carnation family in 12 in. or larger planters. They work well on decks, patios, and balconies.

Flowering Kale and Cabbage

Brassica oleracea

When, Where, and How to Plant

Plant flowering kale and cabbage in very early fall when the temperature is cool, and transplants are available. In the southern part of our state in Zones 8 and 9, flowering kale and cabbage may provide winter color all through the season till spring heat arrives. In Zones 6 and 7, it is still worth planting because of its spectacular early fall colors. For best color, do not plant in the shade or in heavy clay soil without first improving with organic matter. To improve soil, blend 3 in. of high-quality organic matter with the top 3 in. of existing soil. Insert transplants no deeper than they were originally grown in the container. Firm the soil, water thoroughly, and apply root stimulator. After all planting is complete, mulch with 3 in. of bark mulch. If planting in containers, use a light-weight potting soil.

Growing Tips

Very little pruning is required. Remove unsightly leaves. Apply sufficient water to ensure moist growing conditions, but do not overwater. Maintain a season-long mulch layer. If a season-long encapsulated bedding plant fertilizer was applied at planting time, no additional fertilization is necessary.

Care

Cabbage loopers or aphids may visit your flowering kale and cabbage but normally are not serious problems. Should controls be necessary, visit your local garden centers for pest control advice.

Companion Planting and Design

Flowering kale and cabbage are striking additions to your landscape when used near entries or any place you want eye appeal and accent. One of the best uses is in masses of a single color. You might also use them to outline beds of other cool-season plants such as calendula, pansies, or dianthus. Flowering kale and cabbage also work well in large containers as a central focal point or as part of a mass color pot. Soft purple-gray foliage is a good mixer with blue and purple pansies and violas and the silver foliage of dusty miller.

I Suggest

For the best effect, place in mass plantings during the fall after the summer temperatures have cooled.

Sometimes you will find flowering cabbage or kale listed as "edible." Of course taste is a subjective matter just as beauty is in the eye of the beholder. Since my taste may not be the same as yours, try the taste of flowering cabbage or kale and see if you like it. Some folks feel it is a bit too bitter. Flowering kale and cabbage normally are sold as white, pink, or mixed. The Northern Lights series is available in white, pink, rose, and mixed. 'Cherry Sundae' is available in patterns of carmine and cream. Sometimes described as looking like snowflakes, flowering kale is available in 'Red Peacock', 'White Peacock' and 'Nasoya'.

Other Common Names

Ornamental Cabbage, Ornamental Kale

Bloom Period and Seasonal Color

Fall, spring, and (mild) winter foliage in white, carmine, purple, and cream, and soft grays.

Mature Height × Spread

10 to 18 in. × 10 to 12 in.

Geranium

Pelargonium × hortorum

Every year when springtime rolls around, my wife, Judy, needs to have some geraniums. I'm sure that if you have a chance to enjoy their beauty, you will want some too. Geraniums may be grown as bedding plants in masses or in individual containers such as large terra-cotta pots, planters, and hanging baskets. While red tends to be the traditional color of geraniums, today there are wonderful varieties of coral, pink, white, and blends. Some geraniums, called scented geraniums, not only come with small blossoms and colorful/interesting foliage but are also scented. Take a look at some of the more unusual types such as Martha Washington geranium, Pelargonium × domesticum.

Other Common Names
Bedding Geranium, Common Geranium

Bloom Period and Seasonal Color
Spring, summer and fall blooms in pink, red, bronze, maroon, white, and salmon.

Mature Height × Spread
12 to 24 in. × 8 to 18 in.

When, Where, and How to Plant

Plant 4 or 5 in. potted geraniums in the early spring after all danger of frost is past. Some plant references will refer to the geranium as a full-sun plant. In our Texas heat, plant geraniums where they receive morning sun only, but shade them from the hot, west, afternoon sun. Plants grown this way should provide long bloom periods. But even some of the plants grown in shaded areas will stop blooming in midsummer due to our tremendous heat. In order for geraniums to do well, do not plant them in poorly drained areas or heavy clay soil but plant them in well-drained, improved beds. Incorporate 3 in. of high-quality organic matter into your existing native soil. Remove the geranium from the container and insert into the soil to the depth of the plant's soilball. Firm the soil, water thoroughly, and apply root stimulator. After planting, mulch the planting area with 3 in. of bark mulch. When planting in containers, use a lightweight potting soil.

Growing Tips

Remove spent bloom heads to ensure continuous blooming throughout the season. Water thoroughly, taking care not to overwater—geraniums will not tolerate a wet soil. Maintain a 3 in. layer of bark mulch throughout the entire growing season. Geraniums need to be well-nourished in order to do their best. Apply a slow-release, granular-type, or encapsulated fertilizer that will last throughout the growing season.

Care

I have experienced no serious pests with geraniums.

Companion Planting and Design

Geraniums can be successfully grown in containers. I have grown them in 14 in. terra-cotta pots and have had some as long as five years. They work well in terra-cotta, plastic, or even in wooden planters that you may design yourself. Geraniums are excellent in window boxes and are often associated with the cottage garden image of white picket fences and front porches.

I Suggest

Unlike in other parts of our country, geraniums, grown for their blooms, are not considered full sun, summer annuals due to Texas' intense heat and sun. Enjoy them in the cooler spring and fall periods, and provide some shade for them during the summer.

When, Where, and How to Plant

Plant impatiens transplants in the spring approximately two weeks after all danger of frost has passed. Plant in a shady planting bed that will be easy to water and has been improved with moisture-holding soil. Mix a combination of compost and brown sphagnum peat moss, using about $1^{1}/_{2}$ in. of each with 3 in. of native soil tilled together. Insert your transplants into the well-prepared bed at soilball depth. Water thoroughly. Apply root stimulator and mulch the bed. Mulch with 3 in. of bark. When planting in containers, use a lightweight potting soil and plant at the same depth.

Growing Tips

Midsummer pruning may be necessary with impatiens to improve overall structure. Maintain a moist soil throughout the growing season. Drip irrigation will help maintain even soil moisture throughout the growing season, even saving you up to 50 percent on your water bill. Overwatering could cause the fleshy stems and plant crown to rot. Maintain a 3 in. layer of mulch to conserve soil moisture. Impatiens respond quite favorably to seasonal applications of fertilizers.

Care

Mealybugs, slugs, and snails may visit, but I have not had a serious problem with any insects on these plants.

Companion Planting and Design

The shorter varieties make excellent border plants that are dense and rounded. Use these low-growing varieties in a border with taller varieties of coleus as background plants. Both have similar watering requirements and make interesting statements of color. Window boxes in shady locations are often successfully filled with impatiens. Impatiens are often used in large masses beneath trees and to fill void spaces in shaded shrub plantings.

I Suggest

Enjoy the super colors of impatiens during the spring and early summer in shady areas only. I prefer the New Guinea types myself because of both colorful foliage and blooms. Some varieties of New Guinea impatiens, *Impatiens hawkeri*, include 'Blake', 'Spectra Salmon', and 'Tango'.

One of the most enjoyable plants in my shade area gardening experience is impatiens. If you haven't already, try this very colorful and popular plant in the shaded areas of your garden. While some plant guides state that impatiens may be used in full sun, they obviously are not referring to our Texas region. While shooting a television show in Winnipeg, Canada one July, I had an opportunity to see impatiens grown in full sun. They were magnificent. The colors were outstanding and the foliage was gorgeous—but that was Canada. Impatiens may be used in beds of single colors, most striking in a landscape. They are also extremely effective in hanging baskets or other containers.

Other Common Name
Sultana

Bloom Period and Seasonal Color
Spring to frost blooms in white, red, scarlet, mauve, orchid, purple, pinks, orange, rose, and bi-colors.

Mature Height × Spread
6 to 18 in. × 10 to 14 in.

Marigold

Tagetes spp.

Marigolds are without a doubt my favorite annual blooming plant. Mom and Granny Miller started their marigolds from seeds. Marigolds have been grown for centuries in various cultures, and today, there are even more interesting forms and exciting colors available. I like the various looks marigolds can impart in the landscape. Borders are colorful with these bloomers, and backgrounds may be made striking. They will take the full Texas sun and keep on blooming. Some go by the name mari-mums. This is a name coined by the Texas Agricultural Extension Service. Because of their diversity in heights, widths, and bloom color, make sure your retailer is aware of your specific needs.

Other Common Names
Mari-Mum, African Marigold, French Marigold, American Marigold

Bloom Period and Seasonal Color
Early summer through fall blooms in orange, yellow, mahogany, gold, lemon, near-white, and blends.

Mature Height × Spread
6 to 36 in. × 10 to 18 in.

When, Where, and How to Plant
Marigolds are subject to frost and freeze, so don't plant until all danger of frost has passed. They are easily grown from seed and are fast growing. I like to purchase marigolds that are ready to set out. I don't necessarily look for those that have lots of buds or blooms—just nice, dark-green transplants that are short, compact, and healthy. Marigolds require full sun at least six to eight hours per day. Improve sandy or clay soil by adding 3 in. of quality organic matter, tilled into the native soil. Insert the transplants into your improved bed, no deeper than the soilball. Firm the soil, water thoroughly, and apply root stimulator. After the planting is complete, apply a 3-in. layer of bark mulch. Plant in containers at the same depth.

Growing Tips
Remove old blooms to encourage more flowering. Water sufficiently to prevent soil dryness and to ensure good growth and blooms. Do not over-water. Maintain even soil moisture with 3 in. of bark mulch. Marigolds benefit from a fertile soil. Use fertilizer as needed.

Care
When it gets hot and dry late in the season, spider mites may visit your plants. Snails and slugs may occur on young plants. If they become a problem, visit local garden centers for the best control possibilities.

Companion Planting and Design
Marigolds offer an effective mass of color in the garden at a low cost. Short, bushy varieties, such as 'Queen Sophia', work well in hanging baskets. All marigolds thrive in containers, but because of their vigorous nature, the smallest container I recommend is 12 in. diameter. As a side note: 'Discovery' and 'Voyager' are often labeled as Mari-Mums and may be labeled as such at your local nursery.

I Suggest
One of my favorite varieties is 'Queen Sophia', a free bloomer with abundant foliage. If you have been discouraged by spider mites on your marigolds, plant during September for great color during late fall to frost. Other marigold varieties include 'Cracker Jack' in gold and vanilla, 'Moonbeam', 'Sumo', 'Aurora Yellow Fire', and 'Golden Gate'.

Morning Glory

Ipomoea purpurea

When, Where, and How to Plant

Plant morning glories in springtime after all danger of frost is past and the soil is warm. Morning glory seeds start very easily when directly sown into the soil. A well-drained location and sandy soils are preferred. Plant in a location with a minimum of six hours of full sun. Seeds planted directly will germinate in seven to thirty days. Germination can be hastened by nicking each of the large seeds with a pocket knife, grinder, or hacksaw, or soak seeds twenty-four to forty-eight hours in warm water. These plants will not tolerate wet or poorly drained locations, or heavy soils that are not amended. To improve your heavy soils, incorporate 3 in. of high-quality organic matter into the top 3 in. of the soil. When planting transplants, insert in prepared bed no deeper than they were originally grown in their containers. Firm the soil, water thoroughly, apply root stimulator, and mulch with about 3 in. of bark mulch. Use lightweight potting soil for container planting.

Growing Tips

No pruning is necessary, but you may wish to train your morning glory to grow in a specific direction by tying the vine to a structure with a plastic stretch tie or nylon stocking. Water as necessary to prevent wilting. Morning glory requires a minimum amount of nutrition. One application of rose fertilizer early in the spring is beneficial.

Care

Morning glory is virtually insect and disease free. If grasshoppers or other pests visit your plants, take a trip to your local retailer for appropriate controls.

Companion Planting and Design

These plants are extremely useful for summertime flowering screens. They may be used on any type of structure such as trellises, mailboxes, gazebos, or fences, and are often used for quick shade on porches, or to shade hot, western exposures. Rapid growth and easy culture make for a quick summer screen. The 'Heavenly Blue' variety is truly an outstanding heavenly blue, like no other flower.

I Suggest

Plant these colorful vines in locations where they may be viewed from inside your home as well as out in the landscape. They are great fun for the little gardener.

Since the 1700s, morning glories have been grown by Texas gardeners. You won't find an easier flowering annual vine to grow. And there are many different colors and forms of morning glory to choose from. Those in frost-free areas remain year after year and are called perennials. The plants in areas where they are not hardy (and will freeze out in the wintertime) are called half-hardy perennials and are grown as annuals. Some to try: I. nil, I. purpurea, I. alba, I. tricolor, and the cultivars 'Mini Sky-Blue', 'Scarlet Star', 'Heavenly Blue', 'Roman Candle', 'Early Call', 'Pearly Gates', and 'Scarlett O'Hara'.

Bloom Period and Seasonal Color

Spring, summer, and fall to frost blooms in white, purple, pink, red, blue, scarlet, and crimson.

Mature Height × Spread

8 to 30 ft. × 12 ft. or more

Pansy

Viola × wittrockiana

Pansies are a long-time staple of Texas gardens. If you are new to our area and want to plant pansies at the beginning of summer—don't do it. Spring or summer planting works fine if you are in Indiana, the North-eastern states, or Canada, but not in Texas. Pansies provide outstanding fall, winter, and early spring color in Zones 7, 8, and 9. In Zone 6, they are super in the fall and spring. They are most striking in the landscape when one color is used in a mass, as often seen at botanical gardens. Some of the larger-flowered varieties are 'Burning', 'Clear Sky Primrose', 'Crown Scarlet', 'Yellow Splash', 'Flame Princess', 'Blackberry Rose', 'Frost Rose', 'Pink Shades', 'Raspberry Rose' and 'Silver Princess'.

Bloom Period and Seasonal Color
Fall, winter, early spring blooms in white, blue, mahogany, rose, yellow, apricot, purple, violet, lavender, orange, and bi-colors.

Mature Height × Spread
8 to 12 in. × 12 in.

When, Where, and How to Plant
The best time to plant pansies is early fall when transplants are available and when nighttime temperatures have cooled to approximately 60 degrees Fahrenheit. Do not attempt growing pansies from seed. Even though their appearance is often awful after a hard freeze, a little sunlight and time will have them popping right back up and they will continue to grow and bloom right through the winter. Do not plant pansies in shaded areas or where the soil drains poorly. Blend 3 in. of high-quality organic matter with the top 3 in. of your existing soil. Set transplants approximately 6 to 8 in. apart, in a checkerboard pattern for outstanding impact. Plant no deeper than the soilball depth. Firm the soil around the transplants, water thoroughly, apply root stimulator according to the label directions, and mulch planting area with 2 in. of bark mulch. To grow pansies in containers, fill with a loose, lightweight potting soil, and follow the same procedures as in ground plantings.

Growing Tips
Deadheading encourages more flowering and tidies up the pansy. Maintain a moist soil during the growing season to ensure better blooms, health, and vigor. Nutrition may be supplied by the use of various fertilizers.

Care
Aphids, slugs, or snails may visit your pansies. Try your local garden center for several control possibilities.

Companion Planting and Design
Pansies are good companions with spring bulbs such as daffodils and tulips, and other blooming spring annuals such as alyssum, violas, and spring phlox. Pansies make colorful masses among rocks and informal paths in rock gardens. They are an inviting addition at the entryways to our homes. They work well in large containers in areas that need some splash of color during the fall, winter, and early spring.

I Suggest
Plant groups of single colors. Do not plant a 'hodge-podge' planting with these beauties.

Periwinkle
Catharanthus roseus

When, Where, and How to Plant

The best time to plant periwinkles is in the spring after all danger of frost is past. Periwinkles are versatile, but they do have some specific planting requirements that must be met. Do not plant in heavy clay soil, wet locations, poorly drained locations, or heavily shaded areas. To do their best, periwinkles need a location providing full sun at least six hours per day, and a well-draining soil that is fertile yet moist. Till or blend 3 in. of organic matter into the top 3 in. of your existing soil. Set the new transplants into the prepared bed at the same level they were growing in their containers, and firm the soil. Water thoroughly, apply root stimulator according to label directions, and mulch thoroughly with 2 to 3 in. of bark mulch. To plant in containers, fill near the top with a premium-quality, lightweight potting soil. Plant as when planting in beds.

Growing Tips

Water often enough to prevent soil dryness and ensure good growth and bloom all season long. Periwinkles need to be nourished throughout the entire growing season with a quality fertilizer.

Care

No pruning should be necessary. In my years of growing periwinkles, I have had no insect or disease problems.

Companion Planting and Design

I use solid white periwinkles in large black plastic containers of a 10- to 15-gallon size with copper plants in the center. This combination gives lasting outstanding color. Plant along entryways or driveways. They work equally well in large containers on a deck, around a pool, and near water features. There are sprawling, cascading varieties suitable for containers, such as 'Rose Carpet' and 'Magic Carpet'. Periwinkle is also great in various bed applications. Whether used as border plants or cascading down rock gardens, you will find them very useful in the home landscape.

I Suggest

When I have visited with gardeners, homeowners, and new-to-Texas arrivals, I have noticed their difficulty in adjusting to our long, hot, and sunny growing season. Annual vinca or periwinkle is the perfect annual gardening remedy.

If you happen to be looking for a heat- and sun-tolerant plant that will provide color throughout the entire season, periwinkle is the answer. Periwinkles are truly "Texas flameproof" and continue to bloom and do well in spite of all the heat. When looking for a plant that virtually anyone can grow—even the black thumbs among us— try the almost foolproof periwinkles. Often used in mass to create outstanding groundcover and filler effects, these plants work equally well when container grown. Some periwinkles to try in your home landscape include 'Apricot Delight', 'Pacifica Red', 'Parasol', 'Peppermint Cooler', 'Velvet Rose', 'Tropicana', and 'Terrace Vermilion'.

Other Common Name

Annual Vinca

Bloom Period and Seasonal Color

Spring, summer, fall blooms in white, pink, purple, hot pink, deep rose, and bright lavender.

Mature Height × Spread

6 to 12 in. × 12 to 24 in.

Petunia

Petunia × hybrida

My experience with petunias in Texas is that the single varieties such as 'Summer Madness' and 'Carpet' tend to be more heat resistant. Petunias are usually a cool-season plant in Texas. They prefer the cool spring, early summer, and early fall for growing. If you are looking for petunias that grow all season, ask your local garden center for heat-resistant varieties. Otherwise, grow these gorgeous annuals in the cooler seasons of the year in containers or landscape beds. Among the many varieties are 'Merlin', 'Big Daddy', 'Blue Sky', 'Celebrity Pink Morn', Cloud Mix, 'Flame Carpet', 'Madness Plum Crazy', 'Pastel Salmon', 'Plum Purple', 'Starship', 'Summer Sun', Summer Cascade series, Ultra Star series, 'White Magic', 'Double Delight', 'Caprice', 'White Swan', and in the Wave™ series, 'Pink Wave™' and 'Purple Wave™'.

Bloom Period and Seasonal Color
Spring, summer, fall blooms in pink, salmon, red, rose, burgundy, violet, lilac, cream to pale yellow, and variations.

Mature Height × Spread
6 to 18 in. × 12 to 24 in.

When, Where, and How to Plant

The best time to plant petunias is very early spring when transplants are available—approximately two weeks after the last average killing frost in your area. Some gardeners also enjoy planting petunias in very early fall. Petunias will resist light frost and remain until the first hard freeze. In order for petunias to thrive, plant in a moist, fertile soil that drains well. Add organic matter in the form of brown sphagnum peat moss, compost, and ground-bark mulch. Add approximately 1 in. of each one of these three to the top 3 in. of your soil. Blend thoroughly, and you will have a bed approximately 6 in. deep, ready for petunia planting. Remove your selected petunias from their containers, and insert them soilball-deep into the prepared bed. Firm the soil well, water thoroughly, apply root stimulator, and mulch the entire planting with approximately 2 in. of bark mulch. When planting in containers, fill within 2 in. of the top with a premium lightweight potting soil.

Growing Tips

Water petunias sufficiently to maintain a moist, but not wet, soil throughout the entire season. Nutrition can be added through one of several fertilizers applied once at planting.

Care

Minimal pruning is required, though deadheading can be beneficial. My petunias have suffered no pest problems. For help with any chewing pest, visit your local nursery.

Companion Planting and Design

Petunias work well as beds of color early in the year or even during early fall. They are very much at home in mixed annual and perennial beds. Cascading varieties such as 'Cascade Pink', 'Cascade Red', 'Cascade White', and the Wave™ series are often used in hanging baskets or in large containers. The most striking petunia effect is accomplished by using many of one variety or color together. Grandiflora cultivars have fewer, but larger blooms, while multiflora cultivars have an abundance of smaller blooms.

I Suggest

One of my favorite varieties is 'VIP'. This old-fashioned, lightly fragrant, single petunia is on my A+ list.

Portulaca

Portulaca grandiflora

When, Where, and How to Plant

Plant portulaca in the spring after all danger of frost is past. Moss rose can stand the heat—even in nearly pure sand locations. While moss rose is quite tolerant of relatively dry areas, it will not tolerate prolonged wet-soil conditions. Don't even think of planting in poorly drained soil or full shade. To improve the soil, add organic matter in the form of compost, ground bark, or brown sphagnum peat moss. Add approximately 1 in. of one of these three ingredients to the soil. Till the organic matter into the top 3 in. of soil for a bed fit for moss rose through the entire season. Remove your transplants from their containers and insert them to the depth of the top of the soil-ball. Firm soil, water thoroughly, and apply root stimulator. After planting is complete, mulch planting area 1 to 2 in. deep. When planting in containers, fill with lightweight potting soil near the top.

Growing Tips

Water enough to prevent soil dryness and to ensure good growth and great blooms throughout the entire season. The fleshy plants can be damaged with overwatering. Apply fertilizer throughout the season.

Care

No pruning is necessary to maintain a good-looking bed; however, cutting back terminals will induce branching, thus more blooms. The cut terminals may be tucked into soil and may root and grow. Through decades of plantings, I have experienced no insect problems with moss rose, nor am I aware of any pests.

Companion Planting and Design

Portulaca is marvelous in outlying beds in the sunny locations of your home landscape. It works well as a container plant just as it did in Granny Miller's big dishpan. It may also be grown successfully in hanging baskets of all sizes. Moss rose is ideal for hot rock gardens and along sunny borders, trails, and paths.

I Suggest

Use these varied and versatile plants in your favorite colors or single colors in mass plantings in beds, in pots, or in baskets for season-long color.

Granny Miller always had moss growing in her Indian Creek, TX, garden. Years later, I found out that the "moss" Granny grew was portulaca, moss rose, or rose moss—though it was just moss to her. It is an extremely easy-to- care-for plant, and Granny's container of choice was an old dishpan. Portulaca is an excellent choice for Texas gardens—tough, versatile and durable. It will even thrive in pavement cracks.

Other Common Names

Moss Rose, Rose Moss

Bloom Period and Seasonal Color

Spring to fall blooms in bright colors and pastels of white, red, cerise, rose pink, orange, and yellow.

Mature Height × Spread

4 to 12 in. × 8 to 12 in.

Salvia
Salvia splendens

There are over 750 different types of salvias around the world. In Texas, the one we think of as the bedding salvia is called Salvia splendens, *red salvia. It is a striking plant when used in the home landscape. Salvia may be used in masses in a sunny location where the soil drains well. It is not a color plant for heavily shaded areas, but it will tolerate some light shade. It is equally striking when used in containers twelve inches or larger, and I have seen them used in masses inside hanging baskets for an outstanding color combination with a dark-green basket. You may also wish to try* Salvia farinacea 'Victoria', *a violet-blue relative.*

Other Common Names
Scarlet Sage, Red Salvia

Bloom Period and Seasonal Color
Spring to fall blooms in white, pink, rose, red, violet, burgundy, salmon, purple, or cream.

Mature Height × Spread
6 to 12 in. × 8 to 10 in.

When, Where, and How to Plant
Plant salvia in the early spring after all danger of frost is past. *Salvia splendens* requires a well-drained, rich, moist soil. Do not plant in hot, difficult-to-water, dry locations or in poorly drained, wet, shady locations. For best results, plant this species of salvia where it will receive morning sun with some afternoon shade. Red forms are best in full sun, while pastel forms tend to do best in partial shade. Incorporate 3 in. of high-quality organic matter into the top 3 in. of soil. Remove plants from their containers, and insert into the soil at soilball level. Firm soil and water thoroughly. Apply root stimulator, and mulch the entire planting 3 in. deep. When planting in containers, use lightweight potting soil and plant at the same depth as in-ground plantings.

Growing Tips
Be sure to maintain even soil moisture. A drip irrigation system can help in this process. To help maintain and conserve soil moisture and to moderate some of the extremities in soil temperatures, be sure to maintain about a 3-in. layer of bark mulch over your planting throughout the entire season. Properly nourished salvia will survive stressful situations. Apply the fertilizer of your choice according to label directions.

Care
Pinching spent bloom spikes may be necessary to maintain a more compact and desirable plant. This will also ensure better growth and continued flowering during the late summer and early fall bloom period. Spider mites may appear during hot, dry summers. Visit local retail garden centers for proper pest controls.

Companion Planting and Design
Salvia is often used in masses in parks of all sorts. Experiment with mass plantings in your home landscape. Plant salvia in entryways and yard beds. Use in containers on decks, gazebos, or by swings.

I Suggest
Try one of my favorites, *S. coccinea*, 'Lady in Red'. There are also white and pink/salmon varieties of *S. coccinea*. Mexican bush sage, *S. leucantha*, should be in everyone's landscape.

Snapdragon
Antirrhinum majus

When, Where, and How to Plant

Plant snapdragons transplants in the fall as a cool-season annual or to enjoy in late winter/early spring until our summertime heat takes them out. Snapdragons need a very rich, moist, well-drained soil. Do not plant in dry, heavy clay, or poorly drained soils. Snapdragons do best in daylong full sun, but they will perform satisfactorily with six to eight hours of sun per day. Till 3 in. of high-quality organic matter into 3 in. of existing soil. Install snapdragons in the improved bed no deeper than they were growing in the containers and firm the soil around them. Water thoroughly, apply root stimulator according to label directions, and spread 3 in. of bark mulch over the entire area. If you are planting in containers, use a premium-quality, lightweight potting soil filled to within 2 in. of the pot's rim. Plant at same depth as in-ground plantings.

Growing Tips

Water sufficiently to maintain a moist soil, but don't overwater. Provide good nutrition by fertilizing according to directions.

Care

Removing spent blossoms is beneficial to the long-term bloom of snapdragons. Rust may be a problem for snapdragons. Tender, new growth may be visited by aphids, but this is not usually a serious problem. Visit local garden centers for pest controls.

Companion Planting and Design

Group shorter varieties in plantings for mass effect or as border plants. The taller varieties work very well as background with shorter snapdragon varieties or pansies in front. Create all sorts of effects by simply using various types, colors, and sizes available at your local retailers. Color, sizes and varieties all may vary yearly, so be on the look-out for new ones to try each year. Grow in containers near an entryway or any other place that you would like some outstanding color in the cooler season.

I Suggest

We have always enjoyed the dwarf types of snapdragon. Let me know how you like them.

Many flowering annuals used in Texas landscapes are also extremely popular in the rest of the country. Among these are zinnias, marigolds, petunias, and snapdragons. In my years of giving gardening talks for children, I have learned that the snapdragon is a clear favorite. Children think they are very "neat" and enjoy planting and opening the flowers for a look inside. If you have little gardeners around, let them plant some snapdragons in the fall or early spring. Some excellent varieties include 'Madame Butterfly', 'Giant Forerunner', 'Liberty', 'Black Prince' (a dark, almost black-colored selection), 'Lipstick' (a "lipstick" red variety), 'Monarch', 'Purple King', 'White Wonder' (a classy white variety), 'Double Sweetheart', 'Dwarf Trumpet', Dwarf Bedding mixed, 'Floral Showers', 'Lavender Bicolor', Little Darling mixed, 'Peaches and Cream', and 'Royal Carpet'.

Bloom Period and Seasonal Color

Fall and early spring blooms in red, white, yellow, orange, maroon, fuchsia, carmine, and pink.

Mature Height × Spread

6 to 4 ft. × 6 to 8 in.

Sunflower

Helianthus annuus

Years ago I was in Winnipeg, Canada, on a road trip taping a television show. The production crew was stunned when they saw the gigantic fields of sunflowers in the area. If you have ever seen a field of sunflowers in full bloom—stretching as far as the eye can see—you know the striking effect of which I speak. Sunflowers are great for children, too. I love to get the little gardeners involved in planting, and you won't find a better flower for those little bitty fingers. There is a wonderful sunflower variety called 'Teddy Bear' that gets about two feet high and has six-inch ultra-double blossoms. And what child doesn't like Teddy bears?

Other Common Name
Annual Sunflower

Bloom Period and Seasonal Color
Summer and fall, dark centered, single, semi double, or double daisy-like blooms in gold, lemon, bronze, mahogany, and white.

Mature Height × Spread
18 in. to 10 ft. × 2 ft.

When, Where, and How to Plant
Plant seeds directly in the soil after temperatures are consistently above 70 degrees Fahrenheit, day and night, for approximately two weeks. Plant in the landscape where there is a minimum of six hours of full sun with shade the rest of the day. Do not plant in heavily shaded, poorly drained, or damp locations. To grow sunflowers in heavy clay soil, improve the soil by incorporating approximately 4 in. of organic matter into the top 4 in. of the soil. Follow the directions on your seed packages for proper spacing and depth. Plant smaller varieties in 5- to 20-gallon containers filled with lightweight potting soil. Young sunflower seedlings are somewhat cold tolerant, allowing early planting in spring and late planting in summer. Plantings may be made as late as August, and the fast growing plant will still flower and produce seed, and be around for Halloween.

Growing Tips
Sunflowers are drought tolerant and will grow under adverse conditions. To prevent wilting and dryness and to have great-looking sunflowers through the entire blooming season, supply sufficient moisture. Fertilize sunflowers at planting time with a season-long encapsulated fertilizer, or use specialty type granular, liquid, or water-soluble fertilizers as needed.

Care
Pruning is usually not necessary. The larger varieties may require some staking and tying. The smaller varieties may benefit from the removal of spent blossoms to encourage additional blossoms. Some chewing insect pests, including grasshoppers, may visit your beautiful sunflower plantings. Consult your local garden center for appropriate controls.

Companion Planting and Design
Sunflowers may be used with other summer color annuals, shrubs, or perennials. Plant in a mass to create a fun "forest" for the little ones. Graduated plantings of a few inches to several feet may be completed with this one annual. I recommend visits to local nurseries on a "hunt" with your young ones to see which varieties and heights are available.

I Suggest
Let your children plant some sunflower seeds and see their enjoyment when the seeds break the ground, grow, and bloom. It's great!

Verbena

Verbena × hybrida

When, Where, and How to Plant

Plant verbena approximately two weeks after all danger of frost is past in a sunny location where it will receive a minimum of six hours of full sun in well-drained soils. Don't plant in heavily shaded, poorly drained, or wet areas. Incorporate 3 in. of high-quality organic matter into the native soil. Remove transplants from containers and insert into prepared bed at the same level they grew in their containers. Firm the soil around the soilball, water thoroughly, and apply root stimulator. Add 3 in. of mulch on top of the finished bed. Use a lightweight potting soil for container plantings and plant at the same depth as above.

Growing Tips

Maintain a moist soil to achieve optimum growth and bloom, but don't overwater. Use encapsulated bedding plant fertilizers that last for an entire season at planting time. Apply liquid, water-soluble, and specialty granular fertilizers as needed throughout the season.

Care

Pruning is usually not necessary, but removing spent blooms can be beneficial for encouraging new grown and flowering. Verbenas may be visited with powdery mildew if planted in areas where the air movement is poor and they are kept too damp. To prevent this, plant in areas where air quality is good and avoid watering foliage. Verbena is easy to grow, with few insect pests.

Companion Planting and Design

Use verbena in any type of bed planting, whether you are looking for a colorful garden or an edging plant. Verbena makes a vivid groundcover, complementing background seasonal annuals and perennials. The low, massive plant is well suited to embracing rocks and growing along gravel walks and paths. Due to its trailing nature, verbena also makes a wonderful hanging basket and is particularly useful if you have limited space or want to create a vertical effect. Terra-cotta, ceramic, metal, plastic, or wood containers work equally well. Try verbena in window boxes or planters in sunny areas.

I Suggest

Plant the widely available hybrid verbenas but don't forget natives such as Prairie verbena.

Some verbena, such as prairie verbena, grows wild throughout our state—though most varieties found today in garden centers are hybrids. The hybrid varieties have greater vigor, form, and many more blooms and colors. Verbena is great for border planting or hen used in masses to create a spectacular annual groundcover effect that lasts throughout the entire season. Verbena provides a variety of color in areas of your garden where a relatively low, trailing plant is needed. The grayish or deep-green foliage is often aromatic. Verbenas have been around for decades. While not as upright as other annuals, they are super when filling in areas or cascading. Try 'Sangria', 'Trinidad', 'Blaze', 'ShowTime', and the 'Spirit of 76'—a mixture of red, white, and blue.

Other Common Name

Common Garden Verbena

Bloom Period and Seasonal Color

Spring to fall small clustered blooms in white, pink, red, purple, magenta, wine, blue, apricot, salmon, and bi-colors.

Mature Height × Spread

4 to 12 in. × 12 to 18 in.

Wax Leaf Begonia
Begonia Semperflorens-Cultorum Hybrids

Wax leaf begonias are the annual bedding plants of choice for Texans who wish to have color in the shade or sun from the same plant that will last the entire season. I've been growing wax leaf begonias for over two decades, and I continue to enjoy the many different choices on the market today. Foliage color ranges from bright green to dark green, to green with various colors in the foliage, such as bronze, mahogany, and chocolate brown. They are excellent top-quality bedding plants for edging in the home or commercial landscape. Just about anyone can grow wax leaf begonia. If you feel that your thumb is less than green, give this easy plant a try this season.

Other Common Names
Fibrous-Rooted Begonia, Wax Begonia

Bloom Period and Seasonal Color
Spring, summer, and fall blooms in white, red, pink, and blends.

Mature Height × Spread
6 to 16 in. × 8 to 12 in.

When, Where, and How to Plant
Plant wax leaf begonia in early spring when transplants become available and two weeks after the last killing frost date. Wax leaf begonias are not usually planted from seed in the home garden. Plant wax leaf begonias in rich, deep, fertile, and moist soil. Do not plant in poorly drained soil, wet locations, or areas that are difficult to water. Plant in soil that has been well amended with at least 3 to 4 in. of organic matter. Set plants into improved soil no deeper than originally grown in their containers, and firm the soil. Water thoroughly, apply root stimulator, and then mulch bare soil with approximately 2 to 3 in. of bark mulch. For container planting, use a lightweight potting soil, and fill the container up to 2 in. from the rim.

Growing Tips
Maintain a moist soil throughout the entire growing season, but do not overwater. Maintaining a thick layer of mulch will keep soil moisture even. Season-long, micro-encapsulated bedding plant fertilizers applied at planting time work well for wax leaf begonias. Apply liquid, water-soluble, and granular fertilizers as needed throughout the entire growing season.

Care
Remove any spent blossoms or damaged leaves to dress up the plant. Slugs or snails may visit wax leaf begonias, but they usually are not a serious problem. Visit your local garden centers for several control options.

Companion Planting and Design
Use as bedding plants around walkways and in landscape beds or as edging plants with taller-growing plants as background. Use to add color in your landscape and where space is limited, like a deck or patio. Begonias are attractive when interplanted with caladium (in the shade) and other summer annuals such as verbena, marigold, and periwinkle (in the sun).

I Suggest
If you live in an apartment, townhouse, or condominium that has an area for some containers, grow your favorite color of wax leaf begonias in single color plantings in pots for a dramatic, colorful effect.

Zinnia

Zinnia elegans

When, Where, and How to Plant

Plant zinnias in your home landscape in the spring, two weeks after the last frost. Zinnias will not tolerate poorly drained soil. Don't plant in shady areas or locations where air movement is insufficient. Plant in well-drained soil that is fertile and moist. Blend in 3 in. of high-quality organic matter, including brown sphagnum peat moss, ground-bark mulch, or compost, with the top 3 in. of your existing soil. Remove the plants from their containers, and insert into the bed at the depth that they were originally grown. Firm the soil. Water thoroughly, apply root stimulator according to label directions, and mulch bare soil with 3 in. of pine bark mulch. When growing them in containers, make sure you use lightweight potting soil filled to within 2 in. of the top and planted at the same depth previously described.

Growing Tips

Maintain even soil moisture, but don't allow your zinnias to become extremely dry or wet. Use season-long encapsulated bedding plant fertilizer, liquid, water-soluble, or specialty granulated fertilizers throughout the season.

Care

Remove spent blossoms to keep your zinnias blooming during the season. Plant zinnias in beds that drain well and have good air movement. Tall zinnias may require staking due to the weight of their blooms in wind and rain. Zinnias may have powdery mildew if air circulation and drainage are poor. Leaf miners also visit occasionally. If this becomes a problem, visit your local garden center for controls.

Companion Planting and Design

Spectacular when massed as a bedding plant, zinnias also work well with other annuals such as marigolds and salvias. Use in entryways or as background plants in your garden to create an outstanding effect. The old-fashioned zinnia is much at home in cottage gardens, or in a row in the vegetable garden for cutting. Zinnias are summer delights with their many vivid colors and constant butterfly companions.

I Suggest

I prefer the dwarf varieties of zinnia planted in large groups in the garden. Dwarf varieties also work well in containers. 'Thumbelina' is a dwarf variety you can try, and 'Cut and Come Again' is a special favorite of butterflies.

Zinnia is the most popular seed-grown bedding plant in America. While at the end of the alphabet, it is tops when it comes to producing results from seed. My granny, your granny, everybody's granny, at some time or another has grown zinnias. If you haven't personally tried this ever cheerful and easy plant, I encourage you to do so. They are widely available at retail gardening centers in a broad assortment of types and colors, from the low-growing dwarf types to the taller standard types. Zinnias perform well in locations with full sun, good air circulation, and soil drainage. If you are looking for an easy plant for your children to try, don't forget zinnias, from seeds or transplants.

Other Common Name

Old Maids

Bloom Period and Seasonal Color

Summer and fall blooms in red, orange, rose, cherry, pink, salmon, lavender, gold, yellow, cream, white, green, and bi-color.

Mature Height × Spread

6 to 40 in. × 6 to 12 in.

Bulbs, Corms, Rhizomes, and Tubers *for Texas*

Children love to plant bulbs, corms, rhizomes, and tubers. With a size that makes them easier to plant than most seeds and some transplants, they are small enough for little fingers to handle and are easy to grow and enjoy. Traditionally, we lump bulbs, corms, rhizomes, and tubers together and call them "bulbs," but there are important horticultural differences among them.

Bulbs are tough. With proper selection and location, some bulbs will survive with minimal care. There are old homesites where nothing remains, yet flowers from bulbs appear each year for us to enjoy as we drive by.

There are native bulbs as well as imports, although imported bulbs are the ones found most often at local garden centers. Bulbs may also be obtained through seasonal catalogs. Catalogs offer a vast selection, especially if the gardener is looking for a particular variety. Make sure what is advertised in the catalogs will grow well in your area.

One thing that makes bulbs, corms, rhizomes, and tubers unique is that they have bloom seasons or color seasons. Some bloom in early spring or late summer, others in the fall. Be sure you understand the blooming time of the plants you're considering. It's sometimes said, "If it blooms in the spring or summer, you dig, divide, transplant, or plant in the fall. If it blooms in the fall, then you dig, divide, transplant, or plant in the spring." Some bulbs, such as tulips, are usually best treated as annuals—planted each year. Caladium bulbs may freeze or rot if left in the ground. Others such as day-lilies and Iris grow and multiply, and thus will need dividing every three or four years.

Daylily

Because of our lack of long cold winters, certain bulbs benefit from being chilled. Leave the bulbs in the bottom of a refrigerator below 45 degrees Fahrenheit for about six weeks. Two types of popular bulbs that require refrigeration are hyacinths, *Hyacinthus orientalis*, and tulips, *Tulipa* spp. Be certain that the bulbs remain dry in storage. Do not store with any vegetables or fruits, which release ethylene gas and will kill the flower buds in the bulbs. After chilling is complete, plant immediately to avoid losing the chilling effect. Because of these chill-

ing requirements, most tulips do not repeat well in Texas. Texas gardeners often make the decision to treat tulips as annuals in their gardens.

Bearded Iris

Some plants in this chapter, including gladiolus, *Gladiolus* hybrids, or glads, are best lifted and stored indoors for the winter and then replanted the following spring. For example, Caladium, *Caladium bicolor*, a tropical plant grown for its colorful foliage, benefits from being lifted out of the ground for the winter. Caladium does not tolerate cold soils well, especially soils that tend to be poorly drained.

Store bulbs, corms, rhizomes, or tubers, in a cool, dry location that has good air circulation. Bread trays, citrus bags, and ladies' nylon stockings all work well as storage containers. Do not seal them in a plastic bag. Drainage is very important for successful long-term growth of most corms and tubers, so make sure your bed is well prepared and drains thoroughly before planting. Soil beneath trees may be compacted, indicating poor aeration and interior drainage. To assure drainage cultivate generous amount of organic matter, such as brown sphagnum peat moss into the soil.

Some narcissus tend to naturalize easily and thrive in many locations as if nature intended it to be there. Gardeners who intend to naturalize jonquils often just toss handfuls of the bulbs into the air and plant them wherever they land!

Most bulbs, rhizomes, corms, and tubers are best grown in full sun; however, spring bulbs usually do well beneath deciduous trees, as the trees are void of foliage during their productive time. Select firm bulbs without rot, mold and discoloration.

If your gardening space is limited, or if you choose to grow bulbs for indoor use, try growing them in containers. This is referred to as "forcing bulbs." The grower usually forces the bulbs to produce blooms out of season. It is delightful to have hyacinth on the dining table in January, or festive amaryllis blooms available for the holiday season. Almost any type of container will work, and the bulbs may be grown in gravel, premium lightweight potting soil, or other medium. Those bulbs assuring success include hyacinth, paperwhite narcissus, and amaryllis. Bulbs that may be forced or grown in containers out of doors include tulip and daffodil.

Caladium
Caladium bicolor

Heart-shaped caladiums have been in use by gardeners since the 1800s, if not earlier. My first experience growing these colorful beauties was in 1971 when I was employed by a nursery which literally sold thousands of these beauties. Since not many blooming plants thrive in shaded areas, I often recommend the planting of caladiums. Not only will they provide outstanding color that lasts well into the summer, but they work just as well when grown in containers as they do in well-prepared beds. I have continued to use caladiums through the years and have always found them relatively easy to grow. Today, there are even sun-tolerant varieties.

Other Common Name
Fancy-Leaved Caladium

Bloom Period and Seasonal Color
Summer foliage color in blends of green, white, pink, red, and metallics.

Mature Height × Spread
12 to 16 in. × 12 to 18 in.

When, Where, and How to Plant
Do not plant your caladium tubers until nighttime temperatures are consistently above 65 degrees Fahrenheit for two weeks, and 70+ degrees Fahrenheit is even better. Most caladiums do best in shaded areas, although light morning sun may not be harmful. If you wish to plant caladiums in sunnier locations, I strongly suggest you try the strap-leaf, sun-tolerant varieties. Before planting, improve your soil and make sure it drains thoroughly. Do not plant caladiums where soil drainage is poor or in difficult-to-water locations. If your soil is heavy clay, be sure to improve it thoroughly before planting by blending 3 in. of organic matter with the top 3 in. of existing soil. Place tubers approximately 1 to 1^1/$_2$ in. below the surface of the soil and water thoroughly. When planting from pots, remove plants and place them in holes no deeper than the soil depth of the containers. Firm well, apply root stimulator according to label directions, water thoroughly, and mulch bare soil with 3 in. of bark mulch.

Growing Tips
Maintain moist growing conditions at all times. Caladiums benefit from fertilization programs. Apply fertilizer according to label directions. Water-soluble, liquid, specialty, and encapsulated slow-release forms all work well. Do not overfertilize.

Care
Prune out all flower stems as they emerge, but no other pruning is necessary. Slugs or snails may visit your caladiums. If they become a problem, go to your local retail garden center, which should offer several control solutions.

Companion Planting and Design
Caladiums may be used in background plantings or in beds of ferns, English ivy, ajuga, liriope, azalea, aucuba, or other shade-loving plants. They are good mixers with shade-loving annuals such as impatiens and wax leaf begonias. They also work well as edgings and look good in various sizes of containers and baskets.

I Suggest
Don't forget to also experiment with some of the newer strap-leafed types that are sun tolerant. Caladiums can create the same band of color from shade to partial sun/shade and into full sun.

Canna
Canna × generalis

When, Where, and How to Plant

Cannas are best planted in the springtime after soil temperatures reach 60 degrees Fahrenheit and higher. Do not plant in the fall. While cannas will survive rather harsh conditions, they prefer a deep, moist, rich soil. Plant in full-sun, well-drained locations that are relatively easy to water. Prepare your soil before planting canna rhizomes. Blend 4 in. of organic matter with the top 4 in. of native soil. Plant rhizomes approximately 4 in. below the soil surface, spacing them from 18 in. to 3 ft. apart. If you wish to plant from containers, set the plants in individual planting holes no deeper than the soilball. Firm the soil around the rootball, water thoroughly, apply root stimulator according to label directions, and mulch bare soil with approximately 3 in. of bark mulch.

Growing Tips

Maintain moist growing conditions for best results. Drip irrigation is well suited to cannas, and maintaining a 3 to 4 in. layer of mulch will help conserve soil moisture. Fertilize in the springtime after new growth begins, using encapsulated, slow-release, specialty granular, liquid, or water-soluble fertilizer according to label directions. Reapply as desired.

Care

Prune out each bloom stalk as blooms complete their show, and cut off and remove plants' tops after the fall killing freezes. No other pruning should be necessary. Slugs, snails, and leaf rollers may visit your cannas. If these pests become problems, consult your local retail garden center for control options. Remember to read and follow label directions on any product you use to control pests.

Companion Planting and Design

Cannas may be grown in beds with other bulbs, annuals, and perennials or in stand-alone beds. The most striking effect comes from mass plantings in multiple rows. With their various colors and sizes, a color palette can be created with beds of these easy-to-grow favorites.

I Suggest

Because of their relative ease and good chance of success, cannas are excellent for the little gardener. Plant any of the dwarf types in groups of seven or more.

Cannas, while native to tropical and subtropical America, have been grown here since Colonial times. Today, we can find cannas growing on old homesites where little or no maintenance occurs. Cannas were originally grown for their striking foliage. The foliage is still interesting, but breeding has resulted in many different bloom colors. For full-sun locations, you won't find a plant that's more colorful or easier to grow, whether planted directly in the ground or in large tubs. Retailers often carry cannas in a range of sizes. The standard can be quite tall (up to seven feet), while the dwarf runs from two to three feet. Before purchasing, be sure to ask how tall your selected varieties will grow in your location.

Bloom Period and Seasonal Color

Spring and summer blooms in yellow, orange, pink, red, coral, and cream.

Mature Height × Spread

18 in. to 8 ft. × 18 to 24 in.

Crinum
Crinum spp.

Crinums have been successfully grown by Texas gardeners since the 1800s and have been a staple in many old-fashioned country and cottage-type gardens. My Granny Miller raised crinums with minimal care and water in her dry country garden in Indian Creek (Brown County), so they must be tough and durable plants! Crinums can often be found growing on their own in woods, pasture areas, meadows, old homesites, and cemeteries throughout Texas. With many types and varieties to try, they are one of the easiest and most rewarding true bulb plants to grow. Among the varieties are 'Sacramento', 'Empress of India', '12 Apostles', 'Carroll Abbott', 'Gowenii', 'Ollene', 'Peachglow', 'Sangria', 'Cloud Davis', 'Mrs. James Hendry', and 'Ellen Bosanquet'.

Bloom Period and Seasonal Color
Spring and summer blooms in white, dark or pale pink, cream, and wine.

Mature Height × Spread
1 to 4 ft. × 2 to 3 ft.

When, Where, and How to Plant
Plant crinums in the springtime after soil temperatures have warmed to 60 degrees Fahrenheit or higher. Planting too early may cause bulb rotting. Crinums may also be planted through the summertime and early fall. Select a location where the bulbs will not be disturbed for several years. They prefer a loam soil that drains well and do best when planted in an area with a minimum of six hours of full sun. Plantings usually take a year or two to establish and flower freely. This is important to remember when dividing and transplanting. Plant in well-prepared beds. Incorporate approximately 4 in. of organic matter into the top 4 in. of native soil. Dig individual planting holes and set the bulbs tops even with the surface of the soil mix. Firm the soil well, water thoroughly, apply root stimulator according to label directions, and mulch with 3 in. of bark mulch.

Growing Tips
Water as necessary to prevent soil dryness. Maintaining a 3 to 4 in. layer of mulch will conserve moisture. As new growth begins in the springtime, fertilize with water-soluble, encapsulated slow-release liquid, or specialty granular fertilizers. Reapply as necessary during the growing and blooming season. Crinum respond with larger and more blooms if well nourished.

Care
Remove spent bloom stalks after blooming is complete. Snails or mealybugs may appear on occasion. Consult your local retail garden center for control possibilities.

Companion Planting and Design
Plant crinums in old or country cottage gardening themes. They may also be grown successfully in tubs and with other summer bulbs. They are good mixers with summer perennials and annuals. With their coarse foliage, crinums make bold accents and are desirable around landscape pools.

I Suggest
While crinums may be relatively difficult to locate, they are certainly worth the effort. Mine are currently growing in three different locations—in a bed with crape myrtles, a large bed with other bulbs and perennials, and a raised western exposure lightly shaded by a catalpa.

Daylily

Hemerocallis spp. and hybrids

When, Where, and How to Plant

Daylilies are so tough and durable they can be dug, divided, and planted any time of the year in Texas. But a good rule of thumb is: If it blooms in the spring and summer, dig, divide, and transplant in the fall. Fall planting of daylilies' tuberous roots provides very good results, but very early spring planting also works well. For best results, plant daylily tuberous roots in deep, rich soils that have been improved with organic matter. Incorporate 3 to 4 in. of organic matter into the top 3 to 4 in. of existing soil. Plant tuberous roots approximately 2 in. deep, spaced 24 in. apart. Do not crowd the plantings as they multiply quickly with good care. Firm the soil lightly. After planting, water thoroughly, apply root stimulator, and cover bare soil with 2 in. of bark mulch. Daylilies may also be set out as transplants in improved soil. Dig individual planting holes no deeper than the top of the soilball. Insert the plant after removing from containers. Firm the soil, water thoroughly, apply root stimulator, and mulch as described.

Growing Tips

Water as necessary to prevent wilting. This is important during the blooming periods. Fertilize in springtime as new growth begins with granular, slow-release, premium-quality rose fertilizer.

Care

Remove spent stalks after blooming is complete. Daylilies have few pests, however they may be damaged with aphids and thrips in spring and grasshoppers in late summer. Visit your local nursery for appropriate control aids.

Companion Planting and Design

The versatile daylilies may be used as bedding plants for mass plantings, or planted in tubs in any landscape location. Because of their various bloom colors, patterns, and heights, daylilies may be utilized in large and stunning plantings of their own. They are good planted with dwarf cannas, iris, other perennials or bulbs, and late spring and summer annuals.

I Suggest

My wife, Judy and I currently enjoy 'Aztec Gold' and 'Stella d'Oro' hybrids. Both are dwarf hybrids that bloom more freely and longer than the old standard varieties.

Daylily is a member of the lily family that may be grown in all areas of Texas. In today's daylily market, you can find literally hundreds, if not thousands, of varieties available. It's an old-fashioned plant that you may find growing in abandoned locations, but it's also found in the most modern gardens with new and improved varieties. They are often used in municipal and botanical garden plantings in addition to home gardens. They will grow in almost any type soil, full sun or lightly shaded areas. Daylily is easy to plant and grow, providing nearly 100 percent assurance of success. As a result, it's very kid-friendly.

Bloom Period and Seasonal Color

Spring, summer, or early fall blooms in yellow, orange, red, pink, apricot, lilac, cream, or white.

Mature Height × Spread

1 to 4 ft. × 1 to 2 ft.

Gladiolus
Gladiolus spp. and hybrids

When looking for a great cut flower to incorporate into your garden plantings, gladiolus should be at the top of your list. Florists prize these summer-blooming plants because of the cut blooms' long life and ease of use in arrangements. There are close to 300 hybrids and cultivars of gladiolus worldwide. Many are native to South Africa. One of the more hardy varieties is G. byzantinus, considered hardy in all Texas zones. G. × colvillei, sometimes called "dwarf baby glads," is hardy in Zone 7 southward. Some cultivars are 'Amanda Mahy', 'Peach Blossom', and 'Spitfire'.

Other Common Name
Glads

Bloom Period and Seasonal Color
Spring and summer blooms in all colors except true blue.

Mature Height × Spread
18 in. to 6 ft. × around 12 in.

When, Where, and How to Plant
Plant gladiolus corms in the springtime after soil temperatures warm to 60 degrees Fahrenheit. Plant approximately every two weeks through the midsummer to ensure continuous bloom and color from gladiolus during the normal growing season. Gladiolus prefer a deep sandy loam. If growing in heavy clay, add organic matter to the soil to a minimum depth of 6 in. Plant corms in well-prepared beds. Incorporate approximately 3 in. of organic matter into the top 3 in. of existing soil. Place corms approximately 4 to 6 in. deep and space 4 to 6 in. apart. Cover the corms and mulch the planting area with 2 in. of bark mulch after the plants sprout and appear.

Growing Tips
Water to maintain a moist soil. Do not allow to dry, especially during blooming periods. Fertilize at planting time with long-lasting, slow-release, rose fertilizer placed approximately 2 in. below the corm, or fertilize through the growing season with liquid or water-soluble fertilizers according to label directions. Keep soil loose around the plants so it will be receptive to watering and feeding.

Care
Staking is usually required with the taller varieties to prevent them from becoming top heavy. Thrips may become a problem during warm days. If they do, visit your local retail garden center to find the best control possibilities.

Companion Planting and Design
Glads are often used in formal cutting gardens or vegetable gardens. Use the dwarf varieties with plantings in and among some lower-growing varieties of other plants. Try *G. alatus*, which normally grows 4 to 10 in. high and has red and yellow flowers. Plant it in a rock garden with good drainage. The tall varieties tend to work best grouped together in cut flower gardens. My wife and I grow some in a bed of angel trumpet. The tall glads stand regal as background border plantings mixed with seasonal annuals and perennials.

I Suggest
Be prepared to stake the taller growing varieties. Bamboo stakes and plastic stretch tie tape work well for this activity.

Hyacinth
Hyacinthus orientalis

When, Where, and How to Plant
Plant in the late fall as soon as garden areas are prepared and bulbs are available. Plant in garden locations with thoroughly improved soil, where they will receive a minimum of six hours of full sun. Hyacinths favor shade from our hot, western, afternoon sun. Do not plant in locations that are difficult to water, in heavy clay soils that are not amended, or in damp locations. Incorporate approximately 3 in. of organic matter into the top 3 in. of existing soil. After bed preparation is complete, plant individual bulbs approximately 4 in. deep and mulch 2 in. deep. Water thoroughly and apply root stimulator according to directions.

Growing Tips
Water as necessary to prevent soil dryness. This is especially important during blooming and growth cycles. Fertilize at planting time with approximately 1 teaspoon of premium-quality, long-lasting rose food, placed 1 in. below the bulb. Fertilize existing beds in the spring as new growth emerges. Use water-soluble liquid or granular fertilizers as directed.

Care
Cut away the bloom stalk upon completion of flowering. No other pruning should be necessary. *H. orientalis* is generally considered free of insects and diseases.

Companion Planting and Design
Hyacinth has a pleasing look in garden settings when used in groups or as a border. When grown in the home, *H. orientalis* will reward you in early spring with its faithful bloom and fragrance. Try one or more inside by growing in hyacinth glasses—containers made especially for this purpose. They're fun to grow and anyone can do it. The stiff, formal appearance of the blooms lends them to formal plantings. Hyacinths are most showy in large drifts combined with other spring bulbs, flowering trees, and shrubs.

I Suggest
Start several bulbs of hyacinth indoors at different times during the fall. Hyacinths diminish in size of bloom from year to year, thus new plantings should be added to the garden to assure quality blooms.

There is nothing like the heady, perfumed fragrance of hyacinths in bloom. Some sources say that H. orientalis came to us through Europe from the Eastern Mediterranean during the early 1500s. Stunning in mass plantings, as an addition to a border, or as an indoor forced plant, all types and colors have a wonderful fragrance. Some of the unusual bloom colors, such as deep tangerine, mauve, and beet purple may be a little difficult to find. Blues, pinks, lavenders and whites are the colors of some hyacinth cultivars that are often used indoors and for garden plantings. H. orientalis albulus, the 'Roman Hyacinth', has white to blue fragrant blooms. Several stems arise from each bulb with open blooms.

Other Common Name
Dutch Hyacinth

Bloom Period and Seasonal Color
Late winter and spring blooms in white, pale yellow, pink, red, and blue to purple.

Mature Height × Spread
8 to 12 in. × 6 to 8 in.

Iris

Iris spp.

Iris is a long-time staple in Texas gardens. The rhizome type is hardy in all of Texas and the one grown most often. Bearded iris are classified miniature dwarfs, standard dwarfs, intermediate, miniature tall, and tall, with heights ranging from three to twenty-seven inches. While there are many beautiful hybridized varieties of iris on the market, be sure to ask your local garden center if the varieties you want will grow well in your landscape. Some varieties will die quickly in our warm Texas climate. Most iris are grown in Washington State and Colorado, and while there are many varieties adapted to Texas, there are many that are not. Obtain desired selections from local gardens and local garden club sales when possible.

Other Common Names
Bearded Iris, Flags

Bloom Period and Seasonal Color
Spring blooms in all colors.

Mature Height × Spread
3 in. to 4 ft. × 12 to 16 in.

When, Where, and How to Plant
According to The Texas Iris Society, the iris is so tough it can be dug, divided, and transplanted any time of the year. My wife and I set out the rhizomes and plant in the fall. Iris will grow in almost any type of soil, but for best results, plant in prepared beds. It needs a minimum of six hours of full sun per day. Incorporate approximately 3 in. of organic matter into the top 3 in. of your soil. Install rhizomes level with or about 1 in. below the soil surface and no deeper, firm the soil, water thoroughly, apply root stimulator according to label directions, and mulch with approximately 1 to 2 in. of bark mulch. Note: In relatively heavy soils, plant rhizomes at soil level and cover with an inch of mulch. Do not plant the iris too deeply; leave the upper rhizome showing, with soil firmed around it.

Growing Tips
As new growth begins in the springtime, fertilize with a premium-quality, long-lasting, slow-release rose fertilizer. Water thoroughly as needed. Keep soil moist but not wet.

Care
Do not prune back the blades or leaves severely. Iris needs to retain all its leaves as long as possible in order to manufacture the plant food that will be stored in underground structures for next year's blooms. Cut away spent bloom stalks after all blooms have opened and completed their show. Prune damaged or dead leaves as needed. Iris borers or grasshoppers may visit your planting. If the pests become a problem, inquire at your local retail garden center for best controls.

Companion Planting and Design
Smaller varieties may be used in mass plantings for borders or as groundcovers. Taller-growing varieties make excellent cut-flower plantings. Iris may be utilized in beds of cannas and daylilies or in stand-alone plantings. Iris are attractive as large massive drifts in lawns and borders.

I Suggest
Select the variety or varieties whose colors you like and plant where they can be seen. They are super in cut flower arrangements!

Narcissus
Narcissus spp. and hybrids

When, Where, and How to Plant

Plant narcissus in the fall in well-drained soils at locations receiving full sun or partial shade. Narcissus may be planted beneath deciduous trees as the trees are void of foliage and allow sun when the narcissus are productive. Avoid poorly drained soil or areas that are difficult to water. If the soil at your location does not drain properly, or if it is very hard and compact, add approximately 3 in. of organic matter to the top 3 in. of native soil. Plant bulbs at approximately twice the depth of their height in prepared beds. Firm the soil, water thoroughly, apply root stimulator according to label directions, and cover with 2 in. of bark mulch.

Growing Tips

Water as necessary to prevent soil dryness. Fertilize at planting time with approximately 1 teaspoon of premium-quality, slow-release rose fertilizer placed 1 in. below the individual bulb(s). Fertilize new growth from existing beds in the spring with the same fertilizer according to label directions.

Care

After blooming is complete cut away the bloom stalks. No other pruning should be necessary. Allow the leaves to remain on the plant until they turn yellow or brown. The leaves make plant food in the form of carbohydrates that is stored for next year's bloom. Snails may visit your narcissus planting. If slugs or snails become a problem, visit your local retail garden center for appropriate control measures. Watch for bulb rot in poorly drained locations.

Companion Planting and Design

Narcissus is pleasant to the eye and has a wonderful fragrance. Everyone who visits a home will enjoy the plantings near an entryway. Use narcissus as bedding or border plants, as well as in woodland plantings, rock gardens, and containers. Bulbs for naturalizing are usually offered at bargain prices in catalogs. Use in mass plantings in order to create a "knock your socks off" color effect in the springtime.

I Suggest

Use some members of the narcissus genus for indoor color and fragrance by forcing in containers.

Nothing says spring to Texas gardeners like narcissus. It's among the most popular of all bulb plants we grow. It is called jonquil, daffodil, or narcissus—all three names are correct. The group name is Narcissus, and jonquils and daffodils are both narcissus. Usually the name jonquil refers to the very small-blooming, almost grasslike, narrow-leafed plant. The names daffodil and narcissus are often used interchangeably. Whichever name you use, there are many different varieties. Not all varieties repeat flowering year after year in Texas where winters are mild. Some you may wish to try in a Texas garden are 'Lucifer', 'Carbineer', 'Ceylon', 'Rustom', 'Pasha', 'Mount Hood', 'Ice Follies', 'Peeping Tom', 'Golden Dawn', 'Cheerfulness', 'February Gold', 'Thalia', 'Pink Champion', 'Suzy', 'King Alfred', and 'Fortune'.

Other Common Names
Daffodil, Jonquil

Bloom Period and Seasonal Color
Late winter and spring blooms in yellow, gold, orange, white, red, and pink, plus bicolors.

Mature Height × Spread
3 to 18 in. × 6 to 8 in.

Spider Lily

Lycoris spp.

Spider lily, or magic lily, is known as the plant that seemingly comes from nowhere to make wonderful blooms in late summer and early fall. These flowers are often used around the bases of trees and in woodland settings where they do an outstanding job of providing color. They come into bloom during our long, hot, dry summers after a thoroughly drenching late-summer/fall rain. Spider lilies appear on graceful stems, totally void of foliage, thus the name surprise lily, or naked lady. L. radiata is coral colored with long upward curving stamens. 'Alba' has creamy white flowers and 'Carnea' flowers are tinted pink. L. squamigera is usually the hardiest variety and has funnel-shaped pink flowers.

Other Common Names
Resurrection Lily, Naked Lady, Surprise Lily

Bloom Period and Seasonal Color
Late summer and fall blooms in red, pink, white, and yellow.

Mature Height × Spread
1 to 2 ft. × 6 in.

When, Where, and How to Plant

Spider lilies are considered relatively unknown as far as bulbs are concerned, and they may be somewhat difficult to locate in the retail garden center. A better source may be a catalog, or a relative or neighbor who wishes to share some with you. Spider lilies tend to do their best in sandy loam soils, but if you have heavy clay, they should grow adequately with soil improvement. When planting in lawn areas, dig individual holes and set bulbs in the ground so the tops are almost even with the soil. Make sure the soil drains properly. For bed plantings, plant in improved soil beds. Incorporate 3 in. of organic matter into the top 3 in. of soil. Plant the bulbs at the same depth you would plant them in the lawn. Water thoroughly and add a root stimulator if desired, then mulch with about 2 in. of bark mulch.

Growing Tips

Water as necessary to maintain moist soil. If planted in beds, mulching will aid in conservation of soil moisture. Fertilize in the springtime with one application of premium-quality, long-lasting, slow-release rose fertilizer according to label directions.

Care

Prune off blooming stalks when flowering is complete. Slugs or snails may visit your planting. If they become a problem, consult your local retail center for the best control possibilities. Follow label directions when using any pest-control product.

Companion Planting and Design

Spider lilies work great naturalized in drifts if left undisturbed, so remember to avoid constant mowing around these areas. They also work well when grouped in beds, and they will multiply readily. These "surprise" bulbs are also attractive planted in groundcover beds, and in the groundcover they are protected from the lawnmower.

I Suggest

Making the effort to find and plant these bulbs because of their ease of care, colors, and "surprise" bloom times.

Tulip
Tulipa spp. and hybrids

When, Where, and How to Plant

Plant tulips in Texas in late fall/early winter. Pre-chill bulbs in the bottom of your refrigerator (nearly all varieties and types) for approximately six weeks before planting. Plant in well-drained soils in sunny locations. In clay soils that drain poorly, incorporate approximately 4 in. of organic matter into your existing soil. Plant bulbs 4 in. deep or at a depth two times their height in your prepared bed. Apply approximately 1/2 teaspoon of premium-quality, long-lasting, slow-release rose fertilizer 1 in. below the bulb and firm the soil. Water thoroughly after planting and mulch bare soil with approximately 2 in. of mulch.

Growing Tips

Water as necessary to maintain moist soil. Do not keep the soil wet, or allow it to become totally dry. Usually fertilizing is required only at planting time. For varieties that do repeat, fertilize once as new growth begins in the springtime with a premium-quality, long-lasting, slow-release rose fertilizer, according to label directions. Cut away bloom stalks once blooms are finished. No other pruning is normally necessary. Aphids, mice, rats, and other pests and organisms may visit your tulips. If they become a problem, check with a local retail garden center for the best control possibilities. Remember to read and follow label directions when using any gardening product.

Companion Planting and Design

The best shows of tulips are created when masses of single colors are used. This technique is often used in public plantings. When planting, try various patterns such as kidney, teardrop, zig-zag, and curved. In small-space areas, plant in planters. Spring annuals such as phlox, pansy, violas, sweet alyssum, and dianthus compliment tulips as well as extend the bloom season long after the bulbs have completed their show. Tulips mix well with other spring bulbs and spring-flowering trees and shrubs such as dogwood and azalea, spirea, quince, redbud, and forsythia. Tulips bring spring charm to rock gardens and garden paths.

I Suggest

In the spring, use cut tulips for indoor color.

When we think about spring-blooming bulbs in Texas, the first to come to mind is usually the tulip. Most Texas gardeners enjoy tulips, but because of the warm climate it's a challenge achieving reliable blooms year after year in most areas. In the cold Panhandle area, temperatures may be cold long enough to allow some tulips to re-bloom successfully. In the remainder of the state, the tulip's beauty may only be enjoyed during one springtime, with sporadic success in the following years. In order to ensure good shows of tulips year after year in Texas gardens, treat them as annuals and replant each year. There are many different types of tulips available, including Darwin hybrids, Parrot, Lily flowered, Fringed, Peony, Triumph, and many others. The best repeat-blooming tulips in Texas are classified as species tulips, such as T. clusiana, lady tulips, and Cretan tulips.

Bloom Period and Seasonal Color

Spring blooms in all colors except true blue.

Mature Height × Spread

12 to 40 in. × 8 to 10 in.

Grasses *for Texas*

We Texans spend more time, energy, effort, and money on our lawns than on any other single item in our home landscape. Lawns are very important to most of us, and we enjoy the special look and feel they bring to our home landscapes. Both lawn grasses and ornamental grasses are included in this chapter.

Multiple Choices

The lawn grass grown by most Texans (especially if they have a full-sun location where children run and play) is Bermudagrass, *Cynodon dactylon*. Centipedegrass, *Eremochloa ophiuroides*, is a great turfgrass for the acid soils of eastern Texas, but will not grow well in the highly alkaline soils often found in the western half of our state. While annual ryegrass, *Lolium multiflorum*, can be planted on bare soil, it is also used in Texas as a temporary cover during our cold season to allow the appearance of green grass on a year-round basis. This is called overseeding. St. Augustinegrass, *Stenotaphrum secundatum*, is known as the turfgrass that will grow in shaded areas—although not in complete shade. For this reason a shade-loving groundcover such as liriope or mondo grass may be used. Tall fescue, *Festuca arundinacea*, is a turfgrass that has recently been promoted in Texas as an alternative to St. Augustine. Tall fescues are primarily northern, cool-season grasses. A few, more heat-tolerant varieties have proved acceptable under close management in the clay soils of Texas. Texans should take a closer look at zoysiagrass, *Zoysia japonica*, because there are some newer varieties that show good results. Look for them at your local garden center or turf grass retailer.

Ornamental grasses may be added throughout your home landscape. In simple mass plantings or in combination with other ornamentals, annuals, perennials, and shrubs, ornamental grass is a valuable, functional plant. It adds interest and beauty to a landscape. There are many different types of ornamental grasses. Maidengrass, *Miscanthus sinensis*, is an ornamental bunch grass often seen growing in striking clumps at the Texas state fair. The white-plumed pampas grass, *Cortaderia selloana*, may very well be the

Grasses in Autumn

Zoysiagrass

oldest, ornamental, clumping grass used in Texas. There is also a pink-plumed variety named Rubra. Fountain grass, *Pennisetum alopecuroides*, is a group of grasses best known as purple fountain grass.

Lawn History, Function, and Tips

Since early American history, lawns were valued and prized as an essential part of the landscape. Thomas Jefferson's homesite, Monticello, is an example of an early lawn that was prized for its beauty. Lawns serve as carpets in our landscapes. Lawns eliminate dust and mud. They help cool the air, hold the soil, and prevent erosion. We lump our lawn grasses into two basic groups, warm-season and cool-season. The only cool-season grass that is reasonably adaptable in most of Texas is some varieties of tall fescue. One may be able to grow Kentucky bluegrass, *Poa pratensis*, under close irrigation in the Panhandle, but this is the only area it could possibly thrive during Texas summers.

When overseeding existing warm-season grasses, we generally use annual ryegrass. However, perennial ryegrass, *Lolium perenne*, may also be planted in late summer to early fall to provide a green lawn through the entire cool/winter season. Most of our grasses are non-native except for currently available selections of buffalograss. You can start a lawn from seed, plugs, sodding, or sprigs, or you may have it hydro-mulched. Don't try starting seeds too early in the springtime when the soil is still too cool for the warm-season, southern lawn grasses. These seeds require a warm soil to germinate properly. Certain parts of the state are better adapted to different lawn grasses than others. Be sure to match your grass selection to your soil type and zone, making sure to understand the care necessary to maintain your new lawn.

Turf is a mat of grass held together by its mat of roots. Some turfgrass, such as the very fine blade hybrid Bermudagrass varieties, are considered high maintenance, while others, such as common Bermuda and centipede, may prove easier to maintain. Lawn and ornamental grasses are available at nurseries and garden centers. Turfgrasses are also sold at specialty retailers.

Caring for Your Lawn

The easiest way to avoid weed problems in your home lawn is to grow a healthy thick turf. Here's one way to accomplish this:

Approximately two to three weeks after the last killing frost in your area, apply your favorite 3:1:2 ratio, long-lasting lawn fertilizer. Reapply approximately every eight weeks through the growing season

Bermudagrass

and once in the fall. The fall application is the single most important application of the year. Don't miss it! Always water thoroughly after applying any fertilizer. Examples of 3:1:2 ratio lawn fertilizer are 21-7-14, 19-5-9, 18-6-12, 15-5-10, and 12-4-8. Water only when needed. Do not set your lawn on a watering schedule. If grass blades are rolling inward from their sides, turning gray-green instead of the normal green, or if the grass lays flat and won't spring back after being walked on, give your lawn a long, deep, drink to a soil depth of six to eight inches. Remove slices of your soil with a narrow bladed shovel to check moisture penetration depth. Mow often enough to remove no more than a third of the grass-blade height every time you mow. A yearly or biannual lawn aeration is especially good for heavy soils. Follow these suggestions for a nice, thick, Texas lawn to enjoy in your bare feet!

If weeds insist on invading your lawn after the above program has been followed for two seasons, then other measures may be taken. The first of these involves using a group of products called pre-emergents. Pre-emergents or weed preventers deny weeds the opportunity to establish themselves in your lawn. The two weed classifications are grassy and broadleaf. Crabgrass and grass burs are grassy weeds commonly found in Texas. Dandelion and chickweed are examples of broadleaf weeds. Henbit and burclover are also broadleaf weeds. Rule of thumb: If it "walks, talks, and acts" like a grass, it's a grassy weed—if it doesn't, it's a broadleaf weed. Like other plants, weeds are classified as annual or perennial. Crabgrass and sandburs are annuals as well as henbit and burclover. Johnsongrass and dallisgrass are perennials.

Most weedy lawn pests are warm-season weeds, but henbit is a cool-season weed, while annual bluegrass is a cool-season grassy pest. Selected pre-emergents or weed preventers will prevent annual broadleaf as well as annual grassy weeds. Check the labels for effectiveness on perennials of either type.

Timing is important when using a pre-emergent to prevent weeds. If applied after weeds are up and growing, it is of little value. To prevent most warm-season weeds, apply approximately two weeks before the last average killing frost or freeze in your area. If spring comes early, you may need to apply the product early. To prevent fall and winter weeds, apply six weeks before the first average killing frost.

If you follow the previously outlined program and suggestions and still have a few tough, pesky perennial lawn weeds, you may want to try a different group of products classified as post-emergent. Most liquids can be spot-applied on troubled lawn areas. Certainly, if you like the looks of some weeds in your lawn (beauty is, after all, in the eye of

Purple Fountain Grass

the beholder) it's your choice whether to remove them or not. See the Appendix for some of the more common problems you may experience with your lawn.

For advice on how to combat diseases and pests, read the care and maintenance sections for the grasses in this chapter. And as always, you may contact me or consult garden center personnel for any additional help you may need.

Bermudagrass
Cynodon dactylon

Used on lawns since the 1800s, Bermudagrass is considered the grass of Texas because it will grow in virtually every area of the state. Bermudagrass grows best in full sun areas—it will not tolerate heavy shade. Grown in high traffic areas such as front lawns, this child-friendly grass spreads by above ground runners and below ground rhizomes. It is the grass used on all athletic turfs and the grass of choice for schools and commercial uses. Some hybrid Bermudagrasses include Uganda, Bayshore, Royal Cape, U-3, Tiffine, Sunturf, Tiflawn, Tifgreen Texturf, Tifway, Toughcoat, Santa Ana, Midway, and Tifwad. The fine textured hybrids form a thick turf and are considered high maintainance.

Color and Texture
Bluegreen with fine texture.

Mowing Height
1 to 1^1/$_2$ in., and 2 in. or taller in mid summer.

When, Where, and How to Plant
Plant Bermudagrass in spring when nighttime temperatures have been consistently above 70 degrees Fahrenheit for two weeks. Plant sod as soon as it is available at local retailers. Plant Bermudagrass in spring, summer, and early fall. To plant sod, measure the area to be planted in square yards. Lightly till the soil, provide drainage, rake, and remove any rocks or debris. Apply a lawn-starter granular fertilizer. Lay the sod with edges flush and water thoroughly. Maintain moist conditions, gradually reducing watering as planting becomes established. To plant seed, measure the area in square feet. Purchase 1 to 1^1/$_2$ lb. per 1000 sq. ft. of hulled seed. Till the area and correct any drainage problems. Sow half the seed in one direction and half at a 90 degree angle to that. No mulching is necessary. Irrigate and maintain moist soil throughout the establishment period. After the first mowing, begin regular fertilizing with 3:1:2 ratio lawn fertilizer. Hybrid Bermudas cannot be seeded and must be established from sod or turf.

Growing Tips
Water to a minimum soil depth of six to eight inches. Begin fertilizing in spring after new growth emerges or approximately six weeks after the last frost in your area. Reapply long-lasting, slow-release 3:1:2 ratio fertilizers about every ten weeks during the growing season, and once again in the fall.

Care
Mow with a sharp-bladed mower. Rotary mowers are acceptable. Bermudagrass may be attacked by brown patch, dollar spot, leaf spots, and other diseases, as well as by grubs, Bermuda mite, sod webworms, army worms, and other insects. Visit your local garden center for controls.

Companion Planting and Design
Use it in sunny landscape areas where you wish to establish a warm-season, tough turfgrass lawn that is sun and wear tolerant. There is no companion planting with Bermudagrass—Bermudagrass spreads by underground runners and may be invasive in neighboring garden beds.

I Suggest
I stay away from the very fine-bladed hybrid varieties. The maintenance required is too intense.

Blue Fescue
Festuca glauca

When, Where, and How to Plant
Plant blue fescue any time of the year. The best planting time is very early spring; second-best time is very early fall. Plant in well-drained, full sun locations. It even grows well in clay soils or sandy soils as long as it is properly drained. Do not plant in heavily shaded areas. Not only does it have a very interesting blue/gray color, but the buff-colored bloom stalks add interest to the landscape. Blue fescue will tolerate many different types of soils. In order to achieve maximum growth, improve the soil slightly. Till approximately 2 in. of organic matter into the top 6 in. of soil. Remove the plants from their containers and plant in individual planting holes no deeper than originally grown in the containers. Backfill with the loose soil mix, water thoroughly, apply root stimulator, and mulch bare soil with 3 in. of bark mulch.

Growing Tips
Water only as necessary to prevent total soil dryness. Fertilize a maximum of twice a year with a long-lasting, granular fertilizer in a 3:1:2 ratio. Examples of this are 15-5-10, 21-7-14, and 18-6-12. Water thoroughly after each application. Fertilize no more than once in early spring and once in early fall.

Care
No pruning is required. In fact, heavy pruning will damage, disturb, or destroy the ornamental shape. Blue fescue has no serious insect or disease problems.

Companion Planting and Design
Blue fescue is wonderful in rock gardens, and it will blend well with Xeriscape plantings where a naturalized look is desired. Not only does blue fescue do well when planted in beds, it also works in large containers. When grown in containers, it is mobile and can be moved on decks or any other places where you want to create a special effect.

I Suggest
Utilize this interesting ornamental grass in southwestern theme gardens or plantings.

Blue fescue makes a very interesting clump planting in a hot, dry location. It's also ideal for a border or mass effect, and is great as an edging plant. Blue fescue will take a small amount of shade, but it does prefer full sun. Poorly drained or wet soil is the worst problem for blue fescue. Do not put blue fescue in areas that have sprinkler systems and are watered frequently, but it's an otherwise tough, durable plant that will take heat and drought. In addition to the standard blue fescue, you may want to try Elijah Blue.

Other Common Name
Ornamental Fescue

Bloom Period and Seasonal Color
Early summer spikes in buff.

Mature Height × Spread
10 to 12 in. × 12 to 16 in.

Centipedegrass
Eremochloa ophiuroides

When looking for an alternative grass to plant in the acid soils of Texas, centipedegrass may work well for you. Centipede is not for alkaline soils and is best adapted to the eastern third of Texas. It's also not recommended for alkaline soils due to severe chronic iron chloris problems. With the proper location, centipedegrass makes a gorgeous, thick, and relatively low-maintenance turf. If you do live in one of these areas, I strongly suggest that you investigate growing centipedegrass. It's a warm-season perennial grass that is spread by above-ground stolens or runners and by seeding. While centipedegrass needs less maintenance than St. Augustine or Bermuda, it does require some upkeep. Perhaps it should be called "reduced-maintenance" rather than "low-maintenance."

Color and Texture
Bright yellow-green with medium texture.

Mowing Height
2 to 3 in. or taller in mid summer.

When, Where, and How to Plant
Establish from seed in early spring after soil and air temperatures warm consistently to 70 degrees Fahrenheit for a minimum of two weeks. Plant centipedegrass in full sun and in areas with good soil drainage. Centipedegrass will exist in lightly or filtered shaded areas, such as beneath tall pine. Don't plant in heavy shade. Centipedegrass is slow to establish from seed as it is erratic in germination, germinating over a long period of time. To plant from seed, till the area, correct drainage if needed, and rake to remove any rocks or other debris. Sow seeds at $^1/_2$ to 2 lb. per 1000 sq. ft. Maintain moisture at the soil level. After establishment and first mowing, water as needed to prevent wilting. To plant sod prepare soil as for seed. Lay sod end-to-end and side-to-side for an instant lawn. Or cut into 6 × 6 in. squares and plant in a 12 in. checkerboard pattern. Maintain moisture to prevent wilting.

Growing Tips
Water to a soil depth minimum of 6 to 8 in. Centipedegrass needs water from time to time during the winter. Sufficient water is required through our blazing July and August temperatures. Specialty centipedegrass lawn fertilizer (15:0:15) is available, which includes iron—necessary to avoid yellowing. Apply as growth begins in spring, twelve weeks later, and once during the fall. If soil tests indicate a lack of phosphorous, 15:5:10 in most cases will also work well. Centipede lawns are sensitive to over fertilization, which may reduce growth and can cause death of the grass.

Care
Mow once per week to maintain an attractive lawn. Centipedegrass is relatively free of pests, but if insects or diseases such as brown patch happen to invade, visit your local retail garden center for control options.

Companion Planting and Design
Centipedegrass should not be used in conjunction with Bermuda or St. Augustine lawns. It should be utilized as a stand-alone grass. Use it to establish any lawn design desired in acidic soils.

I Suggest
Oaklawn is our oldest popular selection. Centipedegrass will not turn as dark green as Bermuda and St. Augustine.

Fountain Grass
Pennisetum alopecuroides

When, Where, and How to Plant

Plant purple, or any other fountain grass in the springtime, after all danger of frost has passed. Plant in a full sun location in improved soil. Till 3 to 4 in. of organic matter into the top 4 in. of your soil. Remove plants from containers, insert them into holes that are no deeper than rootball depth, and backfill with improved soil mix. Water thoroughly and apply root stimulator according to label directions. After the planting is finished, mulch bare soil with about 3 in. of bark mulch. When planting in large containers, use a light-weight potting soil and plant at same depth as stated above.

Growing Tips

Water as necessary to prevent complete soil dryness. While this plant is quite drought tolerant, don't let it go bone dry in mid-July or August. Maintain a 3-in. depth of bark mulch through the entire growing season, especially in July and August. Fertilize with your favorite lawn fertilizer. Those that work well are 15:5:10, 18:6:12, and 21:7:14 slow-release types. Your first application can be two weeks after your initial planting, a second application ten weeks later, and possibly a third early in the fall.

Care

Pruning is not necessary unless you wish to remove any wind- or storm-damaged parts or want to use plumage for indoor decoration. No serious pests affect fountain grass, with the exception of an occasional grasshopper that may stop by for a bite.

Companion Planting and Design

Use in smaller areas for spot or clump-type plant-ings, and accents. It may create a large screen for dividing different areas of your color garden. I like to use it in large containers on the deck in full sun. Ideal for detail garden design, or accents in rock or water gardens.

I Suggest

If you would like some purple in your containers or landscape, try a planting of purple fountain grass.

Fountain grass is sometimes called purple fountain grass because of its purple color. It is a neat, upright, clump-type, grass-like foliage that has a reddish-brown coloring on its outside edge and red rose flower spikes. The spikes may grow as tall as four feet and will decorate the plant through the entire summer— absolutely gorgeous for use in your landscape. Do not plant in heavily shaded areas. These plants are quite drought tolerant and may be used in areas where you rarely have a chance to water. 'Little Bunny' is a dwarf variety that grows only about twelve inches high and is hardy in Zone 7 southward through Zone 9. The dwarf form 'Hamelin' has a long bloom season and is excellent for small areas and containers.

Bloom Period and Seasonal Color
Summer and fall spikes to 4 ft. in red rose.

Mature Height × Spread
10 in. to 3 ft. × 1 to 2 ft.

Maidengrass
Miscanthus sinensis

Maidengrass is an ornamental, perennial, clump-forming grass, with green to silvery to white patterns of color in upright, long, grass-type foliage. In the fall, the foliage may be golden bronze, and the leaves fan-shaped. You might even notice the blossoms have changed to a silvery color. Frost or freeze on the foliage of miscanthus *in wintertime can be quite lovely. I use maidengrass around the southwest end of the house and in our rock garden planting. Our prevailing southwesterly breezes create motion in the plumes of blooms as well as in the grass blades themselves. Maidengrass is a wonderful addition to the home landscape. It is very easy to grow and maintain—virtually trouble-free. Selections include 'Strictus', which has a narrow growth habit for small detailed areas, 'Yaku Jima', a dwarf form ideal for Japanese gardens and containers, and 'Silberfeder', the silver feather grass.*

Other Common Names
Japanese Silver Grass, Zebra Grass

Bloom Period and Seasonal Color
Summer to fall with light colored plumes and golden bronze to tan fall foliage.

Mature Height × Spread
2 to 10 ft. × 8 ft.

When, Where, and How to Plant
Plant maidengrass in the early spring after all danger of frost has passed. Do not plant in heavily shaded areas or where soil drainage is poor. Miscanthus does best in well-prepared soil. With a digging fork or shovel, till or blend approximately 4 to 6 in. of high-quality organic matter into the top 6 in. of soil. Remove plants from containers, dig individual planting holes no deeper than the top of the soilball, install plants in these new homes, and backfill with the loose soil mix. Water thoroughly, apply root stimulator, and mulch all bare soil with about 3 in. of bark mulch. If planting in containers, use a premium-quality, lightweight potting soil and plant at the same depth as stated above.

Growing Tips
Water sufficiently to prevent soil dryness. Maintaining a thick layer of mulch through the entire growing season will greatly conserve your soil moisture, reducing the number of times you must water. Fertilize in the spring as new growth begins, again ten weeks later, once again ten weeks after that, and then again in the fall. Use a premium-quality 15-5-10, 18-6-12, or 21-7-14 fertilizer according to label directions.

Care
Pruning once a year in the very early spring is desirable. Cut the top back to about 6 in. from the ground to remove all the dead growth. No insects or diseases are known to cause problems for miscanthus.

Companion Planting and Design
I enjoy planting it in pockets among our existing landscape plants. Native Texas plants used in combination with miscanthus create interesting effects. Maidengrass can be outstanding in the landscape and may be used in yard beds. I would not use it near entryways or walkways, as it may overpower them. Plant in large containers and areas in rock gardens, courtyard, and patio designs.

I Suggest
Try the variety called zebra grass, 'Zebrinus', for something different. While there are other green and white plants available, none have zebra grass's interesting white markings across the leaves.

Pampas Grass
Cortaderia selloana

When, Where, and How to Plant

Plant pampas grass in early spring. It tolerates all types of growing conditions except heavily shaded or damp areas, and it tolerates most soils except for those that are waterlogged or poorly drained. To plant pampas grass in beds, place the beds away from your home and make them at least 5 ft. wide. Till in 5 in. of high-quality organic matter. For spot plantings, loosen the soil in an area about 3 times the width of the original container. Dig the hole only as deep as the soilball and set the plants in the soil no deeper than the soilball. Backfill with loose soil or improved soil mix. Water thoroughly, apply root stimulator, and mulch heavily with about 4 in. of bark mulch on all bare soil.

Growing Tips

Water sufficiently to prevent soil dryness. For an aggressive-growing pampas grass, fertilize with a long-lasting lawn fertilizer (such as 19-5-9, 21-7-14, or 15-5-10). Apply in early spring as new growth begins, again ten weeks later, and then again in another ten weeks. Fertilize one time in the fall.

Care

You may want to prune pampas grass to remove winter damage. Cut pampas grass to about 12 in. in height early in the spring or very late winter—just as new growth is beginning. This may be done with a small hand pruner or a lopper, but I have seen some folks use a very small chain saw! In most areas of Texas, pampas grass has no serious diseases or insect pests.

Companion Planting and Design

Create a secluded corner in your landscape and pampas grass will give you screening on any side you wish, giving you a private area in which to place a bench, table and chairs, or swing. Treat pampas grass as a secondary plant, not as a major or key visual point. It is most attractive in bloom. It could have winter kill and may not regain its beauty until late summer and fall, depending on the zone you live in.

I Suggest

For a drought tolerant ornamental bunch grass, this family from the pampas of South America is hard to beat. Use them in areas away from pedestrian traffic.

Pampas grass is the oldest, most frequently used ornamental grass in Texas. It has been used for decades in our gardens, as well as for commercial applications. It makes a great privacy screen—but do not plant near the end of your driveway because it may block your view. If you decide to plant near your sidewalk or where you walk frequently, keep in mind that the grass is rather sharp, with razor-like margins. Pampas makes an interesting specimen plant, and it is great for screening out noise and wind. Plant it virtually anywhere in your landscape where you have full sun. 'Pumila', a dwarf pampas grass, grows to about 3 feet. 'Monvin' grows to only four feet. 'Violacea' has pinkish flower plumes in the fall.

Bloom Period and Seasonal Color
Late summer and fall blooms in white and pink.

Mature Height × Spread
6 to 10 ft. × 13 ft.

Ryegrass
Lolium spp.

Ryegrass is overseeded with lawngrasses such as St. Augustine, Bermuda, zoysiagrass, and centipede to maintain a year-round green appearance. The annual ryegrass greens the existing lawn as the permanent grass goes dormant, then dies out with the heat of late spring as the permanent grass begins to green. An exception to this is the perennial ryegrass, Lolium perenne, which may be used successfully year-round in the panhandle area when irrigated—but is a challenge. For a finer-bladed grass with less frequent mowing, perennial ryegrass is for you. Perennial ryegrass is more costly to establish, but the difference in price may be worth it. Perennial ryegrass is commonly used as an annual throughout the remaining portion of Texas. Both types of ryegrass tend to fizzle out as temperatures rise in the spring and summer.

Color and Texture
Medium to dark green with medium texture.

Mowing Height
2 to 2¹/₂ in.

When, Where, and How to Plant
Plant six to eight weeks before the first killing frost. To establish ryegrass for the winter, it is important that you plant early—while the weather is still warm. Ryegrass has difficulty germinating and establishing after cold weather arrives. It establishes well in either acid or alkaline soils, clay or sand. To help establish ryegrass, mow your permanent grass low to the ground at the time of planting. Use 5 to 8 lb. of current-season seeds per 1000 sq. ft. Sow the seeds in two directions, with the second direction at a ninety-degree angle to the first. Water frequently to maintain a moist soil at ground level. After it's established, reduce the watering frequency. If desired, apply a lawn-starting fertilizer at the time of seed sowing. Ryegrass may be seeded on bare soil and is often seeded on unestablished sites to avoid erosion and to establish a quick winter cover.

Growing Tips
To prevent drying and wilting, water as necessary throughout the entire season. Approximately four weeks after first mowing, apply a 3:1:2 long-lasting lawn fertilizer (such as 15-5-10, 21-7-14, or 18-6-12). Apply throughout the growing season—after establishment, mid-season, and then in late winter/early spring. You may choose not to fertilize, if the grass is healthy and growing well.

Care
In order to maintain a manicured lawn, mowing is required throughout the fall, winter, and spring. Make sure that your mower has a sharp blade. Brown patch, leaf spot, and rust may appear on ryegrass. If these diseases become a problem, visit your local garden center for controls.

Companion Planting and Design
Overseed on lawn grasses such as St. Augustine, bermuda, zoysia and centipede. Annual, winter ryegrass with its bright green ushers in the spring season, complementing spring's flowering trees, shrubs, and flowers. Deciduous shade trees are void of foliage in winter, allowing sun; thus, ryegrass does well beneath deciduous trees.

I Suggest
To establish a green lawn for the winter, plant at the proper time. Any variety or type will do the job, but always plant seeds packaged for the current season.

St. Augustinegrass
Stenotaphrum secundatum

When, Where, and How to Plant
Plant St. Augustine in the springtime after all danger of frost is past. To do well, it needs a minimum of four hours of full sun per day, or eight hours of mixed sun and shade. Plant St. Augustine from plugs, blocks, sprigs, or sod. St. Augustine cannot be established by seeding. For an instant lawn, plant solid over the entire area. Or cut up in 6 in. square blocks and plant in a checkerboard pattern, with blocks approximately 6 in. apart. This method will establish a complete lawn in one growing season. Make sure the grade is properly graded so there will be no low areas with standing water. Lightly till the area and rake. Water often during establishment to prevent wilting, then reduce watering frequency.

Growing Tips
Water as needed to avoid prolonged and severe wilt. Fertilize in the springtime as new growth begins or six weeks after the last frost in your area. The 3:1:2 ratio lawn fertilizers often recommended for warm-season grasses work well with St. Augustine. Among these fertilizers are 18-6-12, 19-5-9, 21-7-14, and 15-5-10. Use a long-lasting fertilizer following directions.

Care
St. Augustinegrass is susceptible to brown patch, leaf spot, and gray leaf spot. It's sometimes visited by grubs, chinch bugs, and other unwanted pests. If problems persist, check with local retailers for available methods of control. If the St. Augustine decline (SAD) virus invades your lawn, replant with the virus resistant Raleigh cultivar.

Companion Planting and Design
There are no companions for St. Augustinegrass. It will crowd out Bermuda as well as other grasses. Use as a stand-alone in any type of design desired.

I Suggest
St. Augustinegrass is best utilized for the home-owner wanting a thick lush lawn, but it will not tolerate high traffic areas such as enclosed yards with dogs or pathways. I do not recommend it in large areas due to the high maintenance needed, including the cost of watering, fertilizing, mowing, and insect and disease control.

My Granddad Miller, a long-time dry land cotton and grain farmer from Indian Creek, Texas, said that once he got his St. Augustinegrass established it didn't need any more care than Bermudagrass. St. Augustinegrass has been used since the 1700s in all areas of the southeast and southwest, in Bermuda, and as far south as New Zealand. While it is still generally considered high maintenance, it's a wonderful barefoot grass and great for lying beneath a shade tree. Because St. Augustinegrass doesn't have underground runners or rhizomes like Bermudagrass, it's relatively easy to prevent intrusion into flowerbeds.

Color and Texture
Dark green with coarse leaves.

Mowing Height
2 in. or more in mid summer.

Tall Fescue
Festuca arundinacea

For generations, tall fescue grass has been used success-fully in northern states and in the transitional zone that includes the northern part of Texas. It is utilized as a substitute for shade-tolerant grasses such as St. Augustine and may adapt to heavier soils in northern Texas. Tall fescue requires different management practices than St. Augustine. Do not fertilize during the summer, plant in early fall, and be prepared to sow additional seed each fall. Look for low-growing, heat- and drought-tolerant, disease-resistant, dwarf, turf-type fescue grasses. Do not use pasture types of fescue for lawns. Since their introduc-tion, the tall fescue grasses have been the focus of an active program to breed new varieties that are more heat toler-ant for Southern lawns. It may sound a bit confusing, but now there are "dwarf" tall fescues on the market.

Color and Texture
Dark green with coarse to medium texture.

Mowing Height
2 to 3 in., or taller in mid summer.

When, Where, and How to Plant
Plant tall fescue in the fall. In order for tall fescue to do reasonably well, it usually needs 4 hours of full sun or eight hours of 50 percent sun, 50 percent shade. If all the trees in your yard are deciduous (and their leaves fall), there will be adequate sun-light for fescue. It should continue to do well through the fall and early spring before the trees put out leaves. After your trees put on a new set of leaves, your fescue may begin to thin due to lack of sunlight, but the thinning will probably be more due to the increase of late spring and summer heat. Make sure your area has adequate sunlight prior to planting. Plant tall fescue from seed in well-pre-pared seedbeds. Rototill the area 3 to 4 in. deep. Handrake, removing rocks and debris. Use 6 to 8 lbs. of seed per 1000 sq. ft. Sow half the seed in a north/south direction, the other half in an east/west direction. Water thoroughly and maintain moist soil on the top level. After establishment, watering frequency may be reduced.

Growing Tips
Water as needed to prevent wilting. Fertilize three times during the growing season: once in the early fall, once in late fall/early winter, and once again in late winter/early spring. Apply long-lasting, slow-release fertilizer (such as a 15-5-10, 19-5-9, 18-6-12, or 21-7-14). Water thoroughly after every application.

Care
Tall fescue lawns may have unwelcome visits from fusarium blight, leaf spot, or even brown patch. Insects such as army worms, cutworms, and white grubs may visit as well. Visit your local retail garden center for controls. Tall fescue lawns may thin out in the dry summer conditions common to Texas. To ensure a thicker lawn, apply extra seeds each fall.

Companion Planting and Design
Tall fescue grasses should be used as stand-alone pure plantings. Tall fescue does demand frequent summer watering and for this reason is usually recommended for smaller shaded lawn areas with automatic sprinklers.

I Suggest
A trial planting one season will help to determine if you like its looks year-round.

Zoysiagrass
Zoysia japonica

When, Where, and How to Plant
Plant, or sod zoysiagrass in early spring after all danger of frost has passed and the soil has warmed slightly. Do not plant in heavily shaded areas, locations that are difficult to water, or poorly drained sites. Till 3 to 4 in. deep and make sure the grade drains properly. Rake to remove rocks, sticks, or other debris, and apply a starter fertilizer according to label directions. Install 2 × 2 in. plugs set on 1 ft. centers in a checkerboard style pattern, or place solid sod for an immediate lawn. Zoysia is not seeded.

Growing Tips
Water often enough to prevent wilting. Fertilize once in the springtime as new growth begins and once in the fall using a 15-5-10, 21-7-14, 19-5-9, 18-6-12, or other 3-1-2 ratio lawn fertilizer.

Care
While zoysiagrass grows significantly more slowly than Bermudagrass, it is recommended that it be mowed almost as often to maintain an even turf and to avoid the scalped look. Zoysiagrass is relatively free of insects but may be visited by the common white grub. Brown patch, rust, and leaf spot may visit zoysia, but it usually recovers quickly if proper environmental conditions are established. If these pests or diseases persist, consult your local retailer for controls. Some zoysias are considered high maintainance due to their thick, dense turf, which require dethatching yearly after establishment. A reel mower is best for maintaining an even cut. Zoysia is slow growing, slow to establish, and demands routine watering and fertilization.

Companion Planting and Design
There are no companions to plant with zoysiagrass—the most elite of all southern grasses. Zoysiagrass is recommended for small, detailed garden areas such as Japanese gardens or small courtyards and lawns.

I Suggest
Visit plantings of this pretty grass in real life situations before deciding if this is the grass for you. Although a more expensive initial investment than most other grasses, it is one of the best looking available and lower in water use than St. Augustine.

Zoysia is a beautiful grass that tolerates shade. It's considered exceptionally cold tolerant—more so than other grass species normally grown in Texas. Meyer is an improved strain of the original parentage and has been grown in the United States since the 1940s. It is very slow to establish. If planted in a clean bed where no weeds and grass are growing, 2 × 2 in. plugs placed in a twelve-inch checkerboard pattern may take as long as two years to cover the area. You may choose to put in solid sod on a clean prepared seedbed. Most available varieties include El Toro, Meyer, 'Cavalier', and Emerald. Palasades and Jamur are two of the most preferred but are not always available.

Other Common Names
Korean Lawn Grass, Japanese Lawn Grass

Color and Texture
Dark green with very fine texture.

Mowing Height
1/2 to 1 in. or taller in mid summer.

Groundcovers *for Texas*

Groundcover is the name of the plant group that includes vining and clumping plants, and extremely low-growing plants or dwarf plants. When combined these create a groundcover effect.

Facing the Facts

I frequently receive calls to my radio show from home gardeners who are facing the fact that they can't grow turfgrass under their shade trees. Most grasses considered shade tolerant actually need four hours of full sun per day or eight hours of 50 percent mixed sun and shade. When I suggest that these gardeners remove some trees, I usually hear squeals of protest. I don't like to remove trees either. But there is another solution: groundcovers.

Periwinkle

Groundcovers or groundcover-type plants—creepers, vines, prostrate shrubs, low-growing shrubs, and dwarf shrubs—allow home gardeners to have something green growing under their wonderful, cooling, shade trees. Keep in mind that these plants do not tolerate the foot traffic that is tolerated by turfgrass. However, with a little ingenuity, wonderful pathways can be made through groundcovers. Also, not all groundcovers will grow in heavily shaded areas; some require full sun. Groundcovers are perfect for very steep areas or other "no mow" areas. Look for plants that can weep down the slopes, holding the soil together along with providing an attractive look. In a practical sense, groundcovers reduce maintenance in hard-to-maintain areas in the landscape, such as areas between the drive and house—eliminating having to mow and edge turf. Design-wise, groundcovers can be a unifying element, tying plant groupings together, as well as providing interest and accents of texture, color, form, contrast, and pattern in the garden design. For example, groundcover areas serve as a welcome relief and contrast from often harsh, boring, surfaced areas. Pockets of groundcovers in gravel walk areas can add interest of color, form, and texture.

This chapter covers twelve groundcovers—most of which are commonly used in Texas. For something a bit more unusual, review the segments on sedum, *Sedum* spp., and santolina, *Santolina chamaecyparissus*. Though a bit more difficult to locate than the rest, sedum's and santolina's beauty and versatility in the home landscape are worth the effort.

When choosing groundcovers, it is helpful to first visit several nurseries to inspect groundcover varieties. When choosing one for your landscape, ask questions like: Will this grow in sun? Will it grow in full shade? Is it winter hardy in my area?

Prepare the soil by tilling the area. The planting area must be totally weed and grass free prior to planting. If it is poorly drained or lacks nutrition, add organic matter and slow-release fertilizer. There are materials called erosion mats that can be placed on top of prepared beds to hold the soil in place until your groundcover becomes established. Groundcovers and fertilizers may all be found at your local nursery, along with the assistance of trained professionals.

Non-shrub groundcovers will usually achieve total coverage of an area two seasons after planting from four inch containers on twelve inch centers. The more aggressive plants may accomplish total coverage in one season if planted early in the spring and provided with proper care.

Fertilization helps to encourage the spreading of groundcovers. Begin to apply 18-6-12 or any other slow-release 3:1:2 ratio lawn fertilizer approximately six weeks after planting or as new growth begins. Apply at the same rate as used for fertilizing lawns. Always read and follow label directions, and water thoroughly after each application. You may apply fertilizer to established plantings as new spring growth begins, and reapply each time your lawn is fertilized. Water your groundcover plantings deeply and thoroughly as needed.

Controlling weeds is also important to the successful establishment of groundcover plantings and is especially true for recently planted areas. Mulching with bark will help, but hand-to-hand combat/weeding may be needed to remove persistent weedy pests. Pre-emergents for preventing weeds are available at local nurseries. Remember, always read and follow label directions.

Gray Santolina

Ajuga
Ajuga reptans

Ajuga is a groundcover that grows in all Texas zones, but I recommend you test drive it first in a small area before planting large areas. An excellent addition for rock gardens, ajuga should receive morning sun and shade from the hot western afternoon summer sun. Also known as carpet bugle and bugleweed, ajuga performs well in hanging baskets—especially during its spring blooming period. Look for a possible decline in the tough months of July and August. And finally, wherever you place ajuga, make sure that the soil drains well.

Other Common Name
Carpet Bugle

Bloom Period and Seasonal Color
Spring blooms in white, blue, and rose.

Mature Height and Spread
3 to 8 in. × 1 1/2 to 2 ft.

When, Where, and How to Plant
Plant container-grown ajuga in a well-prepared bed of loam or clay-type soil. Sandy soils are easily improved with lots of organic matter. In clay soil, add approximately 2 in. of high-quality organic matter and blend with the top 2 in. of the existing soil. After beds are completed, plant ajuga at the same level it was grown in the containers. Water thoroughly, apply root stimulator, and cover bare soil with approximately 2 in. of bark mulch. Make sure the soil in which you plant ajuga drains well.

Growing Tips
Water as necessary to maintain a moist soil. Do not keep the soil wet nor allow it to go totally dry. Wet soils can induce rot and other diseases. Fertilize in the springtime with a slow-release rose fertilizer. For maximum benefit, fertilize approximately three times during the growing season. Water thoroughly after every application.

Care
Ajuga normally does not require pruning. Spider mites may visit in hot, dry weather. Wilt disease may occur, usually appearing in the heat of summer and associated with erratic watering. A fungicide should be applied to the total planting when first signs of wilt occur. Consult your local garden center about control possibilities.

Companion Planting and Design
Ajuga is good to use in areas that need a controlled groundcover. Easy to control and maintain, ajuga is attractive, but its colors such as bronze, deep wine, variegated cream, and purple to pink marbling may not blend well with the other hues in your landscape. Its low, spreading growth habit makes it ideal for informal, natural spreading along walks and informal plantings. Ajuga is excellent cascading over low walls or edgings. It is a colorful groundcover mat, offering delightful blue-purple blooms to complement the spring bulb blooms. Ajuga lends itself to detail designs in small pocket plantings and in rock gardens.

I Suggest
Try the different varieties of ajuga in small areas first, before investing in large areas.

When, Where, and How to Plant

Plant Asian jasmine from 4 in., quart-sized, and larger containers. Plant in early spring through early fall. If planting during the winter, use quart-sized or larger plants. Asian jasmine may be grown in sandy soils or heavy clay soils. Do not plant in areas that are difficult to water, poorly drained, or total-shade areas. Asian jasmine will tolerate less-than-desirable soil conditions. For best results, plant it in well-prepared beds. Add 2 in. or more of organic matter to the top 2 to 3 in. of existing soil. Insert plants in the soil no deeper than they were originally grown in the containers, firm the soil, water thoroughly, and apply root stimulator. Mulch bare soil with about 2 in. of bark mulch. If you plant Asian jasmine from 4 in. pots in early spring—arranging them 12 in. on center in a checkerboard pattern and watering and fertilizing properly—full coverage should be achieved at the end of the season.

Growing Tips

Fertilize in the spring and every time you fertilize your lawn. Use the same fertilizer, set at the same application rate. Water thoroughly after application and as necessary to maintain moist soil.

Care

Prune in spring to remove winter-damaged top growth and to even out planting beds. Asian jasmine has no serious pests.

Companion Planting and Design

Do not plant Asian jasmine in beds with dwarf plants, where it will overpower the smaller plants. Asian jasmine is excellent in beds with standard landscape plants. It's also used to accent taller plants such as tall crape myrtles. Asian jasmine is often used beneath trees, in left-over areas in pavement such as parking strips and bands between walks and drives, and in areas too large for plant groupings but not large enough for a lawn grass. The variegated form with cream and green marbled foliage is excellent in large containers or for cascading down a wall or column.

I Suggest

Utilize Asian jasmine in areas where mowing is difficult or dangerous. It's a beautiful groundcover and works well.

Asian jasmine is the groundcover used most often in Texas. Found in many commercial applications and public gardens, it is widely available at garden centers and nurseries. Some varieties of Asian jasmine include 'Asia Minor', (often considered a dwarf form), 'Variegatum' (a variegated form), and 'Nortex' (a variety that has more spear-shaped or lance-shaped leaves than the T. asiaticum). T. jasminoides or star jasmine is a cousin to Asian jasmine, but is not hardy in all areas. Hardy in Zone 8 and southward, star jasmine may be grown on structures or trellises. It's similar in growth habit to Asian, but it has masses of small, star-shaped, lightly fragrant white blooms in the growing season.

Other Common Name
Groundcover Jasmine

Bloom Period and Seasonal Color
Grown for foliage. Turns a slight bronze after freezes.

Mature Height and Spread
12 to 16 in. × 10 ft.

Creeping Juniper
Juniperus spp.

There are many varieties of groundcover juniper in Texas today. Some of the family groupings include J. conferta, J. horizontalis, and J. procumbens. When looking for these plants at your local garden center use the term "groundcover-type junipers." When you find the juniper that you like, ask these questions: "How tall does this specific variety grow in my area? How wide does it spread? Will it take partial shade? What type of soil does it require?" After you receive this information, you will be able to determine which varieties to plant. The following varieties are among those suitable for groundcovers: 'Bar Harbour', 'Plumosa', 'Hughes', 'Youngs', 'Turquoise Spreader', 'Blue Rug', 'Emerald Sea', and 'San Jose'.

Other Common Names
Prostrate Juniper

Bloom Period and Seasonal Color
Evergreen foliage.

Mature Height and Spread
6 in. to 2 ft. × 4 to 8 ft.

When, Where, and How to Plant
Fall is an excellent planting time for Creeping Juniper, but early spring is also good. Do not plant in areas that have poorly drained soil or are difficult to water. Plant in locations where it will receive a minimum of six to eight hours of sun per day and a little shade from the hot western afternoon sun. Junipers will grow in practically any Texas soil. In order to receive maximum benefit from juniper, incorporate approximately 4 in. of organic matter into the top 4 in. of native soil. Install plants no deeper than originally grown in the containers. Do not plant too deeply. Firm the soil thoroughly, apply root stimulator following label directions, and cover bare soil with approximately 2 in. of bark mulch. Spacing will depend on the variety selected.

Growing Tips
Water as necessary to maintain moist growing conditions and achieve maximum growth, but do not overwater. As new growth begins in the spring, fertilize with a long-lasting, slow-release lawn fertilizer with a 3:1:2 ratio. Reapply twice more during the growing season and once again in the fall.

Care
Groundcover juniper normally does not require pruning. Spider mites may visit your juniper during late summer in hot, dry locations. If this occurs, consult your local retail garden center for best control possibilities.

Companion Planting and Design
Plant where you desire a small-leafed evergreen planting that is low growing and relatively easy to maintain. Groundcover juniper looks wonderful when allowed to weep over stone walls. It is excellent for slopes and inclines. It is ideal for rock gardens. Juniper is salt spray tolerant, making it very adaptable for coastal planting. The gray-blue juniper groundcovers are particularly attractive with colorful plants such as barberry and dwarf nandina. Juniper may be grown in planters and containers to cascade over the sides.

I Suggest
Try one or more of these babies when looking for a low maintenance plant group for a difficult to mow area. Shore juniper, *J. conferta*, is one of my favorites.

Gray Santolina

Santolina chamaecyparissus

When, Where, and How to Plant

Plant santolina in the early spring or early fall. Santolina requires good soil drainage and sun in order to thrive. If the soil in your location does not drain well, blend approximately 3 in. of ground bark into the top 3 in. of native soil to make a 6 in. raised bed. After bed preparation is complete, remove santolina from containers and install into pre-dug holes no deeper than the top of the soil-ball. Firm the soil around plants, water thoroughly, apply root stimulator according to label directions, and cover bare soil with 2 in. of bark mulch.

Growing Tips

Remember, do not over water santolina. Water only to prevent soil dryness. Fertilization is usually not required, but one application per year of a slow-release 3:1:2 ratio fertilizer (such as 15-5-10) can be beneficial. Remember to read and follow label directions, and water thoroughly after fertilization.

Care

You may wish to perform minimal shearing of branches that tend to grow out of the compact form. If so, shear once or twice a year. Santolina has no pest problems.

Companion Planting and Design

If you are looking for different plants and ways to utilize them, try santolina cascading down a rock wall, concrete wall, or even over a bed edge raised with railroad ties or landscape timbers. It's especially attractive in rock gardens, mounding over rocks or pea-gravel walks. Gray santolina's fine textured foliage is a distinctive feature and a strong contrast and accent when combined with green foliage. Its unique gray foliage mixes well with colorful annuals and perennials, accenting vivid colors. It is ideal for hot, dry locations. Santolina is relatively short-lived—three to five years in humid areas—becoming somewhat unsightly with age, especially in hot, humid climates.

I Suggest

Try one or both of the green and gray santolina in a southwestern theme garden for a different look.

I have grown both gray and green santolina. It is said, "Beauty is in the eye of the beholder." This certainly is true when deciding between gray and green santolina. They are perfect when you need a bushy-type, low-growing, shrubby groundcover for a hot, dry, full-sun area. Such conditions are ideal for santolina. This is not a plant to be used in shady areas, where air drainage is poor, or where the soil is excessively moist. It grows equally well in sandy or clay soils. I have discovered that if blooms begin to develop and you desire a compact plant, keep the blooms snipped off.

Other Common Name
Lavender Cotton

Bloom Period and Seasonal Color
Summer blooms in yellow.

Mature Height and Spread
1 to 1 1/2 ft. × 3 to 5 ft.

Hardy Fern
Many genera, species, and varieties

Just by their very presence, ferns seem to impart a cooling effect to a landscape. I have a wooded area on my property that has mixed hardwood trees, dogwoods, native hawthorns, redbuds, and other flowering plants, and we are fortunate enough to have a spring that flows through our property nourishing a wide selection of ferns. Ferns are often found growing naturally in shaded areas along our creeks and streams but sometimes sunburn in our Texas sun. Many of these ferns make great groundcovers in heavily shaded areas where grass will no longer grow. The term "hardy" means the plant will withstand the freezing temperatures in a particular zone. Some varieties are more evergreen than others, but most are deciduous.

Other Common Name
Hardy Wood Fern

Bloom Period and Seasonal Color
Evergreen or deciduous foliage. Colors are dark to light green silver, to maroon or cinnamon.

Mature Height and Spread
1 ft. to 3 ft. × spread width.

When, Where, and How to Plant
Plant ferns in early spring. They may be planted successfully in the summer and on into early fall. For best results, plant ferns in shaded areas in soils with lots of organic matter. Incorporate as much organic matter as possible (up to 6 in.), into the soil. One of the best sources of organic matter is brown sphagnum peat moss. After improving the soil, remove your selections from the containers and install into the beds no deeper than they were grown in the containers. Firm the soil, water thoroughly, apply root stimulator, and mulch bare soil with about 3 in. of bark mulch.

Growing Tips
Maintain a moist soil at all times during the growing season. A thick layer of mulch will conserve moisture and enhance fern growth. Fertilize three times during the growing season with granular lawn, water-soluble, liquid, or encapsulated slow-release fertilizer.

Care
Prune out dead parts every spring as new growth begins. No other pruning is necessary. Ferns normally do not have pests. If pests happen to bother a planting, visit a local garden center for control possibilities. Remember to read and follow label directions.

Companion Planting and Design
Plant hardy ferns in formal or informal beds. Use ferns as background plantings with colorful shade-loving plants such as caladiums, spring bulbs, impatiens, or azaleas. They may also be planted in large tubs or planters. *Cyrtomium falcatum*, or Hollyfern, is evergreen in most of Texas, and ideal in shaded planters. Fronds or leaves make excellent indoor decorations throughout the growing season in arrangements with cut flowers.

I Suggest
If you have a spot where nothing will grow due to the heavy shade, these great looking easy-to-grow plants are super.

When, Where, and How to Plant

Plant hosta in early spring. When making your selections, ask the retailer how tall and how wide specific varieties grow in your area. Plant hosta in well-prepared beds with lots of organic matter. Do not plant hosta in sunny locations. Prepare the beds as you do for ferns, incorporating approximately 4 in. of organic matter into the top 4 in. of the soil. After bed preparation is complete, remove your selections from the containers and install in the soil no deeper than they were originally grown. Spacing depends on the variety you have selected. After planting, water thoroughly, add root stimulator according to label directions, and mulch bare soil with approximately 3 in. of bark mulch.

Growing Tips

Water as necessary to maintain a moist soil throughout the entire growing season. Fertilize as new growth begins in the spring with a long-lasting, slow-release lawn fertilizer (such as 18-6-12, 19-5-9, or 21-7-14). Water-soluble, encapsulated, slow-release, or other types of fertilizer may also be used.

Care

Pruning is normally not necessary. Slugs or snails may visit your hosta plantings. If they become a problem, visit your local garden center for the best control possibilities. If slugs and/or snails are already a major problem in your landscape, get the situation under control before planting any hostas.

Companion Planting and Design

Plant hostas in the ground in shady locations or large tubs. Large-tub hosta plantings will provide you with portable color for shady areas. These colorful plants may be grown in the same locations as hardy ferns. Hostas do well in natural, woodland settings, along wooded trails and paths. The hosta's coarse texture and striking colors are accents for the garden, and it lends itself to detail design.

I Suggest

Hosta works well as a winter hardy, colorful plant group for heavily shaded areas. One variety I particularly like is 'So Sweet'.

I often get questions from people who are seeking information on color plants for shaded areas. Hosta is a fine choice for this, and it can be grown singly or in masses to create groundcover effects. It gives great color from its foliage as well as from its blooms. I have seen gorgeous plantings of hosta in the heavy soils of Dallas, Fort Worth, Waco, and Houston, and also in the light, sandy soils of eastern Texas. It will grow in light shade or heavily shaded areas. Varieties of hosta include 'All Gold', 'Crown Jewel', 'Gold Standard', 'Francee', 'Golden Prayers', 'Green Elf', 'Krossa Regal', 'Royal Standard', 'Serendipity', 'Elegance', 'Halcyon', and 'Wide Brim'.

Other Common Name
Plantain Lily

Bloom Period and Seasonal Color
Summer blooms in white and blue, and foliage color in green, chartreuse, gray, blue, and combinations.

Mature Height and Spread
12 to 18 in. × 18 to 36 in. and spreading.

Liriope
Liriope muscari

Liriope muscari is often used to line walkways, pathways, or driveways. It also makes good groundcover, growing in shady locations under trees where other groundcovers will not grow. Its main flush of growth is in the spring. It does not respond well to heavy foot traffic. Use carefully placed stepping-stones as walkways. Some liriope varieties stay rather low, such as 'Lilac Beauty', 'Silver Midget' and 'Silver Sunproof'. Others get quite tall, such as 'Evergreen Giant', 'Majestic', 'Big Blue', and 'Webster Wideleaf'. Be sure you select the right variety to fit your specific application. Liriope is often referred to among gardeners as monkey grass, but according to the Texas Cooperative Extension Service, the name monkey grass "technically" refers only to mondo grass, Ophiopogon japonicus.

Other Common Name
Monkey Grass

Bloom Period and Seasonal Color
Summer blooms in white, lilac, and purple.

Mature Height × Spread
8 to 30 in. × continuous spreads to no specific width.

When, Where, and How to Plant
Plant in early spring after all danger of frost has passed, or in early fall. Incorporate 4 in. of organic matter into the top 4 in. of the native soil. Install selections at the same depth they grew originally. Backfill, water thoroughly, apply root stimulator according to label directions, then mulch the entire bed with 3 to 4 in. of bark mulch. If you wish to plant in 15- to 20-gallon nursery containers or in a hanging basket, plant at the same depth they grew originally and follow the rest of the suggestions for planting in the ground.

Growing Tips
Maintain a moist soil to ensure proper growth. Do not maintain a wet soil nor allow the soil to be continuously dry. Fertilize two weeks after the last average killing frost, then ten weeks later, again another ten weeks later, and then one time in the fall. Use a 3:1:2 ratio long-lasting lawn fertilizer, (such as a 15-5-10, 19-5-9, or 21-7-14).

Care
Prune one time a year, cutting dead outer leaves in early spring before new shoots emerge. Usually there are no serious pests that bother liriope, though grasshoppers may occasionally visit. If they become a problem, look for controls at your favorite nursery.

Companion Planting and Design
Use liriope to line a formal walkway, breaking the harshness of straight edges. It's also used to create natural-form pathways in the landscape and used in planter boxes or large pots. Try growing 'Giant', *Liriope gigantea*, in a large hanging basket, allowing it to weep down the side. Use liriope for detailed plantings, clumps, and groundcover areas in rock gardens, Japanese gardens, and patio areas. Attractive in naturalistic settings to border informal paths.

I Suggest
In Texas landscapes, liriope has long been used to line walkways, but I recommend using taller varieties of liriope in mass or as stand-alone group plantings.

Mondo Grass

Ophiopogon japonicus

When, Where, and How to Plant

Plant mondo grass in very early spring or fall. It does best in well-prepared beds. Blend approximately 4 to 6 in. of high-quality organic matter into the top 6 in. of the existing soil. Remove the plants from the containers, dig individual planting holes no deeper than the top of the soilball, and place the plants into the planting holes. Backfill with a loose mix, water thoroughly, apply root stimulator, and mulch the finished planting with about 3 in. of bark mulch. When planting in containers, use lightweight potting soil.

Growing Tips

Water as needed to prevent wilting. For optimum growth, fertilize in early spring with a 3:1:2 ratio, long-lasting lawn fertilizer (such as 21-7-14, 18-6-12, or 15-5-10).

Care

Shearing or mowing once a year is desirable for maintaining a more compact and uniform look. This is normally done in the spring after all danger of frost and freeze is over. Mondo grass is virtually insect and disease free when properly cared for.

Companion Planting and Design

Mondo grass may be used to line borders or walkways, or you may wish to create a groundcover in shade or partial-shade locations. In heavily shaded areas where turfgrass is not able to grow, mondo will thrive and acquire a deep-green color that looks like grass. You may want to try mondo grass in a hanging basket. It is often used as a groundcover beneath trees and shrub plantings. Mondo grass is excellent for detail designs in rock and water gardens, and for patio and entry area details.

I Suggest

In areas where turf grass will not grow due to heavy shade try the dwarf mondo grass planted in a checkerboard pattern. It should grow and produce a low-growing, grass-like covering that is evergreen.

Mondo grass is an evergreen plant that has multiple uses in our home landscape. It works well in shaded areas. It comes in a dwarf variety as well as standard varieties. Planting in a checkerboard pattern will usually lead to a "grass" look in one to two seasons. Keep in mind that mondo grass is not a turfgrass, so it will not tolerate a lot of foot traffic. If you want a way to move through plantings of mondo grass, carefully place stepping-stones or walks. Do not expose mondo grass to daylong full sun or reflected heat. Morning sun with afternoon shade is desirable.

Other Common Names

Lilyturf, Monkey Grass, Border Grass

Bloom Period and Seasonal Color

Evergreen

Mature Height × Spread

3 to 10 in. × spread width.

Periwinkle
Vinca minor

Vinca minor has smaller leaves than Vinca major. Both types are ideal in woodland locations where dappled sunlight is available throughout the day and moist soil conditions exist. Vinca will take full sun during the morning, but must be shaded from the hot afternoon sun in order to do well. It will also grow in full-shade locations. Vinca, with its dark-green, almost waxy, leaves and colorful blooms, is one of the best groundcovers we have in Texas. The variegated types provide color from both foliage and bloom. Some varieties are: V. major 'Variegata', with white or cream markings; V. minor 'Alba', with white flowers; and 'Variegata', with green and white leaves. 'Bowles' has larger flowers and deep-green leaves.

Other Common Name
Vinca

Bloom Period and Seasonal Color
Spring blooms in white and purple.

Mature Height and Spread
4 to 18 in.

When, Where, and How to Plant
An ideal planting time for periwinkle is very early spring, but early fall is also good. Periwinkle does best in locations that drain properly. It will grow in both sandy and clay soils as long as adequate moisture is available. To achieve maximum benefits, incorporate approximately 2 in. of organic matter into the top 2 in. of the existing soil. Install the plants no deeper than originally grown in the containers. If you buy 4 in. pots in early spring and space the plants approximately 12 in. apart in a checkerboard pattern, you will have complete coverage by the end of one season.

Growing Tips
Water as necessary to maintain a moist soil, especially through the growing season. Vinca is quick to wilt when dry, yet drought tolerant, persisting for years in deserted home sites. Do not overwater, especially in heavy clay soils. Fertilize in spring as new growth begins with a long-lasting, slow-release lawn fertilizer. Use a 3:1:2 ratio (such as 18-6-12, 19-5-9, or 15-5-10), and follow label directions.

Care
Periwinkle normally does not require pruning. One of the few pests to bother periwinkle is caterpillars. In heavy infestations, caterpillars have the potential to strip all the leaves from vinca. If pests cause problems with your periwinkles, visit your local retail garden center to find the best control possibilities.

Companion Planting and Design
You can grow periwinkle in large tubs. Try one or both types in large hanging baskets or other containers. Remember that periwinkle is a groundcover, not a turfgrass, and does not tolerate foot traffic. If passage is required, pathways should be installed. Vinca is ideal for large areas, such as beneath shade trees, as it is fast growing and quick to spread. The new spring foliage and periwinkle-blue blooms are attractive when planted with spring bulbs and dwarf azaleas.

I Suggest
Visit botanical gardens, arboretums, and other public gardens before planting vinca to help determine if you like this plant.

Prostrate Rosemary
Rosmarinus officinalis 'Prostratus'

When, Where, and How to Plant

Plant in early spring (after all danger of frost has passed) or early fall. Plant in sunny areas where the soil drains exceptionally well. A slightly alkaline soil is preferred. All types of rosemary may be grown in containers with great success. If you have a soil location that is poorly drained, raise the bed using several inches of 50 percent ground bark combined with the native soil. Install no deeper than the plants were grown in containers, and firm the soil. Water thoroughly, apply root stimulator, and cover bare soil with approximately 2 in. of mulch.

Growing Tips

Water only when needed to prevent complete soil dryness. Be careful not to overwater. Fertilizing is usually not required.

Care

You may prune to obtain desired shape, but normally no other pruning is necessary. Rosemary does not attract any serious pests.

Companion Planting and Design

Weeping, creeping, or groundcover rosemary in large containers is gorgeous when grown poolside and on decks, balconies, and patios. You may also wish to try it in large hanging baskets. Rosemary serves well as an accent plant. It is a must for herb and kitchen gardens, and ideal for rock gardens.

I Suggest

Give any or all varieties of rosemary a try in a hot, full sun, hard-to-water location. I have one rosemary as large as an average dining room table and love it.

Chicken and rosemary go together like love and marriage, and the rosemary most often used in cooking comes from the bush-type plant, Rosmarinus officinalis. *However, its low-growing cousin works equally well for cooking and makes a gorgeous blooming groundcover in the landscape. Prostrate rosemary provides a multitude of benefits. It smells wonderful, it blooms, it is easy to dry, and it looks great in the landscape. Once you see a hot, dry, full-sun area of prostrate groundcover rosemary, you will wonder why you didn't plant it sooner. In some catalogs and guides, you may see prostrate rosemary listed as a creeping or groundcover form. Other worthwhile varieties of rosemary are* 'Salem', 'Benanden Blue', *and* 'Huntington Carpet'. *Great planting and good cooking!*

Other Common Names
Rosemary, Dwarf Rosemary

Bloom Period and Seasonal Color
Spring/summer blooms in blue.

Mature Height and Spread
2 × 4 ft.

Sedum
Sedum spp.

Sedum is a good choice as a groundcover for a sunny rock garden location. It is excellent in hot, dry Texas locations. Wherever you plant sedum, make sure that the soil drains well. Some varieties die out each year, while others remain evergreen. Ask at your local garden center about the types that interest you. Questions to ask include: "Is it evergreen or deciduous in our area? How tall does it grow? What bloom colors are available?" There is a wide variety of sedums from which to choose—the reference Hortus III *has over six pages of different sedum types. Some varieties that are more readily available include 'Gold Moss', 'Ruby Glow', and 'Red Carpet'.*

Other Common Name
Stonecrop

Bloom Period and Seasonal Color
Spring, summer or fall blooms in yellow, red, pink, pink-purple, and bronze-pink.

Mature Height and Spread
4 to 18 in. × 12 in.

When, Where, and How to Plant
Plant in early spring or early fall. Plant sedums in your landscape in any location where you want a succulent, fleshy-looking groundcover. Do not plant in shady locations or poorly drained soils. Very little soil preparation is necessary, except in poorly drained soil. Plant transplants no deeper than they were grown in their containers—be very attentive to planting depth. Firm the soil around your transplant, water thoroughly, apply root stimulator according to label directions, and cover bare soil with 2 in. of bark mulch.

Growing Tips
Water as needed to prevent total soil dryness, but do not keep wet. Fertilize once in the spring as new growth begins with a long-lasting, slow-release rose fertilizer.

Care
Sedum normally does not require pruning, except to cut back old flower stems that may appear unsightly. Sedum is usually pest-free. If a problem with pests develops, visit your local retail garden center for control possibilities. Remember to read and follow label directions.

Companion Planting and Design
Rock gardens are just one application for sedum. It may also be used for a groundcover elsewhere. Try sedums in large pots, hanging baskets, or other containers. Because of similar cultural needs, santolina is an excellent companion plant for sedums. Sedums work well laced along gravel or natural, sunny walks or trails.

I Suggest
I am currently growing 'Goldmoss' sedum in a raised bed at the base of tall althea, allowing it to trail over the rock used to construct the raised bed. Try something similar. It's easy!

Wintercreeper
Euonymus fortunei

When, Where, and How to Plant

The ideal time to plant euonymus is early fall. Early spring is also a good planting time. Wintercreeper *Euonymus* is extremely easy to grow, but do not plant it in hot, dry places, areas with reflected heat, or locations that are difficult to water. It should not be planted in heavily shaded areas or poorly drained soil. Improve the soil by incorporating 3 in. of organic matter into the top 3 in. of the soil. Plant individual plants no deeper than originally planted in the containers. Firm the soil around individual plants and water thoroughly. Add root stimulator according to label directions, and cover bare soil with 2 in. of bark mulch.

Growing Tips

Do not keep wet, and do not allow the soil to become dry. Fertilize in spring, as new growth begins, with a long-lasting, slow-release 3:1:2 ratio lawn fertilizer. Examples include 15-5-10 and 18-6-12. Remember to read and follow label directions, and water thoroughly after each application. Apply again around June 1 and once again in the fall.

Care

Pruning is usually not required; however, cutting back tip or terminal growth will help form a denser planting. Water as necessary to maintain moist soil. Scale insects may visit euonymus. If this becomes a problem, apply dormant oil during the winter season according to label directions.

Companion Planting and Design

For something unusual or wild looking, try euonymus in large hanging baskets. The relatively large leafed 'Coloratus' may be successfully used to secure the soil. Spreading euonymus is ideal on slopes and on difficult to maintain inclines.

I Suggest

Wintercreeper is ideal for Texas gardeners in the high plains or panhandle areas of Texas where it is often difficult to establish groundcovers.

I first came into contact with euonymus *when I grew the variety 'Coloratus' as production manager at a wholesale nursery in 1972. It's easy to propagate, easy to grow, and works beautifully in the landscape. If you have relatively large areas that need a winter-hardy groundcover, wintercreeper is an answer. Make sure it has plenty of room to grow and the soil drains well. Wintercreeper* Euonymus *grows particularly well in the Panhandle area where other groundcover-type plants may have difficulty surviving the harsh winters. 'Coloratus' changes color with the seasons. After a few hard frosts or freezes, its green leaves take on various shades of maroon, purple, and bronze.*

Other Common Name
Spreading Euonymus

Bloom Period and Seasonal Color
Evergreen foliage with bronze/purple tints after freezes.

Mature Height and Spread
6 in. to 2 ft. × 2 to 8 ft.

Native Grasses, Shrubs, Trees, and Vines *for Texas*

There's absolutely no place like Texas—and no natives like Texas native plants! This chapter will cover native grasses, shrubs, trees, and vines. Some of the best and easiest-to-grow native Texas plants have become standards in the nursery industry as well as our home landscapes. Cenizo, or Texas sage, *Leucophyllum frutescens*, has become widely available across the state. Additional shrubs including American beautyberry, *Callicarpa americana*, perhaps are less widely known but super in the landscape. I have been growing one planting of American beautyberry for nineteen years and it looks great. This is especially so during late summer and early fall when it is loaded with tight clusters of purple berries. Outstanding!

Southern Magnolia

Choices that Stop Traffic

Autumn sage, *Salvia greggii*, is another native plant that does beautifully in well-drained Texas soils. *Salvia greggii* not only is easy to grow but also offers us bloom color in sunny spots. The large native shrub wax myrtle, *Myrica cerifera*, has also become a welcome addition to our landscapes. I grow a planting of this native as a screen, and it works well. If you are looking for a native, tall growing (up to twenty feet) shrub to utilize as a specimen, screen or other application, wax myrtle will work well for you. It performs well in clay or sandy soils in urban and rural landscapes.

I write garden columns for several publications in the state and do live call-in radio shows as well. My readers and listeners often ask for my recommendations for fast-growing shade trees. I don't recommend these types of trees. Most, such as Arizona ash, *Fraxinus velutina*, tend to be loaded with problems. If you want to plant an ash, then look for Texas ash, *Fraxinus texensis*, a high quality tree that is native to Texas. For outstanding fall color, plant a sweetgum, *Liquidambar styraciflua*. If you're a fan of elm trees, try the cedar elm, *Ulmus crassifolia*. Most people become instant fans of this gorgeous native Texas elm in their landscape. All of these native trees normally have fewer problems than some imports.

If vines are your passion, a native vine with an exotic-looking blossom is the maypop or passion vine, *Passiflora incarnata*. At garden shows these actually stop traffic as visitors inquire about them with a mixture of excitement and wonder.

For you "Hummers" lovers, a planting of coral honeysuckle, *Lonicera sempervirens*, is highly recommended. Hummingbirds love this baby!

If you like wisteria, but are concerned about it taking over your landscape, try Texas wisteria, *Wisteria macrostachya*. It has wonderful flowers and is much easier to manage than the imported wisterias. This beauty works well on garden structures out in the landscape, including, but not limited to, arbors, perolas, and arches.

The native grass currently used in most of Texas is buffalograss, *Buchloe dactyloides*. It is sun-, heat-, and drought-tolerant. It is not shade-tolerant and normally is not recommended for the higher rainfall areas of East Texas. Buffalograss should work well for you in full sun areas that are only occasionally mowed.

Remember that there are nurseries that specialize in native Texas plants. For more research on Texas native plants, I suggest you contact the Native Plant Society of Texas (see page 252 for contact information). The NPSOT is an excellent source for more recommendations. Find a chapter near you, and have fun with our native Texas plants!

Redbud

Agarito
Berberis trifoliolata

Agarito grew in the mesquite woods of Brownwood, my hometown and the county seat of Brown County. We called these interesting native shrubs "agarito berries" because of their edible berries. The berries were a bit difficult to harvest, due to the spiny leaves, but they had a nice red, tart juice, and we enjoyed them. We also looked for agarito berries when visiting my grandparents in the Keys Crossing area at Indian Creek, along the Colorado River. Even today, in certain Texas stores you will find jelly made from agarito berries. Its leaves can turn reddish or yellow in the fall and remain that way till new growth begins in the spring. Agarito is hardy statewide.

Bloom Period and Seasonal Color
Blooms yellow in spring and produces red berries.

Mature Height × Spread
3 to 6 ft. × 3 to 6 ft.

When, Where, and How to Plant
Plant agarito in early fall or early spring in a well-drained location that receives full sun, or at least six hours of full sun. It will grow in sand or clay soils but do not plant in heavily shaded areas or soils that tend to stay damp. To use agarito as a landscape shrub in beds, a thorough tilling of the soil is all the preparation that is necessary. If you wish to plant in a poorly drained location, plant the shrubs in raised beds to which you have added lots of organic matter and other drainage materials. Remove agarito from its container and plant in the soil no deeper than it was growing in its original containers. Planting too deep is sure death. Firm the soil well around the root system, water thoroughly, apply root stimulator, and cover bare soil with about 3 in. of bark mulch.

Growing Tips
Water only as necessary to prevent complete soil dryness. Do not overwater. Fertilize no more than one time per year with a premium-quality, slow-release rose fertilizer.

Care
Prune agarito if desired, but it's much better to allow it to grow to its natural shape. Agarito is considered pest-free.

Companion Planting and Design
Use agarito in landscape beds as foundation plantings, specimens, or mass plantings. They are super in a Xeriscape.

I Suggest
Using this prickly native Texas shrub wherever a minimum of water is available. *B. repens* or creeping barberry is dwarf and usually grows less than a foot tall. *B. swasey,* known as Texas barberry or Texas mahonia, may grow in the five- to seven-foot height range. Both are easy to grow.

American Beautyberry

Callicarpa americana

When, Where, and How to Plant

Plant American beautyberry in early spring or fall in a spot where it will have plenty of room to grow. If you wish to plant two or more, space them about 5 to 8 ft. apart. American beautyberry has the ability to grow in various types of soils. It will grow in sand, loam, and clay, as well as in soils that are rather acrid, alkaline, or calcareous. It will also grow in fairly moist areas. American beautyberry will grow quite well in our native soil, but if you decide to do some soil preparation, do it as if you were making up a bed for any other landscape plant. Loosen the soil in an area several times wider and no deeper than the soilball. Remove the plant from its container, place into its individual planting hole, backfill, and firm the soil. Water it thoroughly, apply root stimulator, and cover bare soil with about 3 in. of bark mulch.

Growing Tips

Water as necessary to prevent soil dryness, especially during the months of July and August. The most important time to have moist soil is during the blooming and fruiting stage. Fertilize one time as new growth begins in the spring and once again in the fall with a premium-quality, slow-release granular rose fertilizer.

Care

It can grow as tall as 10 ft., although in our landscape it usually grows around 7 ft. To help make it more compact, cut it back very severely at the beginning of each season just before spring growth. This pruning is simply a matter of taste and choice. We have had no insect or disease problems with American beautyberry.

Companion Planting and Design

Use American beautyberry as a specimen plant or among perennials or other landscaping. I do not recommend it as a foundation plant, because it is deciduous. However, its show of unusual color makes it worth planting in a secondary location.

I Suggest

Plant one of my favorite native shrubs, the purple species *Callicarpa americana*, and let me know what you think.

Ah, American beautyberry. Judy and I get more compliments and comments on our American beautyberry than on any other plant we have in the large bed near our back entry, a southwestern location. It's growing in a rocky location among other native and imported plants, and it's spectacular. It receives plenty of morning sun and some shade from the hot western afternoon sun. We allow it to grow as it should be grown, reaching a relatively large size with weeping, arching branches and clusters of bright purple berries. Beautyberry also comes in white, but I prefer the purple. The white variety is C. americana 'Lactea', and has abundant creamy white berries. It grows under the same conditions as the standard American beautyberry. American beautyberry will grow throughout Texas.

Other Common Name
French Mulberry

Bloom Period and Seasonal Color
Summer blooms in greenish white. Purplish berries in late summer to early fall.

Mature Height × Spread
4 to 6 ft. × 5 to 8 ft.

Buffalograss
Buchloe dactyloides

Buffalograss is a great grass of the plains that helped to nourish the buffalo herds and was used by settlers to build sod homes. Buffalograss is not for everyone, but for an extremely low-maintenance lawn in full-sun locations you should consider this native grass. Buffalograss usually grows in the four- to six-inch range and spreads by seed or above-ground runners. It does best in areas that receive less than 30 inches of rain per year. Two main areas where buffalograss is not recommended are east Texas and the Gulf Coast prairie areas. Buffalograss will adapt to all other areas of Texas. If you wish to have a low-maintenance turfgrass near entrances or along a drive, buffalograss is a good choice.

Color and Texture
Blue-green with fine texture.

Mowing Height
2 to 3 in. or taller.

When, Where, and How to Plant
Plant in the early spring after soil and air temperatures warm to 70 degrees Fahrenheit. Plant sod as soon as it is available at local retailers. Plant buffalograss in clay soils. To establish from seed, measure the area in square feet. Lightly till the area, correct drainage problems, and rake to remove any rocks or debris. Sow $^3/_4$ to 4 lb. of treated seed per 1000 square ft. Sow one half of the seed in a north/south direction and the remaining half in an east/west direction. No mulching is required. Water thoroughly and maintain moisture. As the seeds germinate and plants establish themselves, reduce watering. To plant sod repare soil as for seed. Lay the sod end-to-end and side-to-side in a solid mat for instant effect. As an option, divide it into strips no smaller than 6 × 6 in. and plant in a checkerboard pattern, 12 to 16 in. apart. The lawn should establish within one season. Water as needed to prevent wilting.

Growing Tips
Water thoroughly and deeply. Little to no fertilization is necessary.

Care
Buffalograss does not require mowing, but you may want to keep it at 2 to 3 in. high. Buffalograss is free of pests. Very little watering and fertilizer is required.

Companion Planting and Design
Buffalograss is a top-notch grass to hold the soil on steep areas you don't want to mow. It works in Xeriscapes of native Texas plants where the soil is conducive to successful long-term growth. Plant buffalograss alone as other grasses will invade it. Buffalograss is slow growing and lies close to the soil surface; therefore, the fine bladed grass requires little mowing. It is considered less refined in appearance than other grasses but requires very little maintenance. For this reason, it is often used in large, semi-maintained areas. Not a polished looking lawn grass. May turn straw colored in mid to late summer, as it tends to go semi-dormant in heat.

I Suggest
Prior to planting buffalograss take a look at some plantings of the native strain plus some selections such as 609 and Prairie before determining if it is the turf grass for your needs.

Carolina Jessamine

Gelsemium sempervirens

When, Where, and How to Plant

Carolina jessamine grows best when planted in spring or fall. It will grow in full sun and shady areas, though blooming is reduced in the shady areas. For best bloom and overall growth, plant in locations that receive six to eight hours of full sun. It will grow in sandy, loamy, and clay soils, will tolerate damp conditions, and has moderate drought resistance. To achieve maximum growth, improve the native soil by incorporating organic matter into the planting area, combining approximately 3 in. with the top 3 in. of your soil. This will make a well-prepared bed approximately 6 in. deep. For training on a structure, plant one gallon containers to start on the vine. Set containers approximately 4 ft. apart to cover a solid wall, and insert plants no deeper than they were grown in their containers. Firm the soil well around them, water thoroughly, apply root stimulator, and cover bare soil with about 3 in. of bark mulch.

Growing Tips

Water sufficiently to prevent soil dryness, especially important in July and August. Maintain a 3 in. layer of bark mulch around the root system year-round. After blooming has completed in the spring, fertilize with slow-release granular rose fertilizer. Reapply your selected fertilizer mid-season and again in the fall. Remember, follow directions and water thoroughly after each fertilizer application.

Care

Prune and train as necessary to meet specific goals. Keep in mind that Carolina jessamine tends to grow rapidly, especially in early spring after bloom is complete, so pay close attention to directing and training. Elastic stretch tie is wonderful for tying Carolina jessamine to any structure. Carolina jessamine has no serious pests.

Companion Planting and Design

You may grow Carolina jessamine on trellises or other structures, and in large tubs or planters on your deck or balcony. It may be trained in specific patterns if desired. It may also be used to cover the ground and spill over falls and slopes.

I Suggest

Planting Carolina jessamine on a vertical structure to show off its color. It's easy to achieve and very attractive.

Gelsemium sempervirens is an excellent native vine for Texas gardeners. It's the most widely used vine in our landscapes, and perhaps the most widely used vine of any type, imported or native. I have it growing on two large trellises on the west side of our home. The trellises go from the ground up to the eave of the house, are fastened directly to the wall, and are covered with Carolina jessamine. It's a beautiful show and also helps conserve energy for us by acting as a heat barrier during the summer. Two varieties are 'Pale Yellow', and 'Pride of Augusta', which is double flowered and early blooming. Carolina jessamine is hardy in Zones 7 to 9.

Other Common Names
Carolina Jasmine, Yellow Jasmine

Bloom Period and Seasonal Color
Late winter- to early-spring blooms in yellow, with evergreen foliage the remainder of the year.

Mature Height × Spread
Vine to 20 ft. in any direction.

Cedar
Juniperus virginiana

I was fortunate to have Granddad and Granny Miller for many years. At Christmas the tree they used was J. virginiana. Judy and I have also used cedars in our own home as holiday trees. If you truly want to do a "Country Christmas," a cedar tree is the type to use. In Brown County where I grew up, cedar trees are cut for fence posts and sawed into lumber. Female trees tend to be more blue-green in color, and they are the only ones that produce berries. There are many cultivars, including 'Cupressifolia', 'Idyllwild', 'Manhattan Blue', 'Glauca', and 'Skyrocket'. Some are trees, while others are classified as shrubs; all are J. virginiana. It's important to note that many people are allergic to cedar. J. virginiana is hardy in all Texas zones.

Other Common Name
Eastern Red Cedar

Bloom Period and Seasonal Color
Nonshowy blooms in summer with evergreen foliage.

Mature Height × Spread
20 to 40 ft. × 20 to 30 ft.

When, Where, and How to Plant
Plant container-grown selections anytime, but fall is best, followed by early spring. Midsummer is not the best time to plant, due to heat and drought and shock to the root system during its growing season. Cedar trees will grow in all types of Texas soil, as long as it is well drained. Don't plant them in wet soils or in shady locations. No special soil preparation is needed. Loosen the soil in an area two- to three-times wider than the soilball, but dig the planting hole only soilball deep. Remove the plant from the container and place it in the hole. Backfill with loosened soil, water thoroughly, and apply root stimulator. Mulch bare soil with 3 to 4 in. of bark.

Growing Tips
Cedar requires minimal watering when the tree is establishing itself. Cedar trees respond well to fertilizer. A three-times-a-year program should work well. Apply long-lasting, slow-release, premium-quality 3:1:2 ratio lawn fertilizer (such as 21-7-14 or 15-5-10) according to label directions. Apply the first treatment as new spring growth begins, ten weeks later, and during the fall season. Water thoroughly after each application.

Care
It's best to allow cedars to maintain their natural form. If you prune, do so during the spring. Don't severely prune branches that have no foliage or they will fail to produce new foliage. Spider mites, bagworms, juniper scale or blight, and cedar apple rust are potential problems.

Companion Planting and Design
Cedar trees may vary widely in size and shape. These evergreens work well for windbreaks, privacy screens, and as a specimen. They are drought tolerant once established and work well in a Xeriscape. They produce heavy shade but groundcover may be used in their shadow. Cedars are a good transitional plant to unify natural plantings and more formal groupings.

I Suggest
Visit the Texas Hill Country to see these plants in their native habitat. For a more even row (as in a screen) or where a blue tint is desired, try 'Manhattan Blue'.

Cedar Elm

Ulmus crassifolia

When, Where, and How to Plant

Plant cedar elm any time of year from containers no larger than the 20-gallon size. The ideal planting time is fall or very early spring. If you buy a tree in a container larger than 20 gallons (or in a very large ball), have a landscape contractor plant it for you. When you do plant, dig the hole no deeper than the depth of the soilball, but make sure it's significantly wider and be sure to loosen up that soil. DO NOT add any soil amendments. Remove the plant from its container and set in the planting hole. Backfill and water thoroughly. Construct a berm to hold water. If necessary, stake temporarily to prevent top movement. Cover bare soil with 3 in. of bark mulch and apply a root stimulator.

Growing Tips

Water as necessary—especially during the two-year establishment period—to prevent soil dryness. After the tree has been in your landscape one year, fertilize it three times a year. Try a premium-quality, slow-release lawn fertilizer with a 3:1:2 ratio. Apply once in the spring when new growth begins, once in the fall, and once in mid-season.

Care

Prune to shape the cedar elm in very early spring as new growth begins. Elm leaf beetles may visit your tree, but in most cases they are not a big problem.

Companion Planting and Design

Plant anywhere that you wish to have a top-quality shade tree. A prime location is on the west side of your home. Because the tree is deciduous, it can help lower your energy bills by providing shade in summer and allowing the sun to strike your home during the winter after it has lost its leaves.

I Suggest

Try this native Texan if you want an easy-to-grow, tough, and durable deciduous shade tree in the landscape.

If you like elm trees but want to avoid elm diseases, cedar elm is the tree for you. (Cedar elm is resistant to Dutch elm disease). It is found growing naturally in some of the central areas of Texas, but it is adaptive to all areas of the state. I've seen it growing quite well in heavy clay soil as well as in very light sandy soils. It's a very strong, absolutely gorgeous tree with built-in wind resistance. Because of its spread of forty to fifty feet and its oval upright crown, it can be used very successfully in urban landscapes. It will even stand some compaction of the soil it grows in. Cedar elm is hardy statewide.

Bloom Period and Seasonal Color
Fall leaf color in yellow.

Mature Height × Spread
60 to 80 ft. × 40 to 50 ft.

Coral Honeysuckle
Lonicera sempervirens

If you love the excitement hummingbirds bring to the home landscape, you should plant coral honeysuckle. Not only does coral honeysuckle attract hummingbirds, it also attracts many admirers, and it's easy to grow on any type of gardening structure. We currently have a planting growing on a structure that I built on a wall with one-inch chicken wire on the east side of our home. Planted with gallon-sized containers of coral honeysuckle four feet apart, in two years it was solid from top to bottom and remains absolutely loaded with blossoms. Coral honeysuckle is easy to find at your local retail garden center, but make sure that you specify this native plant; it's less rambunctious than imported types. Coral honeysuckle is hardy statewide.

Other Common Name
Trumpet Honeysuckle

Bloom Period and Seasonal Color
Spring, summer blooms in clusters of small, coral, trumpet-shaped blooms. Foliage is round leaves in a blue-gray-green color.

Mature Height × Spread
Vine to 20 ft. in any direction.

When, Where, and How to Plant
Plant honeysuckle in early spring so it will have the entire growing season to establish itself. A preferred planting area for coral honeysuckle is eastern exposure and shade from the hot west afternoon sun. While it will grow in full sun, it will need supplemental irrigation in order to maintain the looks of its foliage. It will grow in sandy, loam, or clay soils, and will even grow in some areas where drainage is poor. If you wish to help its establishment and maintain a more luxurious growth habit, prepare your soil well. Add several inches of organic matter to the top 6 in. of the native soil. You may use compost, brown sphagnum peat moss, ground-bark mulch, or some of each. After bed preparation is complete, dig individual planting holes no deeper than the plant soilball. Install the plants in their new homes, firm the soil well, and water thoroughly. Apply root stimulator according to label directions, and spread with 3 in. of bark mulch.

Growing Tips
To prevent soil dryness, water as necessary throughout the growing and blooming season. The most critical time is during July and August. Maintaining a thick bark mulch will greatly conserve soil moisture. Fertilization may be necessary during the early establishment period and any time extra nourishment is needed. If planted in rich, deep soils, fertilization is seldom necessary.

Care
Prune and train as necessary to reach desired goals. Tie to growing structure with elastic stretch ties. There are no serious pests.

Companion Planting and Design
If you like to have blooming plants that require minimal care, but do not have a lot of square footage, try coral honeysuckle on wires or other upright structures. It also does well when allowed to weep over rock walls.

I Suggest
If you want to attract hummingbirds, plant this interesting vine.

Flowering Dogwood
Cornus florida

When, Where, and How to Plant

Plant dogwood in early fall or early spring from containers. Soil drainage is important to the long-term growth and overall health of dogwoods, so make sure the soil drains well, wherever you plant the tree. Dig the planting hole no deeper than the depth of the tree soilball, but you may dig it several times wider. Loosen the soil, install the tree in the planting hole, and backfill. Water thoroughly, apply root stimulator, and mulch bare soil with about 3 in. of bark mulch.

Growing Tips

Water your dogwood to prevent soil dryness. Because of their shallow root systems, dogwoods cannot tolerate soils that are dry for prolonged periods of time. Maintaining a layer of mulch approximately 3 to 4 in. deep is a good way to help keep the root system in good health. Fertilize no more than twice a year, once in the spring as new growth begins and once in the fall. Use a premium-quality, slow-release azalea/camellia-type fertilizer. Don't over-fertilize these trees.

Care

Prune to maintain a desired shape; early-spring pruning after blooming is recommended. Leaf spot may visit your planting of dogwood, especially in areas of high humidity and poor air circulation and drainage. Reduce leaf spot by planting in areas with good air movement. Sometimes bores will attack dogwood if the tree is under stress. Reduce bore attack by keeping the tree healthy. Should insects or disease become a problem, visit your local garden centers for controls.

Companion Planting and Design

You don't need a large yard to group several dogwoods together in a multiple planting. There's nothing more showy in a home landscape than a group of dogwoods beneath some tall-growing oak trees or elms. Plant dogwood in a patio area near your home, near garden structures, or on the border of your landscape.

I Suggest

Try growing one of the white varieties in a container, and planting it in the fall. I only recommend landscape plantings in acidic soils.

Where I live, native dogwoods bloom in and among mixed hardwoods, along with redbuds and native hawthorns. It is quite a spectacular sight. Dogwoods grow naturally in the soils of East Texas and will grow throughout our state if given well-prepared soil and proper care. If you are not willing to do what is necessary to the soil for dogwoods, don't plant them or you will be disappointed. There are varieties such as 'Cherokee Chief', which has dark-pink flowers; 'Cloud Nine', a heavy-blooming white variety; 'White Cloud', a well-established, heavy-blooming variety; 'Spring Song', a rose-red blooming variety; 'First Lady' with its variegated foliage; 'Rubra', with pink flowers; and 'Welch's Junior Miss', a pink-flowered variety. I recommend a springtime visit to Palestine, TX, when its Dogwood Festival is in progress. Flowering dogwood is hardy statewide.

Bloom Period and Seasonal Color

Spring blooms in white, red, and pink with red/orange fall leaf color.

Mature Height × Spread

20 to 30 ft. × 25 ft.

Oak

Quercus spp.

There is no group of trees more proper for Texas land-scapes than the oak. Oaks come in many different sizes, types, shapes, and colors. To determine the best varieties adapted to your location, visit local garden centers for in-depth information. Be prepared to tell them your soil type, and soil pH. Ask the retailers about the particular tree's origin and its exact identity. This is especially important when selecting certain live oaks. Live oaks that were selected, grown, and produced in the Gulf Coast area, for example, may not survive in the High Plains area because of the difference in temperatures. Pin oak, water oak, and willow oak should not be planted in alkaline soils. Oaks are hardy statewide, depending on variety.

Bloom Period and Seasonal Color
Non-showy blooms in spring with green, red, and reddish orange leaves.

Mature Height × Spread
20 to 100 ft. × 15 to 80 ft.

When, Where, and How to Plant
Plant oaks in the early fall or very early spring. Dig the planting hole several times wider than the soil-ball, though the hole should not be deeper than the depth of the soilball. Loosen the soil, backfill with the loosened soil, water thoroughly, apply root stimulator, and cover bare soil with about 3 in. of bark mulch. Stake temporarily if necessary.

Growing Tips
Water during early establishment to prevent soil dryness, especially during July and August. Fertilize throughout the growing season with slow-release 3:1:2 lawn fertilizer. I like to fertilize once in the spring as new growth begins, perhaps once during mid-season, and once again in the fall. Some 3:1:2 ratio lawn fertilizers are 21-7-14, 19-5-9, and 15-5-10. My oak trees grow 3 to 4 ft. per year.

Care
Prune to maintain the natural shape of your oak tree. The preferred time for pruning is in early spring as new growth is beginning. Some oak trees may have insect and disease problems, but if your trees are kept healthy and vigorous, these will be kept to a minimum or will be non-existant. If insects or diseases do become a problem, visit your local garden center for the best control possibilities.

Companion Planting and Design
You may wish to try planting deciduous varieties—such as Shumard red oak or bur oak—on the west side of your home. These oaks will provide shade during the hot time of year, and after the leaves fall off, the sun will strike your home to warm it in the winter.

I Suggest
I like several oak varieties, but if I had to pick a favorite, it would be the live oak, *Q. virginiana*. A runner-up is the Texas red oak, *Q. texana*.

Passion Vine

Passiflora incarnata

When, Where, and How to Plant

Plant passion vine in spring after all danger of frost has passed. Plant in any location where the soil drains well. If your soil is heavy or poorly drained clay, raise your bed several inches with a good organic mix as if preparing a bed for bedding plants. Do not plant in poorly drained areas, full shade, or areas that are difficult to water. Special soil preparation is not necessary. In poorly drained areas (or if you wish to have a raised bed), add several inches of organic matter, such as compost, brown sphagnum, peat moss, ground-bark mulch, or a combination of these. Four in. of these materials blended with the top 4 in. of your soil is a good mix for growing any flowering or vining plant. Plant in individual holes no deeper than the plants were growing in their containers. Firm the soil well, water thoroughly, apply root stimulator, and cover bare soil with 3 in. of bark mulch to complete the planting.

Growing Tips

Water as necessary to prevent soil dryness and maintain a moist soil. Fertilize as new growth begins in the spring with your favorite type of fertilizer that is high in the middle ratio number. Remember to read and follow label directions when using any product, and water thoroughly after fertilizer application.

Care

Prune only as needed to achieve your training goal. Normally pests and diseases are not a problem with passion vine. If you happen to have problems with them, take a trip to your local garden center for advice on the control.

Companion Planting and Design

Passion vine may be used with other vining plants, or at the back of screening-type shrubs that will allow the vine to grow up and above them. It will also grow on any structure, including fences, pergolas, gazebos, and lattice.

I Suggest

Try one or more of these exotic beauties in your landscape or in a large container with a trellis. My daughter says, "Papa, they look alien," and I must admit their blooms are exotic.

Passiflora incarnata is known by several names to Texas gardeners, including passionflower, passion vine, and maypop. In most Texas zones it will die down each year, then spring up easily the following spring and grow to its normal size, producing the blossoms that so many people admire. In good-quality soils it branches readily and gives outstanding re-growth, with more vines and blooms every year. It will grow up walls with some assistance and will also run along the ground. Its long tentacles act as holdfasts to attach the stems to whatever structures they are growing on. Passion vine is wonderful near an outdoor seating area where you wish to enjoy its blooms. P. lutea, a small yellow variety, is also available. Passion vine is hardy in Zones 7 to 9.

Other Common Names
Passion Flower, Maypop

Bloom Period and Seasonal Color
Summer blooms in pale to pinkish lavender, blue, yellow, and purple.

Mature Height × Spread
Vine to 20 ft. or more in any direction.

Pecan
Carya illinoiensis

I just love pecan pie—especially my wife's—and pecan shade trees. If you love "Texana," you ought to have at least one pecan tree on your property, for it is the Texas state tree. I grew up in Brown County where a lot of pecans are grown. Across the Colorado River south of Brownwood in the San Saba area, you will find tremendous pecan orchards. There is even a pecan variety called 'San Saba'. There are over a hundred varieties of pecans on the market today. If you want to grow pecan trees for shade and pecans for pies, visit your garden center to get the best locally adapted varieties. These include 'Choctaw', 'Desirable', 'Cheyenne', 'Caddo', 'Shawnee', 'Kiowa', 'San Saba', 'Stewart', and 'Sioux'. Pecan trees are hardy statewide.

Bloom Period and Seasonal Color
Non-showy spring bloom. Fall foliage in yellow.

Mature Height × Spread
60 to 125 ft. × 100 ft.

When, Where, and How to Plant
Plant container-grown pecan trees in the fall or early spring. Plant bare root or packaged selections during your zone's dormant season. You'll find that pecan trees grow satisfactorily in clay soils as long as the soil is deep and drains. It's a mistake to plant these trees in damp, wet, or otherwise poorly drained areas. Don't plant in shallow or rocky soil. No special soil preparation is necessary. Dig the planting hole no deeper than the depth of the plant's soilball, but you may dig it several times wider. After installing your plant, backfill with loosened soil, water thoroughly, apply root stimulator, and cover with 3 in. of bark mulch. Stake temporarily if necessary.

Growing Tips
Drip irrigation is often employed to prevent soil dryness. Maintaining a thick layer of mulch around the root system will conserve soil moisture. Fertilize throughout the growing season. You may use slow-release 3:1:2 lawn fertilizer (such as 21-7-14, 19-5-9, and 15-5-10). There are also specialty fertilizers for pecan trees available as well. In certain areas of the state with highly alkaline soils, supplemental spraying of the foliage with zinc may be necessary. Tip and fact sheets on proper fertilization and care of pecan trees are available at your County Agent's office.

Care
Prune to maintain strong branching and to remove dead wood. There are several insects and diseases that may visit your pecan trees including aphids, webworms, and casebarer. I recommend you pick up a pecan spray schedule from the local Texas Agricultural Extension Service office for advice on these and others.

Companion Planting and Design
Plant pecan trees in your landscape where they will have sufficient room to grow. Ask the local garden center about the varieties you plan to select. Ask questions regarding the potential width and height of the tree. Space your tree away from driveways, pools, your home, and other structures.

I Suggest
Looking at 'Choctaw' and 'Desirable' varieties because they are widely available and produce good pecans.

When, Where, and How to Plant

Plant pine trees in early fall, though early spring is also a good time. Depending on the variety selected, pine trees will grow in light and sandy soils to heavy clay soils. No special soil preparation is necessary. Dig individual planting holes wider than the soilball of the transplant, but not deeper, and loosen the soil. Do not add any additional soil amendments to the planting hole(s). Install plants, backfill with the soil, and water thoroughly. Apply root stimulator according to label directions, spread 2 in. or more of bark mulch around the planting area, and stake temporarily if necessary.

Growing Tips

Water as necessary, especially during establishment. Fertilize approximately three times throughout the growing season with your favorite granular fertilizer. Slow-release 3:1:2 ratio lawn fertilizers work well. Remember to water thoroughly after each application. Examples of 3:1:2 ratio lawn fertilizers are 15-5-10, 18-6-12, and 19-5-9.

Care

Prune to remove dead wood and maintain desired shape. If pests become a problem, go to your local garden center for the best controls. Pests could include pine bark beetles and pine tip moths. Contact the local Texas Agricultural Extension Service office in your county for tip or fact sheets on pine trees used in the home landscape. Healthy pine trees have few problems with insects and diseases.

Companion Planting and Design

Planting location depends on the desired application as well as the ultimate height and width of the tree. Smaller pine trees, such as 'Pinon', may be planted very close to your home. Some of the larger-growing varieties may need to be spaced farther away. Some tall-growing pines can create a windbreak when planted in multiple rows, or you may wish to use a small variety for a patio tree. Pines will also work in a Xeriscape.

I Suggest

Before planting pines you should know your soil's pH—then select any pine that is suited for your region.

When many of us think of naturally occurring pine trees, the East Texas pine automatically comes to mind. It's true that our heaviest pine forests are in East Texas, but pines also grow in West Texas, at Big Bend, and in the Panhandle. Certain pines will even grow in all areas of the state. Perhaps you favor a clump or group planting of them in your landscape simply because you like the look and the smell of pine. Other gardeners like the soothing sound of wind blowing through the trees. Make sure you understand the growth habit and characteristics of selected pine trees before purchasing. Some pine trees grow relatively fast while others are slower. There are also some imported pine trees that adapt well to Texas landscapes. Pines are hardy statewide.

Bloom Period and Seasonal Color

Non-showy blooms in the spring. Evergreen foliage.

Mature Height × Spread

20 to 125 ft. × 15 to 70 ft. or more.

Redbud
Cercis canadensis

After we Texans have been indoors for what seems like a long winter, we are ready to see some spring color. Redbud always does a great job of satisfying this need! Redbud blooms early before getting dressed for the summer in its heart-shaped leaves. C. reniformis 'Oklahoma' or Oklahoma redbud's foliage is soft pink when it emerges; then it changes to a rich shiny green. The leaves of C. canadensis 'Forest Pansy' are scarlet-purple while emerging, changing to maroon as they mature for the summer. I know it seems odd, but there is a "white" redbud—C. canadensis 'Alba', or white-flowered redbud. Check out these possibilities: 'Oklahoma', C. canadensis var. texensis or Texas redbud, and C. canadensis var. mexicana or Mexican redbud. Redbuds are hardy statewide.

Other Common Name
Eastern Redbud

Bloom Period and Seasonal Color
Spring blooms in pink with fall foliage in yellow.

Mature Height × Spread
15 to 30 ft. × 15 to 25 ft.

When, Where, and How to Plant
Fall, winter, or early spring plantings are preferable. I wouldn't plant in July, August, or even early September. Plant in moist, fertile, well-drained soil. Do not plant in heavily shaded areas or spots with poorly drained or wet soils. No special soil preparation is needed. Loosen the soil wider than the soilball, and dig the planting hole no deeper than the soilball. Place in the planting hole. Backfill with loosened soil, water thoroughly, and apply a root stimulator. Mulch bare soil with 3 to 4 in. of bark mulch after planting is completed. Stake temporarily if necessary.

Growing Tips
After redbuds are established, water only during dry periods to help maintain healthy trees. Fertilize four times a year with a premium-quality, long-lasting, slow-release 3:1:2 ratio lawn fertilizer (such as 15-5-10, 18-6-12, or 21-7-14) according to label directions. Apply first when new spring leaves begin to emerge, then ten weeks later, again in ten more weeks, and finally during the fall. Water thoroughly after each fertilizer application.

Care
Prune when young to prevent narrow, weak-angled branches. Very little pruning is needed afterwards. The fast growing redbud is relatively short-lived (twenty to twenty-five years). Aphids may occur on spring foliage. Visit area retailers for controls.

Companion Planting and Design
Use redbuds singularly as lawn trees, specimens, courtyard, or patio plantings. They also work well near yard swings, decks, gazebos, or other garden structures. In group plantings they provide a great spring show. They mix well with and complement flowering dogwood trees, *Cornus florida*, in semi-shady locations. Their scale works well with single-story structures, and they may be placed relatively close to those structures without damage to foundations. Redbud can be used to line drives and walks without damage.

I Suggest
Take a look at the redbud's foliage up close. Be sure to compare the differences in foliage to determine which one you prefer. 'Oklahoma' is my personal favorite.

Sage (Autumn)
Salvia greggii

When, Where, and How to Plant

Plant *Salvia greggii* in early spring or early fall. It prefers full sun all day long (a minimum of six hours), but if it must be in shade part of the day, make sure it receives shade from the hot west afternoon sun. *Salvia greggii* requires no special soil preparation other than making sure the soil drains well. For planting in native soil, dig the hole several times wider than the plant's soilball, but no deeper. Remove the plants from their containers, set in the planting holes, and backfill with the loosened soil. Water thoroughly, apply root stimulator, and cover with 2 in. of bark mulch. This plant is normally said to be winter hardy in Zone 7b southward, but we live in Zone 7a and have enjoyed these beauties for seven years without winter damage.

Growing Tips

Water as necessary to prevent soil dryness, but do not over-water or keep wet. You may fertilize one time per year using a premium-quality, slow-release granular rose fertilizer.

Care

Prune rather severely in early spring to encourage new growth and maximize bloom possibilities. To encourage even more blooms, the plants may be pinched, trimmed, or cut back periodically throughout the growing season. There are no serious insects or disease problems for autumn sage except for those that arise from poorly drained soils.

Companion Planting and Design

When put together in masses to create a tall groundcover-type effect it makes a spectacular planting. If you like Texas landscape plants but your space is limited, try *Salvia greggii* in large containers. It gives outstanding color when placed along walkways going into your home. This Texan is great in a Xeriscape planting.

I Suggest

Any of the colors you personally like will do well. Best impact is obtained in mass plantings of single colors.

Salvia greggii, or autumn sage, is a true member of the sage family. It has wonderful foliage whose fragrance becomes obvious when you simply brush by the plant. It will grow in clichéd soils—limestone, clay, and sandy—if it is well drained. The flowers are only about one inch in size, but extremely colorful. Note: Salvia greggii may grow into a relatively woody plant, become more shrublike, and reach three feet in height. Under these conditions it is often used as a shrub. Cut radically to approximately four inches. Allowed to re-grow, it is called a native flowering perennial. However you classify it, Salvia greggii is a great native flowering plant for any Texas landscape. Various selections come in orange, pink, red, white, and purple.

Other Common Name
Salvia

Bloom Period and Seasonal Color
Spring to fall blooms in white, pink, purple, and red.

Mature Height × Spread
1 to 3 ft. × 3 ft.

105

Southern Magnolia
Magnolia grandiflora

Nothing speaks to Southern gardeners like Magnolia grandiflora, or the Southern magnolia. It's one of the oldest ornamental trees used in our landscapes. It's native to acid soils, but it does well in deep clay soils if moisture is adequate. Because Southern magnolia puts out such dense shade, it's difficult to grow plants beneath it. I have had several requests from callers to my radio shows and readers of my garden columns about what to grow under magnolias. The best solution is to not plant anything under magnolias, and allow the branches to reach the ground. Magnolias can be dominant in the landscape and have the ability to be an outstanding pyramidal-shaped, long-lived, quality tree when selected, planted and cared for properly. They are hardy in Zones 7 to 9.

Other Common Name
Bull Bay Magnolia

Bloom Period and Seasonal Color
Summer through fall blooms in white with evergreen foliage.

Mature Height × Spread
50 to 100 ft. × 30 to 50 ft. or more.

When, Where, and How to Plant
Plant Southern magnolia in the fall or early spring in deep soils. It will grow in sandy soils and clay soils as long as adequate moisture is present, and it prefers a relatively fertile soil. Southern magnolia requires no special soil preparation as long as the soil is deep and fertile, and adequate moisture is available. Dig the planting hole no deeper than the tree soilball. Remove your selection from the container and install it in the planting hole. Backfill, water thoroughly, apply root stimulator according to label directions, and cover bare soil with 3 in. of bark mulch. Stake temporarily if necessary. Not recommended for planting in rocky, shallow soils. Avoid limestone areas.

Growing Tips
Water as necessary to prevent soil dryness. If you have a location that is difficult to water, do some plumbing and set up a drip irrigation system. Do not plant near existing trees or structures or in very shallow soils, especially if it would be difficult to apply supplemental irrigation. Fertilize approximately three times during the year with the same type of granular fertilizer used on azaleas, camellias, or gardenias. Apply in the spring as new growth begins, mid-season, and once in the fall. Always water thoroughly after application.

Care
Prune only dead or damaged limbs and leaves. Do not prune off lower limbs, as this would change the entire growth habit of the tree. Allow the limbs to reach the ground. There are no serious pests attracted to Southern magnolia.

Companion Planting and Design
It can become a wonderful feature in your landscape when placed properly, but since part of its root system is very near the soil surface, I would not recommend planting it close to a house. This is the type of tree one plants to the side of a landscape, allowing it to grow to its full potential.

I Suggest
Give this tree plenty of room and watch it grow!

When, Where, and How to Plant

Plant sweet gum trees in the fall. Spring planting is fine, but fall selection will allow you to determine the leaf color before you plant. Sweet gum will grow in loam or clay soils as long as the soil is deep and moist. Do not plant in shallow soil or in areas that are difficult to water. Sweet gum trees require no special soil preparation, other than making sure the soil is deep, is relatively fertile, and has sufficient moisture. Dig the planting hole no deeper than and several times wider than the tree soilball. Install in the planting hole, backfill with soil only, and water thoroughly. Apply root stimulator according to label directions, and cover bare soil with 3 in. of bark mulch. Stake temporarily if necessary.

Growing Tips

Water to prevent soil dryness. Sweet gum is a tree for relatively moist growing conditions, so plant where you can easily supply moisture when needed. This is especially true in July and August. Fertilize once in the early spring as new growth begins, once mid-season, and once again in the fall. Use a slow-release 3:1:2 ratio lawn fertilizer (such as 19-5-9, 18-6-12, or 21-7-14).

Care

Prune to remove dead branches; no other pruning is usually needed. Tent caterpillars and aphids may visit your tree. In hot dry seasons, spider mites may become a problem. If any of these pests invade your planting, take a trip to the local garden center to research the best control possibilities. Keep sweet gums in good health and you should have few insect problems.

Companion Planting and Design

Because of falling debris and the tree's size potential, do not plant it next to existing structures, walkways, or patios. Use as a specimen tree in west locations in the landscape or as part of a very large landscape bed.

I Suggest

Seekout the fruitless variety if you want to avoid the sweet gum balls.

The highways of East Texas display fall color with naturally occurring plantings of sweet gum. One highway section with excellent fall color is Highway 19 between Athens and Canton. My listeners and readers often want to know about good-quality shade trees that are long-lived and fast-growing. Sweet gum meets all of these requirements. It grows not only in East Texas soil, but also in heavy clay, as long as the soil is deep and the trees do not grow over limestone. Use it away from the home, out in the landscape where the sharp sweet gum balls that fall after leaves drop will not be a problem. Some named varieties are 'Palo Alto', 'Festival', 'Autumn Glow', and 'Burgundy'. Sweet gum is hardy statewide.

Bloom Period and Seasonal Color

Non-showy spring bloom with fall foliage in yellow, red, reddish orange, and burgundy.

Mature Height × Spread

45 to 50 ft. up to 100 ft. × 60 ft.

Texas Ash
Fraxinus texensis

The best ash selection for use in our state is Texas ash. If you are looking for a small- to medium-sized tree that is tough and durable and provides outstanding shade as well as great fall colors, I highly recommend it. Arizona ash is used in developments and is widely available, but it lacks the Texas ash's drought tolerance and is considered a "trash tree." Texas ash is a relatively fast-growing, strong, good-quality, and long-lasting tree. Be warned, there are male and female ash trees. If you are concerned about fruit drop and seeds germinating, make sure the retailer knows that you want only male selections. Other acceptable ash trees include white ash, F. americana, and green ash, F. pennsylvanica. Texas ash is hardy statewide.

Bloom Period and Seasonal Color
Spring, non-showy bloom. Fall foliage in yellow, copper, tangerine, rose, and lime.

Mature Height × Spread
35 to 50 ft. × 25 to 35 ft.

When, Where, and How to Plant
Texas ash may be planted at any time during the year, but fall is best. Plant Texas ash anywhere there is sufficient room for it to grow into its normal shape. Make sure the soil is deep for best overall growth. While Texas ash will grow in rather harsh conditions—such as restricted root zone areas and even compacted soil— plant in locations that have better soil for best results. Texas ash needs no special soil preparation. Simply dig the planting hole the same depth as the soilball, though you may dig it several times wider. After the planting hole is complete, remove your selection from the container and install in the hole. Backfill with the loosened soil, water thoroughly, apply root stimulator, and cover bare soil with 3 in. of bark mulch. Stake temporarily if needed.

Growing Tips
Water as necessary—especially during initial establishment—to prevent soil dryness. After establishment, Texas ash is extremely tough, durable, and drought-resistant. Fertilize once in spring and once in fall. Use a slow-release granular fertilizer (such as 15-5-10, 18-6-12, or 21-7-14). Remember to water thoroughly after each application.

Care
Prune to remove dead or damaged limbs and correct growth habit. Aphids have been known to visit ash trees. If they become a problem, ask your local garden center for controls.

Companion Planting and Design
Texas ash works well in urban lots that are rather small. Plant Texas ash where its fall colors may be easily viewed from the home, and where its dense shade will benefit the home through the summertime. Its leaves will fall off when the weather turns cold, allowing the sun's warmth to strike your home during the winter, thus conserving energy. This ash tree will work in a Xeriscape planting.

I Suggest
Plant Texas ash when you need a fast-growing quality shade tree.

Texas Mountain Laurel

Sophora secundiflora

When, Where and How to Plant

Container grown native plants may be planted anytime. The best time to plant is the fall, or late winter/early spring. Texas mountain laurel is slow growing and does not transplant as easily as other native plants. It requires the least amount of root disturbance as possible at planting time. It may take one year or more for the plant to establish itself. After establishment, Texas mountain laurel is very easily grown in well-drained locations. Do not plant in poorly drained or heavily shaded locations. No soil amending other than for drainage is needed; however, the plant will respond to well prepared soil. I suggest 6 in. of organic matter in a landscape bed, blended with the top 8 in. of native soil. Dig individual hole(s) no deeper than soilball depth. Place mountain laurel in planting hole, backfill, and water thoroughly. Apply a root stimulator according to label directions, and mulch all bare soil 3 to 4 in. deep.

Growing Tips

Do not keep the soil wet or damp. Provide extra irrigation when needed if optimum growth is desired. You may fertilize with your favorite tree or shrub fertilizer. I fertilize most blooming plants, including shrubs, with a rose fertilizer twice to three times in the spring and once in early fall. Always read and follow label directions when using any gardening aid, including fertilizers. Some callers to my radio show say "watching Texas mountain laurel grow is as exciting as watching paint dry." While considered a slow growing native plant, it will respond to improved soil and supplemental water and fertilizer.

Care

Texas mountain laurel is a low care plant and pest free. If any pest is brave enough to visit your plant, have the invader identified at local nurseries and then take a recommended course of action.

Companion Planting and Design

Texas mountain laurel works well in any full sun, well drained location with other natives—including salvia greggii, Texas sage, and agarito. They all are best used as a focal point in beds away from the foundation of a home.

I Suggest

At this time there are no known varieties.

For drought tolerance, no pests, and ease of growing, our native Texas mountain laurel is hard to beat. It naturally occurs in central to south and west Texas in limestone areas, but will grow state wide in Zones 8a to 9b. I am growing one in Zone 7b, which some say is "gardening on the edge." My wife and I are growing a blue one. Its beautiful—almost grape-like—clusters of fragrant blooms remind us of old grape sodas, such as Nu-Grape® and Grapette®, and the good memories that came with them. For deep green foliage with grape soda fragrance give this baby a try. Remember: Texas mountain laurel beans are toxic. Teach children not to put the beans—or parts from any other plant—into their mouths.

Other Common Name
Mescal Bean

Bloom Period and Seasonal Color
Spring blooms in blue grape clusters with evergreen foliage.

Mature Height × Spread
6 × 12 ft. to 25 × 6ft.

Texas Sage
Leucophyllum frutescens

I love our plantings of Texas sage. We have the standard gray and green types. If you live in an area that receives a minimal amount of rainfall, wait until we have one of our nice drenching rains. After the rain, stand back and watch the blooms on Texas sage—they will be absolutely outstanding. I have seen this magic occur in municipal landscapes as well as along medians and highways where the reflected heat is tremendous. Texas sage always stands up to the task. After a rain, there are blooms everywhere—people stop to look and point at the beauty. If you are going to grow only one native Texas plant, choose Texas sage. It is hardy in Zones 7b to 9.

Other Common Name
Cenizo

Bloom Period and Seasonal Color
Summer blooms in white, pink, and purple.

Mature Height × Spread
4 to 8 ft. × 4 to 6 ft.

When, Where, and How to Plant
Plant cenizo in the spring or in the fall. Plant Texas sage anywhere in the landscape that has a minimum of six hours of full sun. It does extremely well in full sun, all day long. It can take only a little shade. Cenizo will grow in any of our native Texas soils as long as they are well drained. Dig the planting hole several times wider than the plant's soilball, but no deeper. Remove the plants from their containers, place in the holes, backfill, and firm the soil well. Water thoroughly. After watering, apply root stimulator, and cover bare soil with 2 in. of bark mulch.

Growing Tips
Water as necessary throughout the growing season to prevent complete soil dryness. Remember, do not overwater. You may fertilize if desired. I suggest a premium-quality, slow-release rose fertilizer applied according to label directions.

Care
Texas sage is a relatively pest-free plant. In the eight years we have been growing it, we have encountered no insects or diseases. Minimum to no pruning is recommended.

Companion Planting and Design
Texas sage may be used as a foundation planting in full sun locations. I like it best in mass plantings in the landscape with native perennials.

I Suggest
Try cenizo as an accent planting in either the green or gray foliage. This shrub is super in a Xeriscape planting. If you want something easy and different in your landscape, try 'Silver Cloud' or 'Rain Cloud'. Both can grow to a height of 3 ft. 'Green Cloud' can grow up to 8 ft., and has green foliage. These varieties may be more difficult to locate but are worth the hunt.

When, Where, and How to Plant

The ideal planting time for Texas wisteria is during the spring when you can find it in bloom; fall planting is also acceptable. Till or otherwise loosen the soil in beds or other planting locations where your selection of Texas wisteria will be planted. Dig planting holes the same depth as the plant's rootball. After planting, backfill, firm the soil, water thoroughly, apply root stimulator according to label directions, and cover bare soil with 3 in. of bark mulch.

Growing Tips

Water as necessary to prevent complete soil dryness. Fertilization is usually not required.

Care

Prune and train as necessary to reach your desired goal. There are no insects or diseases associated with Texas wisteria.

Companion Planting and Design

Texas wisteria displays clusters of blooms after foliage appears. The dark, shiny green leaves showcase lilac and purple blooms. If you have a full sun area on the west side of your home and you wish to create a lattice shaded area, cover that structure with Texas wisteria. Plant it in any location you wish to have a good-looking, easy-to-grow vine with fragrant blossoms. It works especially well on arbors, although pergolas, gazebos, and arches, are all likely candidates for Texas wisteria.

I Suggest

When building structures for Texas wisteria use dimension lumber and heavy lattice panels. Do not plant on lightweight structures. When purchasing Texas wisteria, make sure you choose a color you like by making your selections from plants in bloom. Like Texas mountain laurel, Texas wisteria's sweet grape fragrance makes me think of the old grape sodas I remember.

You may like the looks and fragrance of wisteria, but may be a bit worried that imported varieties will get out of hand and take over the entire yard. Your fears are not unfounded. Sometimes wisteria can turn into Frankenstein. One planted before the turn of the century in California has over a million blooms on it annually. Texas wisteria can be managed much better than the imported wisterias. The blooms are smaller, but it has nice, dark-green, glossy foliage. The combination of blooms and leaves make this quite a showy plant. There are no selected cultivars or named varieties of Texas wisteria. Simply ask for Texas wisteria or Wisteria macrostachya. *It may be more easily found at nurseries that specialize in native Texas plants.*

Bloom Period and Seasonal Color

Spring blooms in lilac and purple.

Mature Length

Vine to 20 ft. in all directions.

Turk's Cap
Malvaviscus arboreus var. *drummondii*

Turk's cap is a rather large, spreading herbaceous shrub. In South Texas it is more woody than it is in North Texas, where it dies down to the ground, comes back every year, and acts more like a large perennial. It's one native Texas plant that will grow in shaded areas. We are able to enjoy the beauty of the plant itself, plus it attracts hummingbirds and butterflies! M. arboreus var. drummondii is the Turk's cap grown most often in Texas. M. arboreus is a species with larger leaves and blooms. If you want to create a backyard habitat, be sure to include Turk's cap. My planting is extra special because it came from my Granny Miller before she went to spend time with the "Big Gardener." Turk's cap will grow in all areas of Texas.

Other Common Name
Bleeding Heart

Bloom Period and Seasonal Color
Spring through fall blooms in red. Occasional red, almost apple-shaped fruits/seed pods.

Mature Height × Spread
2 to 6 ft. × 3 to 5 ft.

When, Where, and How to Plant
Turk's cap is easy to start with transplants, layering, or from seed. Plant Turk's cap in early spring after the soil is warm. It will grow in sunny locations as long as it has adequate soil moisture. Turk's cap will grow in clay, loam, sand, or any mixture of these three types as long as the soil is moist and well drained. To enhance overall growth, you may wish to improve the soil by incorporating 3 in. of organic matter into the top 3 in. Dig planting holes no deeper than the soilball, and insert the plants in the holes. Firm the soil, water thoroughly, apply root stimulator, and mulch 3 in. or so with a bark mulch.

Growing Tips
For maximum growth, water as necessary to maintain a moist soil. Turk's cap benefits from having a well-mulched root system. Fertilize two or three times throughout the growing season to maximize blooms. I fertilize with a long-lasting, slow-release rose fertilizer.

Care
Once new growth begins in the spring, remove any growth that was killed by winter freezes. No other pruning is required. Turk's cap is usually not bothered by serious insect or disease problems. Some herbaceous plants die to, or nearly to, the ground each year, and regrow the following growing season. Turk's cap may follow this pattern in all areas of Texas which receive hard killing frosts and freezes.

Companion Planting and Design
This shrub works well planted in and among other landscape plants. We have planted ruellia at the base of our Turk's cap, with bouncing bet and other easy-to-grow perennial plants around it. This Texas native shrub should not be used in a Xeriscape.

I Suggest
When looking for a little red in a dapple shady landscape give the *drummondii* variety a try. It is more widely available than the larger leaved/ bloomed species *M. arboreus*.

Virginia Creeper
Parthenocissus quinquefolia

When, Where, and How to Plant

Ideal planting times are spring or early fall, but you can plant Virginia creeper any time of the year, as it is extremely durable. Virginia creeper will grow in virtually any type of Texas soil, including clay and sand, as long as the soil is well drained. It will also grow in heavily shaded areas, dappled shade, part shade, or full sun. Because it is adaptable to heavily shaded areas where St. Augustinegrass won't grow, it can come to the rescue and provide needed vegetation cover. Simply loosen the native soil. If you are going to plant a large bed, you will need a tiller. After soil is prepared, plant Virginia creeper at the same depth it was growing in the container. Firm the soil, water thoroughly, apply root stimulator, and cover bare soil with 3 in. of bark mulch.

Growing Tips

Water as necessary during establishment. After establishment, occasional watering to prevent soil dryness is advisable. Fertilization is usually not required. If you wish to enhance or speed the growth of Virginia creeper, be aware that it does grow vigorously in response to fertilization. It also responds well to a moist soil conditions.

Care

Prune as required to maintain desired shape and size. This plant has no pests.

Companion Planting and Design

Virginia creeper may be used as a thick groundcover that requires mowing only once a year. When used as a vine on large garden structures, it will provide complete shade in the summer and gorgeous color in the fall, and it will allow sunlight in during the winter. I think the best application for Virginia creeper is on large garden structures, but it can also be used in expansive areas, used underneath trees, and allowed to weep over stone walls with great impact. When growing underneath groups of trees, it helps create a "woodland" effect.

I Suggest

Take a look at this large leaved deciduous native Texas vine at local nurseries. It works well with tall, solid brick walls with narrow beds, as often found with commercial structures.

Consider Virginia creeper if you need a vine to provide complete coverage of a cottage. It's also excellent for use on walls or structures—it will help save money on air-conditioning when it is planted on the west side of your home. It requires no spraying, no fertilization, and little watering after establishment. You may wish to do some pruning, training, or directing of its growth. Virginia creeper has no known toxic effects and is a wonderful native vine. There are no known named varieties at this time. A first cousin, Boston ivy, P. tricuspidata, covers the campuses of many Ivy League universities. Virginia creeper is hardy statewide.

Bloom Period and Seasonal Color
Fall foliage in red.

Mature Height × Spread
Vine to 50 ft. in any direction.

Wax Myrtle
Myrica cerifera

Wax myrtle generally prefers a moist soil when grown in its native habitat in woodlands and often grows on top of a moist area or spring. But it also grows in hot medians, alongside our multi-lane highways, and in urban applications. I am growing some wax myrtle on the west side of my well-house. The well-house is painted solid white, so there is reflected heat in this location, but the wax myrtle is flourishing. If you have enjoyed a tall-growing yapon holly and want to try something with similar characteristics, take a look at the tall-growing wax myrtle. I cannot emphasize enough how easy it is to grow wax myrtle and how much I think you will enjoy it in your home landscape. Wax myrtle is hardy statewide.

Bloom Period and Seasonal Color
Evergreen foliage.

Mature Height × Spread
12 to 20 ft. or more × 8 to 16 ft.

When, Where, and How to Plant
Wax myrtle can be planted year-round in Texas. The best time to plant is early fall and second best is early spring. Plant wax myrtle in any type of Texas soil, including sand, loam, or clay; it will even grow in relatively poorly drained areas. It will also grow in sunny or shady spots—provided that it receives dappled, not heavy, shade. Wax myrtle needs no special soil preparation. Dig the planting hole several times wider than the soilball, but only to soilball depth. Loosen the soil and plant soilball. Insert wax myrtle approximately 3 ft. apart in mass plantings. Backfill with loose soil, water thoroughly, apply root stimulator, and cover bare soil with 3 in. of bark mulch.

Growing Tips
For best growth, maintain a moist soil. Fertilize two or three times during the growing season—once as new growth begins in the spring, once in the fall, and possibly once in mid-season. Use a premium-quality, slow-release 3:1:2 lawn fertilizer. Some examples of 3:1:2 lawn fertilizers are 21-7-14, 18-6-12, and 15-5-10.

Care
Prune if you would like to maintain or create a desired shape, otherwise no pruning is required. This plant has no serious insects or diseases.

Companion Planting and Design
Wax myrtle is a good plant to grow with ground-covers and other under-plantings. If you want an extremely tall, dense, low-maintenance screening plant, it will also fit the bill. Wax myrtle may also be grown as a specimen plant.

I suggest
Try one as a specimen planting in the landscape.

Woolly Butterfly Bush

Buddleia marubifolia

When, Where, and How to Plant

Plant woolly butterfly bush in early spring or in early fall. It will grow in sand or nice loam, as well as limestone-type soils, as long as the soil is well drained. It will survive harsh conditions, growing in parts of Texas that receive only 12 in. of rain per year. But to get best results from the plant, grow it in the type of beds where you would plant hollies and other landscape plants. First, incorporate approximately 4 in. of organic matter into the top 4 in. of the soil. After the soil is improved (or at least thoroughly loosened in an area several times wider than the plant's soilball), dig holes no deeper than the depth of the soilball and plant. Backfill with soil, firm, and water thoroughly. Apply root stimulator, and cover bare soil with 3 in. of bark mulch.

Growing Tips

Water as necessary to prevent soil dryness; to maximize growth, maintain a moist but not wet soil. Fertilize two times during the growing season with a premium-quality, slow- release rose fertilizer.

Care

Prune as necessary if you wish to maintain a desired shape, though it is best to allow the woolly butterfly bush to grow naturally. For compactness, you may wish to prune severely one time as spring begins. Woolly butterfly bush has no serious insects or diseases.

Companion Planting and Design

Woolly butterfly bush works well when part of a design around courtyards, patios, or pools, and it grows especially well in large tubs or containers. Its appearance is striking, and it can be combined with other native plants, such as Texas mountain laurel, yapon holly, and wax myrtle, as well as with imported plants. It will also work in a Xeriscape planting.

I Suggest

When trying a woolly butterfly bush, you may want to also try a cultivated variety of butterfly bush such as 'Black Knight' (a dark violet-purple), 'Harlequin' (a reddish-purple), 'Monite' (white) and/or 'Pink Delight' (pink blooms).

The woolly butterfly bush belongs to a larger group (or family) called Logania. In this family there is a wide assortment of plants often referred to as butterfly bush, many of which are fragrant and attract lots of butterflies. The woolly butterfly bush does not bloom as profusely as many of its cousins, but its blooms are interesting, and it is excellent for large border plantings. Just make sure the soil drains well, and the plant receives good air movement and lots of sun. This large family has several cultivated plants. When you visit your local garden center, ask to see their selections of butterfly bush. To see the woolly butterfly bush, be specific and ask for it by name. This plant will grow in all parts of Texas.

Other Common Name
Native Butterfly Bush

Bloom Period and Seasonal Color
Spring and summer blooms in orange.

Mature Height × Spread
2 to 4 ft. × 4 ft.

Native Wildflowers *for Texas*

With Texas's wide selection of annuals and perennials, we have many outstanding landscape native plant choices. The native annuals and perennials are commonly called "wildflowers," and Texas is blessed with them in variety and abundance.

In this chapter I have chosen and assembled detailed gardening information on annuals and perennials. While there certainly are more native wildflowers than the ones on my list, this is an excellent selection of specimens that will thrive in our unique Texas climate.

Just think about the diversity of our climate. We have cold Panhandle winters and an almost-tropical Rio Grande Valley. Texarkana gets forty-plus inches of rain per year, and El Paso gets nine inches. A wide variation in soil types and growing zones exists all over Texas.

Wonderful Colors and Blooms

Everyone is, or should be, familiar with our native Texas bluebonnet, *Lupinus texensis*. Take a look at black-eyed-Susan, *Rudbeckia hirta* var. 'Angustifolia'. Both plants provide wonderful color throughout the long growing season. Clasping-leaf coneflower, *Rudbeckia amplexicaulis*, coreopsis, *Coreopsis lanceolata*, Indian blanket, *Gaillardia pulchella*, and Texas bluebells, *Eustoma grandiflorum*, are other wonderful native flowers available to us.

Depending upon which Texas wildflowesr you select, they have the ability to provide season-long bloom in our Texas environment. Examples of season-long bloomers are rudbeckia, coreopsis, and gaillardia. Try them! Properly selected, placed, and maintained, Texas native flowers are a tough and relatively low-maintenance plant group. Our "wildflowers" are considered adaptable to most landscape situations.

On of my favorite wildflowers is black-eyed Susan, a member of the Rudbeckia family. This pretty flower is sometimes called brown-eyed Susan. I enjoy black-eyed-Susan in a west-facing bed along with salvias, daylilies, and ornamental grasses. It is one wildflower I recommend you try if its colors of golden yellow and dark brown fit in with your other landscape colors. You won't be disappointed.

Purple Coneflower

While a stand-alone planting of Indian paintbrush, *Castilleja indivisa*, will make a great color planting, it is super when utilized in combination with our state flower—the bluebonnet. Bluebonnets are great in large mass plantings as well as beds in the landscape. Make sure your location for

Indian paintbrush and bluebonnets is in a sunny spot that drains well. Central Texas and the Hill Country are both known as great areas to view native Texas wildflower blooms during the spring. These locations are especially good for both bluebonnets and Indian paintbrush plantings. Blue is an unusual color in the landscape, yet most Texans enjoy bluebonnets. For more blue color, I suggest having Texas bluebells in your garden. These tall natives add a special touch. Texas lantana, *Lantana horrida*, is tough enough to grow in all areas of our state. Judy and I have lived in rural Van Zandt County for twenty-three years, and the same planting of lantana has been with us for most of that time.

Coreopsis

People often ask me why a purple coneflower has its name when its blooms aren't purple. I don't have a good answer for this. What I do know is that purple (pink or white) coneflower is an easy-to-grow native perennial every Texas gardener should have in a color planting.

A great resource for Texas wildflower information is the Ladybird Johnson Wildflower Center in Austin. You can call or write them for information on wildflowers, or you can go see this interesting place for yourself. Our Texas Department of Transportation (TXDOT) has information on some of the best locations for viewing wildflowers.

Black-Eyed Susan
Rudbeckia hirta 'Pulcherrima'

Black-eyed Susan is a member of the sunflower's family and is a very easy-to-grow Texas native flower. While some varieties are annuals and others are short-lived perennials, either type will work well in the home landscape in full sun locations. Try black-eyed Susan in difficult-to-water areas that beg for great summertime color. Black-eyed Susan is found in East, South, and Central Texas, often in prairie areas or pinewoods. The two varieties of black-eyed Susan are R. hirta var. pulcherrima, a true annual, and R. hirta var. angustifolia, a short-lived perennial. Both varieties will work well in the home landscape.

Other Common Name
Brown-eyed Susan

Bloom Period and Seasonal Color
Summer blooms in yellow.

Mature Height × Spread
1 to 3 ft. × 6 to 8 in.

When, Where, and How to Plant
The best time to start Texas wildflowers, including black-eyed-Susan, is in the fall. If you decide to set out transplants, put them out in early spring after all danger of frost has passed. Black-eyed Susan needs to be in a well-drained location that receives at least eight hours of sunlight. If you are going to start from seed, prepare the soil by lightly tilling—removing sticks or other debris—and raking. Sow seeds according to package directions, and water thoroughly. Maintain a moist soil until seeds germinate and establish themselves, then gradually reduce the watering. If planting in prepared beds from transplants in the spring, be sure to add a few inches of organic matter to the top 3 or 4 in. of the native soil. After soil improvement is complete, remove your transplants from their containers, and install in the soil no deeper than they were growing in the containers. Firm the soil, water thoroughly, apply root stimulator according to label directions, and cover bare soil with 3 in. of bark mulch.

Growing Tips
Water sufficiently to prevent complete soil dryness, but do not over-water. Fertilize one time during the growing season with a premium-quality, long-lasting rose fertilizer, following label directions.

Care
Cut back old or spent flower stems, unless they are to go to seed for future plants. There are no insects or diseases that plague black-eyed Susan.

Companion Planting and Design
These babies will work well in any type of design using Xeriscape principles. Old-fashioned fragrant, non-native petunias and bachelor buttons are good cultural companions.

I Suggest
Try one or more areas of your landscape with either the annual or perennial forms for easy-growing color.

Bluebonnet

Lupinus texensis

When, Where, and How to Plant

Plant bluebonnet seed in the early fall. Set out transplants in late January through February. Plant bluebonnets in grass-free areas that drain well and have full sun. Do not plant in heavily-shaded or poorly-drained locations. Many people write me or call in to my radio show wanting to know if they can just throw bluebonnet seeds on the ground. Don't waste your money, time, energy, and effort doing this. In order to get a good stand of bluebonnets, vigorously rake the soil and make sure that you have removed the grasses in the area—especially Johnson grass and Bermudagrass. A better option is to lightly till the area and rake with a strong rake. Sow the seeds at a rate of approximately twelve seeds per sq. foot. Treated seeds, also known as scarified seeds, germinate very quickly and thrive with minimal irrigation, while untreated seeds may take as long as three years to germinate. In spring, plant transplants in tilled areas. Plant no deeper than they were originally grown in their containers. Water thoroughly and apply a root stimulator.

Growing Tips

Bluebonnets generally do not require pruning or fertilization. Water as necessary to prevent total soil dryness, especially at initial plant establishment. The grower should allow the plants to die and go to seed to allow for next year's crop. These areas will appear unkempt and untidy in the garden. Consider this when planning your garden design.

Care

Bluebonnets are considered insect- and disease-free by most gardeners. In landscape garden areas where plant concentrations are heavy, there may be problems with pillbugs, doodle bugs, or sow bugs. If this occurs in your plantings, seek pest control help at local nurseries. Remember to always follow label directions.

Companion Planting and Design

Bluebonnets are best planted in drifts by themselves.

I Suggest

The blue bluebonnets. Nothing in the plant kingdom speaks more about the beauty of Texas in the spring than the blue fields of bluebonnets. Try some of the other colors if desired, but always have some blue ones too.

When the bluebonnet was originally designated the Texas state wildflower in 1901, the species of choice was the small L. subcarnosus, which is now considered a less showy species. In 1971, the state legislature designated all bluebonnets the official state flower, from the short ones to the tall. There are 150 species of lupines. All but two are considered annuals. Bluebonnets are members of the Lupine genus. Lupines are found mostly throughout western North America but also in the Mediterranean area. The Big Bend bluebonnet, L. havardii, has been reported to grow as high as three feet. We Texans are fortunate to have the best of the Lupines—the Texas bluebonnet.

Bloom Period and Seasonal Color
Blooms during the spring. Blooms in shades of blue, pink, white and maroon.

Mature Height × Spread
15 to 24 in. × 10 to 12 in.

Evening Primrose
Oenothera spp.

Primrose grows in all areas of our state, though depending on the species, different common names are used. O. speciosa is known as the showy primrose, while O. missouriensis is known as the Missouri primrose. Our fellow Texas gardeners along the coast may be most familiar with the beach-evening-primrose, or O. drummondii. These are all perennial primroses. There is also an annual primrose called stemless evening primrose, O. triloba, and O. lamarckiana is an outstanding annual that is naturalized across the United States. A biannual or short-lived perennial is O. hookeri, often called yellow evening primrose. Either Missouri primrose or showy evening primrose is ideal for a perennial bed in a sunny location. If you prefer yellow, go with the Missouri, but if you prefer light pink, choose the showy primrose.

Other Common Name
Buttercups

Bloom Period and Seasonal Color
Summer blooms in white, pale pink to rose, and yellow.

Mature Height × Spread
6 to 24 in. × 3 ft.

When, Where, and How to Plant
Direct seed primroses in late summer to early fall in well-prepared beds. If fortunate enough to find transplants, plant immediately in prepared beds no deeper than the top of the soilball, water thoroughly, apply root stimulator, and cover bare soil with 2 in. of bark mulch. Transplants may be started in early spring after all danger of frost has passed and temperatures are warm. Whether starting from seed or from transplants, plant in sunny, well-drained locations, according to package instructions. Place transplants in prepared beds no deeper than the top of the soil ball. Firm the soil, water thoroughly, apply root stimulator according to label directions, and cover with 2 in. of bark mulch.

Growing Tips
Water as necessary to prevent soil dryness. Maintaining 2 in. of bark mulch will help to conserve soil moisture. Fertilize as new growth begins in the spring. Apply a premium-quality, slow-release granular rose or water-soluble fertilizer. Allow seed heads to mature to allow for future natural seeding in the garden.

Care
Pruning is not required with the evening primroses, but their appearance will benefit from regular deadheading. Evening primrose has few insect and disease problems. If chewing insects become a problem, visit your local garden center for the best control possibilities.

Companion Planting and Design
Plant along the curb, as border accents, or in meadows and rock gardens.

I Suggest
Try the showy primrose or *Oenothera speciosa.*

Garden Phlox
Phlox spp.

When, Where, and How to Plant

Start garden phlox seeds in very early fall. Set out transplants in the spring. All garden phlox will grow in limestone, loam, or clay, as long as the soil is well drained. Louisiana phlox needs at least 6 in. of good soil and at least six hours of full sun per day. Do not plant in poorly drained or heavily shaded locations, although these plants will benefit from a little shady protection from the hot western afternoon sun. If planting from seeds, prepare the seedbed as for bedding plants with lightly tilled soil. In locations that need more preparation, blend 3 in. of organic matter with the top 3 in. of the existing soil. Sow the seeds according to label directions. Water thoroughly. Install transplants in prepared locations no deeper than originally grown in their containers, and firm the soil well. Water thoroughly, apply root stimulator, and cover bare soil with 3 in. of bark mulch.

Growing Tips

Water as necessary to prevent soil dryness, but do not keep the soil wet. Fertilize in the spring as new growth begins.

Care

Remove spent bloom masses to encourage additional blooms throughout the season. Allow some crops to go to seed to multiply planting. No other pruning is required. While garden phlox has few insects or diseases, if pests do visit your planting, make a trip to your local garden center to find the best control possibilities. In closed areas with poor air movement, powdery mildew may become a problem.

Companion Planting and Design

Garden phlox may be grown as a bedding plant in a landscape bed, or added to your perennial plantings. Early spring-flowering varieties are excellent mixed with spring bulbs, pansies, and spring-flowering trees and shrubs. If you enjoy fragrant phlox, try it in some large tubs or beds near your entryway. For best results, plant in large drifts or masses.

I Suggest

If you enjoy a light sweet fragrance in your landscape, try *Phlox pilosa*.

In addition to the outstanding annual phlox grown in our state, you may wish to try some perennial varieties. P. pilosa imparts a wonderful fragrance to the landscape. It's often called fragrant phlox or prairie phlox. P. divaricata, or Louisiana phlox, will grow in East Texas locations where soil conditions are moist. Although it has the ability to slowly creep, phlox is not overpowering and presents an interesting-looking groundcover when used in small areas. P. nana, also known as dwarf phlox, has an unusual white/pink color. It is somewhat woody around its base, and has bright pink flowers. Perennial phlox include P. divaricata, Louisiana phlox, P. pilosa, fragrant phlox or prairie phlox, P. nana, dwarf phlox and P. nivalis, trailing phlox.

Other Common Names

Phlox, Sweet William, Perennial Phlox

Bloom Period and Seasonal Color

Spring to fall blooms in pink, rose, lavender, and purple.

Mature Height × Spread

20 in. × 1 1/2 to 2 ft.

Indian Blanket
Gaillardia pulchella

Gaillardia, or Indian blanket, happens to be one of my favorite native Texas wildflowers. If you are looking for an easy-to-grow, easy-to-care-for color source in your landscape, you can't go wrong with Indian blanket, which in mass plantings in sunny locations provides breathtaking color. Think you can't grow any Texas wildflowers from seeds? I strongly suggest you try Indian blanket. It grows virtually everywhere in our state. There are several variations of G. pulchella. The perennial G. aristata is extremely drought hardy.

Other Common Name
Firewheel

Bloom Period and Seasonal Color
Blooms late spring and summer with golden yellow-tipped red petals and reddish-brown centers.

Mature Height × Spread
1 to 2 ft. × 10 to 12 in.

When, Where, and How to Plant
Direct seed Indian blanket in late summer to early fall. Set out transplants in early spring after all danger of frost is past. Indian blanket requires at least eight hours of full sun in a prepared bed to perform at its best. Completely remove the vegetation from the area, lightly till, and rake. Seeds must be in contact with the soil in order to germinate properly. After sowing the seeds according to package directions, water thoroughly. Plant transplants in the same locations you would plant any other sun-loving annual, making sure that the soil drains well. Standard soil preparation for any landscape bed will be more than adequate for Indian blanket.

Growing Tips
Water as necessary to prevent soil dryness. Do not overwater. Fertilization is usually not necessary for overall care of Indian blanket. If you decide to fertilize, apply a premium-quality, long-lasting rose fertilizer according to label directions. Water-soluble fertilizers for blooming plants will also work well. Remember to follow label directions when using any fertilizer, and water thoroughly.

Care
Remove spent blooms to encourage a longer blooming season. There are no serious diseases or insects that plague Indian blanket.

Companion Planting and Design
Plant Indian blanket in any location in which you have perennial grasses (such as Bermudagrass) under control. It is attractive in rock gardens, or along natural gravel walks and trails. I have seen outstanding plantings of Indian blanket in Santa Fe, New Mexico, and in all areas of Texas. Use in native theme gardens or wherever a low-maintenance color plant is desirable.

I Suggest
Give these super plants a try from seed this fall, or from transplants early next spring.

Indian Paintbrush
Castilleja indivisa

When, Where, and How to Plant
The best time to direct-seed Indian paintbrush is late summer to early fall in a prepared seedbed. If you are fortunate to find transplants, set them out very early in the spring. Plant Indian paintbrush in and among existing vegetation with special seed-planting drills. If sowed on top of the ground, cut the existing vegetation extremely short. Water sown seeds thoroughly. Keep soil moist until well established, then reduce watering. This beauty will grow in clay, loam, or sandy soil as long as it is well drained. It will tolerate a slight shade.

Growing Tips
If growing as a bedding or landscape-type planting, water as necessary to prevent soil dryness. Mulching will help conserve soil moisture. If you fertilize grass during the growing season where Indian paintbrush will be planted, this will provide adequate nutrition. No other fertilization is usually required.

Care
Pruning is normally not required. There are no serious insect or disease problems with Indian paintbrush.

Companion Planting and Design
The plants may be used in clumps by themselves in landscape beds. In masses, they bring outstanding color to our roadsides and fields. They are also wonderful in mixtures with Texas bluebonnets. If you like experimental gardening, try growing Indian paintbrush in very large tubs, pots, planters, or other containers.

I Suggest
Planting from seed. Seed is widely available and transplants are usually difficult to locate at retailers. There are no known cultivars.

Indian paintbrush will grow on its own root system until it intersects with the root system of another plant, and then it becomes partially parasitic. Seeds of Indian paintbrush are extremely fine—it takes only 1/4 pound of seed to plant an entire acre. Most plants have bracts, the specialized leafy structures that give us the color we enjoy. C. latebracteata, or western paintbrush, is found in West Texas and New Mexico. Purple paintbrush, or C. purpurea, is distributed in Arkansas, Texas, and west to Arizona. In Central and West Texas, C. sessiliflora, or downy paintbrush, grows. C. integra, Southwestern paintbrush, can also be found in Central and West Texas.

Other Common Names
Texas Paintbrush, Scarlet Paintbrush

Bloom Period and Seasonal Color
Spring to early summer blooms in white to slightly green. Bracts display intense color from red to red-orange.

Mature Height × Spread
6 to 16 in. × 4 in.

Lanceleaf Coreopsis
Coreopsis lanceolata

Lanceleaf coreopsis is an excellent drought-tolerant perennial that can grow in full sun locations in all Texas soils. The dwarf and taller varieties can both be found at most garden centers. Enjoy this plant's blooms and its ability to re-seed itself. Lanceleaf coreopsis does have a dwarf variety that is simply called dwarf lanceleaf coreopsis. Its normal height range is sixteen to twenty inches, while the standard lanceleaf coreopsis may reach three feet or more. This is a drought-tolerant perennial and a heavy re-seeder that will bloom for long periods.

Other Common Names
Golden Wave, Tickseed, Texas Coreopsis, Blankets of Gold

Bloom Period and Seasonal Color
Summer blooms in yellow.

Mature Height × Spread
18 to 36 in. × 12 to 18 in.

When, Where, and How to Plant
Sow seeds in the early spring or early fall. Set out transplants in early spring after all danger of frost has passed. Lanceleaf coreopsis will grow in a partially shaded area as long as it receives a minimum of six hours of sun per day. Transplants should be planted in beds that are adequate for growing any bedding plant. To create these beds, incorporate approximately 3 in. of organic matter into the top 3 in. of the existing soil. Install transplants in the planting bed, placing them no deeper than they were grown in their original containers. Space transplants about a foot apart in a checkerboard pattern if you want a solid bed. Firm the soil well, water thoroughly, apply root stimulator according to label directions, and cover bare soil with 2 in. of bark mulch. To start from seeds sown directly in the beds, rake the improved bed to a nice smooth level with your garden rake, and sow seeds according to seed package directions. Lightly firm the media with your hand and water thoroughly with a seedling nozzle. Keep the bed moist until the seeds germinate, then gradually reduce watering frequency. Divide overgrown plantings in fall or early spring. Lanceleaf coreopsis is quick to multiply and easy to transplant.

Growing Tips
Water as necessary to prevent dryness and encourage additional buds and blooms. Fertilize in the spring as new growth begins. Apply any premium-quality rose fertilizer according to label directions.

Care
You may wish to prune out spent blooms to encourage additional blooming, but no other pruning is usually required. Lanceleaf coreopsis has no serious pest or disease problems.

Companion Planting and Design
Lanceleaf Coreopsis is useful in a Xeriscape, landscape color garden or slope, and along sunny garden paths. It works well in stand-alone beds or in combination with other wildflowers, as well as with cultivated/hybrid plants. It is an easy-to-grow container plant, and is attractive in clumps and drifts in the sunny rock garden,

I Suggest
Try the dwarf lanceleaf variety for a drought-tolerant, shorter version of tickseed.

Mealy Blue Sage

Salvia farinacea

When, Where, and How to Plant

To plant mealy blue sage from transplants, set them out in the spring in well-drained beds that receive a minimum of six hours of full sun every day. Beds should be well prepared . Blend approximately 3 in. of organic matter (compost, brown peat moss, or ground bark) into the top 3 in. of the soil. Remove individual plants from their containers, and space them 1 to 2 ft. apart in the bed. Plant in a checkerboard style for a mass effect. After planting, firm the soil, water thoroughly, apply root stimulator, and mulch bare soil with 3 in. of bark mulch.

Growing Tips

Water as necessary to prevent soil dryness and to encourage growth and blooms. Maintaining a 2 to 3 in. layer of bark mulch will help conserve soil moisture. Fertilize one time in the spring with a premium quality rose fertilizer as new growth begins.

Care

Mealy blue sage has no serious insect or disease problems. No pruning is required, but some tip pinching will encourage more blooms.

Companion Planting and Design

Try the mealy blue sage in planters in full sun spots on your deck or patio. Other uses include borders, cut flower gardens, color mixes and meadows.

I Suggest

I have an abundance of scarlet sage, *S. coccinea*, planted in a full sun location around our deck. I also grow Autumn sage, *S. greggii*, in addition to mealy blue.

The sage family has over 500 species; about twenty of these grow wild in Texas. The one most widely distributed across the state is the mealy blue sage, and it's also the most widely available. Our daughter Ashley planted some mealy blue sage together with a few dusty miller plants to create a striking silver and blue combination. It was installed in a bed in full sun, in deep sandy soil. These interesting colored plants are easy to plant, grow, and maintain. For the gardener who would like to use a native perennial plant for blue and purple in the landscape, I recommend the mealy blue sage. Some other types of salvia are cedar sage, S. roemeriana, and Texas sage, S. texana.

Other Common Name
Texas Violet, Mealycup Sage

Bloom Period and Seasonal Color
Late spring and summer blooms in purple and blue.

Mature Height × Spread
2 to 3 ft. × 1 to 1¹/₂ ft.

Mexican Hat
Ratibida columnifera

Mexican hat is a wildflower with a unique look. It can be found in all types of Texas soils and all kinds of habitats throughout our great wildflower state. With fine textured leaves that are very long and narrow, and with yellow-trimmed red blooms, it is often grown in large masses that can be seen from a long distance. As outstanding in the garden as it is in the prairie, this is a vigorous, drought resistant perennial that is hard to beat, and it's outstanding in garden plantings.

Other Common Name
Long-Headed Coneflower

Bloom Period and Seasonal Color
Summer blooms in red with yellow edges, and variations.

Mature Height × Spread
2 to 2¹/₂ ft. × 1 ft.

When, Where, and How to Plant
An ideal time to plant Mexican hat from seed is late summer to early fall. If you are fortunate enough to find transplants, set them out in early spring. Plant Mexican hat in sunny locations that receive at least six hours of sun. For long-term blooming, protect from our hot afternoon sun, but do not plant in heavily shaded or poorly drained locations. For the best chance at success, prepare a seedbed before sowing seeds. Remove any existing vegetation that might provide competition and lightly till the soil. If the soil drains well, no additional improvement will be necessary. If the soil is poorly drained, blend approximately 3 in. of organic matter into the top 3 in. of the existing soil. Sow the seeds according to directions on the package. When using transplants, install them in prepared beds no deeper than they were originally growing in their containers. Firm the soil, water thoroughly, apply root stimulator, and cover bare soil with 3 in. of bark mulch.

Growing Tips
Water as necessary throughout the growing season to prevent soil dryness. In landscape beds, maintaining a moist (not wet) soil will encourage profuse season-long blooming. To conserve moisture, maintain a 3 in. layer of bark mulch. Fertilize as new growth begins in the spring. Slow-release, premium-quality granular rose fertilizer works well.

Care
Deadhead spent bloom to encourage extra blooms and a longer bloom season. No other pruning is usually required. Mexican hat has few problems with insects and diseases.

Companion Planting and Design
This unusual plant makes an excellent cut flower lasting a week or more. It's great planted in drives, lanes, slopes, and cut flower gardens. Plant as a stand-alone group planting or in combination with other native flowers such as black-eyed-Susan, gaillardia, coreopsis, verbena, and lantana.

I Suggest
Try some of this species for fun next season because it's very easy to grow. At personal appearances, I'm constantly asked about easy-to-grow color. Mexican hat is a good choice.

Phlox

Phlox drummondii

When, Where, and How to Plant
Sow seeds in late summer to early fall. Plant seeds in well-prepared seedbeds using package directions. Set out transplants in early spring. Whether from seed or from transplants, for best results plant in sunny locations in well-drained soils. To set out transplants, plant in normally prepared bedding-plant soils that drain well. Plant no deeper than the plants were originally grown in the containers. Firm the soil well, water thoroughly, apply root stimulator, and mulch bare soil with 2 in. of bark mulch.

Growing Tips
Water as necessary to prevent soil dryness. This helps to ensure a better and prolonged bloom. Phlox does not usually require fertilization or pruning.

Care
Insects and diseases are normally not a problem for phlox. In enclosed areas of poor drainage and/or air movement, there is a possibility of powdery mildew. If this occurs, visit your local retail garden center for the best controls. Remember to follow label directions.

Companion Planting and Design
In the spring, try setting phlox out in large containers. They are ideal in floral gardens, planted in masses and drifts. Phlox's mix of colors blends well in mixed annual and perennial borders.

I Suggest
If you enjoy the interesting color and look of phlox (which is sometimes called annual phlox), let them naturally seed themselves. By doing this you should have new seedlings the following year with even more color to enjoy. Seedlings are identified by being sticky, soft and hairy. Should you have too many seedlings in one location, transplant carefully to additional sites and/or share them with other Texans. Plant phlox with bachelor buttons, another easy-to-grow annual.

While there are many types of phlox, this variety is named for Thomas Drummond, who harvested seeds in Texas in 1834. The seeds were transported to England, where plants were grown and named for him. Today's varieties of P. drummondii are cultivars of this same colorful annual. Outstanding groupings of this wonderful Texas plant are present on roadsides and in areas where the soil is sandy. This wildflower is a favorite with many Texas gardeners because of its bright colors and ability to grow in any soil. It is a true "blooming trooper."

Other Common Name
Annual Phlox

Bloom Period and Seasonal Color
Summer blooms in violet, pink, white, and blends.

Mature Height × Spread
8 to 20 in. × 10 to 12 in.

Plains Coreopsis
Coreopsis tinctoria

Plains coreopsis is a member of the Texas wildflowers group often referred to as golden wave—no doubt due to the plant's appearance when in large plantings. Also named fig seed or fig weed, I truly enjoy C. tinctoria for its delicate look, as well as its height. Lanceleaf coreopsis, C. lanceolata, has a normal height of approximately three feet and takes about two years to establish well. C. lanceolata is also available in a dwarf form called dwarf lanceleaf coreopsis. This is a very hardy, drought-tolerant perennial that reaches a height of about sixteen to twenty inches. It is a prolific re-seeder and blooms all summer.

Other Common Name
Golden Wave

Bloom Period and Seasonal Color
Summer to fall blooms in yellow with maroon.

Mature Height × Spread
Up to 4 ft. × 1 1/2 ft.

When, Where, and How to Plant
When direct-seeding, plant plains coreopsis in the late summer to early fall. If you are fortunate enough to find transplants in the spring, plant immediately. Start spring transplants after danger of frost has passed. Plant seeds in a sunny location where competition from perennial grasses such as Bermudagrass has been reduced or eliminated. If planting from transplants in landscaped beds, place in prepared beds as background plantings in early spring. Plant no deeper than they were growing in their containers. Firm the soil, water thoroughly, apply a root stimulator, and mulch bare soil 3 in. deep.

Growing Tips
For continued blooms throughout the season, water to prevent soil dryness, maintaining a 3 in. layer of mulch to conserve soil moisture. Plains coreopsis usually requires no fertilization or pruning.

Care
Deadhead spent blossoms to tidy the plants and expand bloom period. Plains coreopsis is free of diseases and insects.

Companion Planting and Design
Combine smaller native Texas flowers for stunning color combinations that will knock your socks off. I like plains coreopsis in combination with Indian blanket, *Gaillardia pulchella*, and Texas bluebells, *Eustoma grandiflorum*.

I Suggest
Try any of these fun, easy-to-grow -plants. The dwarf red variety, 'Nana' in particular, has an interesting appearance and color.

Prairie Verbena

Verbena bipinnatifida

When, Where, and How to Plant

Sow the seeds in late summer to early fall. Set transplants out in early spring. The plants will grow in clay, limestone, and sand as long as the soil is well drained. Prepare a seedbed by removing any existing vegetation or debris, then tilling the soil and raking. If planting from transplants, you may wish to first incorporate 3 in. of organic matter into the top 3 in. of the existing soil. After bed preparation is complete, remove transplants from their containers and install in the soil no deeper than they were growing in their containers. Firm the soil around the new transplants, water thoroughly, apply root stimulator according to label directions, and cover bare soil with 3 in. of bark mulch.

Growing Tips

Water as necessary to prevent soil dryness, especially when planted in the landscape. Maintaining a thick layer of bark mulch will help conserve soil moisture. Fertilize in the spring as new growth begins. A premium-quality, slow-release rose fertilizer works well. Remember to read and follow label directions and water thoroughly after application.

Care

Pruning is usually not required, though you may wish to remove spent blooms to encourage extra blooming, new growth, and new runners throughout the season. Prairie verbena has no serious insects or diseases.

Companion Planting and Design

Prairie verbena offers striking color and will accent virtually any location. You may plant a pure stand of them in a landscape bed, or plant them with other wildflowers. They may also be enjoyed in specialized locations, such as a rock garden or trailing over the edge of a flower bed.

I Suggest

Try the purple to lavender selections.

Prairie verbena is one of the perennial verbenas that belong to the Verbena family. We have at least ten of these verbenas in Texas, but prairie verbena may be the one most commonly seen. When grown in masses, it is an absolutely breathtaking native wildflower. I have seen it grown successfully in Central Texas and in East Texas, in road ditches and fields of deep sandy soil, and it is extremely easy to grow in the home landscape. The following plants are also known as vervains: V. rigida, tuber vervain, V. brasiliensis, Brazilian vervain, V. halei, Texas vervain, and V. canadensis, rose vervain.

Other Common Names

Dakota Vervain, Common Vervain

Bloom Period and Seasonal Color

Early spring to fall blooms in blue to purple/lavender, and pink.

Mature Height × Spread

6 to 16 in. × 18 in.

Purple Coneflower
Echinacea angustifolia

I am often asked, "Why is it called purple coneflower when most of its flowers are pink?" I really don't have a good answer, except that quite a few blooms have a little bit of purple in them when they first start to form. Some petals tend to hang down and some tend to stand out straight. The central parts of the blooms come in different shapes. Purple coneflower is hybridized, and you will find different varieties at your local retail garden centers. These plants grow best in dappled shade. Also known as echinacea, purple coneflower is an herb which has long been used by some folks to treat ailments. Other species of coneflower are E. purpurea, E. pallida, and E. sanguinea.

Other Common Name
Echinacea

Bloom Period and Seasonal Color
Blooms spring, summer, and into the fall with blooms in white, and light pink to deep rose.

Mature Height × Spread
1¹/₂ to 3 ft. × 2 ft.

When, Where, and How to Plant
Sow seeds in spring after the soil warms up, or in very early fall. Set out transplants as soon as they become available. Do not plant in heavily shaded locations, poorly drained areas, or areas that are difficult to water. Purple coneflower is known to grow in clay, loam, or sandy soils, as long as the soil is well drained. To start from seeds, first prepare a bed. Remove vegetation and debris, till the top 3 in. of soil, and blend about 3 in. of organic matter into the soil. Rake thoroughly, sow seeds according to package directions, and water deeply. If setting out transplants, remove them from their containers and install them in the soil no deeper than they were growing in the containers—about 1 ft. apart in a checkerboard pattern. If you are planting in rows, do a double or triple row for an outstanding look. After planting is complete, firm the soil well, water thoroughly, apply root stimulator, and cover bare soil with 3 in. of bark mulch.

Growing Tips
Water as necessary to prevent soil dryness. To conserve moisture, maintain a 3 in. layer of mulch throughout the growing season. Fertilize with a premium-quality, slow-release rose fertilizer as new growth begins in the spring.

Care
Remove spent blooms and stems; no other pruning is necessary. Purple coneflower has no serious insects or diseases.

Companion Planting and Design
Purple coneflower does best when you install it in mass plantings spaced about 1 ft. apart in a checkerboard pattern. This mass effect looks wonderful in the home landscape. You may wish to try some purple coneflowers in large tubs or planters on a porch where they can receive at least six hours of sun. They may be used as clumped accents among low-growing summer annuals.

I Suggest
The coneflower is an excellent, long-lasting cut flower. Use some of the long-lasting blooms in an indoor arrangement.

Texas Bluebells
Eustoma grandiflorum

When, Where, and How to Plant

Plant bluebells as you would any other bedding plant (i.e. marigolds or petunias), in well-prepared beds in sunny, well-drained locations. When planting bluebells from transplants, transfer in early spring after all danger of frost is past. Though they can tolerate some shade from our hot western afternoon sun, bluebells need a minimum of six hours of full sun every day. Plant no deeper than the plants were originally grown in their containers. Firm the soil, water thoroughly, apply root stimulator according to label directions, and mulch bare soil with 3 in. of bark mulch.

Growing Tips

This is one native Texas plant that responds well to fertilizers, mulching, and supplemental irrigation. Water as necessary to maintain a moist soil for maximum production, growth, and beauty. Maintain a 3 in. layer of mulch throughout the growing season to conserve soil moisture. Fertilize in spring as new growth begins, in mid-season, and then once again in the fall. Premium-quality, slow-release, granular rose fertilizers work well. Other fertilizers such as liquids and water-solubles may be used. Remember to follow label directions, and water thoroughly after applying fertilizers.

Care

Remove spent blooms to encourage more blooms throughout the season. No other pruning is usually required. Texas bluebells normally do not have problems with insects or diseases.

Companion Planting and Design

Texas bluebells may be grown in large tubs, as border plantings, or in combination with other cut flower garden plantings.

I Suggest

Plant this flower as a complement to your borders or as a dramatic addition to your landscape. The Texas bluebell with its hard-to-find hue is a wonderful addition to your garden.

Many consider bluebells one of the most beautiful wildflowers in the state. Prized by gardeners for its hard-to-find blue hue, the bluebell is coveted as a long-lasting cut flower. Sadly, this has contributed to the plant being over-harvested. Fortunately, these plants do exceptionally well under cultivation and are available as seeds or transplants in many retail garden centers throughout Texas. Texas bluebells are a member of the gentian family, which includes meadow pink, Sabatia campestris, and mountain pink, Centaurium beyrichii. A blue-flowered first cousin, E. exaltatum, is often found in the southern half of the state. Remember to do your part—don't harvest bluebells in the wild. Let them produce so we can all enjoy their simple beauty.

Other Common Name
Lisianthus

Bloom Period and Seasonal Color
Summer blooms in blue, purple, and white.

Mature Height × Spread
24 to 30 in. × 8 to 10 in.

Texas Lantana
Lantana horrida

I have grown and enjoyed Texas lantana for decades. It is a low-maintenance plant that will thrive even in areas that are difficult to water, blooming the first year and for many years thereafter. Texas lantana makes an outstanding planting in any full sun location with soil that drains well. It's a very easy plant for first-time gardeners (including the little ones) to grow. I suggest you try growing lantana at a seldom-visited location such as a vacation home where your landscape maintenance is necessarily kept to a minimum. Deer don't like Texas lantana. I live in Texas Zone 7b, and my lantanas have continued to return year after year for more than twenty years. These plantings are truly perennial!

Other Common Name
Lantana

Bloom Period and Seasonal Color
Spring, summer, fall blooms in yellow, orange, red, and combinations.

Mature Height × Spread
3 to 5 ft. × 4 to 8 ft.

When, Where, and How to Plant
Start Texas lantana from freshly gathered mature seeds any time you can find them during the growing season, but no later than the end of August. Or make tip cuttings and root them for a start. Set transplants out in early spring after all danger of frost has passed. Plant lantana in any location that receives a minimum of six hours of full sun, and preferably full sun all day long. Prepare seedbeds by improving the soil with organic matter and raking finely. To set out transplants, dig individual planting holes no deeper than the plants were originally grown in their containers. Because of lantana's wide spread, you can space the plants as far as 4 ft. or more apart and still have a solid mass planting.

Growing Tips
Water as necessary to prevent soil dryness—this will help enhance the blooms. Maintain a thick mulch around the entire root system to conserve soil moisture. Fertilize in the spring as new growth begins. Use one application of a premium-quality, slow-release granular rose fertilizer. Water thoroughly after application.

Care
To encourage new growth beginning at the base and to control size, I prune Texas lantana very severely just as new growth begins in the spring. No other pruning is required, but if the plant becomes too large for your area, it may be pruned successfully throughout the entire growing season. My lantana plantings have never had spider mites, but they may visit your lantana during the hot, dry times of the year. Consult with your local retail garden center for the best way to control pests.

Companion Planting and Design
Lantana serves as a colorful, carefree background or border planting for other summer annuals and perennials. Use lantana alone or in combination with other plants. Due to its size, make sure you have adequate space available, or it may overpower the location. I use lantanas in beds where other drought-tolerant plantings are used. They work great.

I Suggest
Take advantage of lantanas in your landscape. This is one of the easiest to grow drought-heat-sun-tolerant color plant groups Texans have available.

Wild Petunia
Ruellia spp.

When, Where, and How to Plant

Start ruellia in any well-drained location from root divisions or transplants purchased at your local garden center in early spring. It will grow in sand, clay, or loam-type soils. Place it where it will have dappled shade throughout the day, or at least shade from the hot western afternoon sun. As long as it doesn't receive heat reflected off your home or other structures, it should do well in a location that receives morning sun. Plant in prepared bedding soils whose top 3 in. have been blended with approximately 3 in. of organic matter. Set transplants in individual planting holes no deeper than they were originally growing in their containers, spacing them approximately 2 ft. apart. Planting in a checkerboard pattern will give you a mass effect the first year. After planting is complete, water thoroughly, apply root stimulator, and cover bare soil with 3 in. of bark mulch.

Growing Tips

For continuous bloom throughout the season, water as necessary to maintain a moist growing environment. Fertilize in the spring as new growth begins, using a premium-quality, slow-release granular rose fertilizer.

Care

Usually no pruning is required. We have had no insect or disease problems with ruellia.

Companion Planting and Design

Ruellia may be used in pure stands or in combination with other perennials. The lower growing varieties are great border plants. We enjoy a planting of non-native sweet autumn clematis in the same bed with ruellia, along with the native shrub American beautyberry.

I Suggest

For an easy perennial that will bloom every year, try the species along with the hybrid cultivated forms.

My family has enjoyed ruellia for several years. It is planted in beds with a southwestern exposure. Ruellia seems to thrive in this location, receiving lots of morning sun and shaded from the hot western afternoon sun. Unlike many of the petunias that are grown in our gardens, ruellia will bloom throughout the entire season. It's not related to the true petunia family at all, though it is often called a petunia. Ruellia is a member of the acanthus family. Several ruellias may be found at your local garden center, including R. nudiflora, violet ruellia), R. humilis, low ruellia, and R. malacosperma. Try one or all in the landscape. I know you will enjoy them.

Other Common Names

Mexican Petunia, Summer Petunia

Bloom Period and Seasonal Color

Summer to fall blooms in shades of lavender, purple, and pink.

Mature Height × Spread

12 to 30 in. × 12 to 18 in.

Perennials *for Texas*

Want to see the same flowers bloom in your landscape year after year? Be sure to consider low-maintenance perennials. While annuals complete their life cycle in one season and biennials in two, perennials grow and bloom for three years or more. And with a wide range of varieties to choose from, there's a perennial for every landscaping need.

What to Look For

Perennials can bloom in almost every season, as there are varieties for spring, summer, and fall. Some bloom for a very short time and then rest for many months. Some bloom repeatedly during a season, and others bloom continuously. When selecting a perennial, research its bloom season, bloom colors, height, and cultural requirements. It's useful, for example, to know that even though a single daylily bloom will last but a day, each daylily plant will produce a daily profusion of blooms for an extended period.

Texas has a wide range of soils and several hardiness zones. Zones, winds, soils, drainage, sun, care, and varieties will determine whether a perennial planting will be successful. Are the perennials that interest you hardy where you live? Be sure to do your homework and select plants that flourish in your zone. And as always, before purchasing your perennial, be sure to ask about its tolerance to our Texas heat in your particular area. Some winter-hardy, cool-season perennials will simply not thrive in our heat; yet, they are often offered in local garden centers.

Perennial Border

Yarrow

Perennials are prized for being a low-maintenance landscape choice—some nearly maintenance free. However, as with any plant you choose for your garden, care requirements should be a priority for selection of perennials for the home landscape. Remember that you may have your perennial for a long time.

Some perennials are grown for their colorful foliage, not for their blooms. Among these are dusty miller, *Centaurea cineraria*, and artemisia, *Artemisia abrotanum* (also known as wormwood or southernwood). Both plants provide interesting foliage, color, and texture that accent other perennials or annuals in the home landscape. Four-o'-clocks, *Mirabilis jalapa*, is an old-fashioned perennial that is easily started from seed and will grow all over Texas. These plants are tough, durable, low maintenance, and fragrant. Ruellia, *Ruellia brittoniana*, is easy to start from divisions by carefully dividing and separating the plant. The divisions will bloom during their first season. Members of this very tough and easy-to-grow family may also be started from seed. And don't forget perennials like garden mums, chrysanthemum cultivars that are grown for their outstanding fall color. Some plant people suggest growing them as annuals, but in most of Texas we can enjoy them year after year. I've enjoyed our planting for more than ten years, which makes our bed of "mums" truly perennial.

Some perennials are native plants that have been selected and cultivated for the home landscape. See the native chapters (pages 90 through 133) for more information. I have selected a dozen perennials to try in your home landscape. In each genus you will find many varieties. Visit your local retail garden center to look over their selection of perennials.

Chrysanthemums

Coral Vine
Antigonon leptopus

My first sight of coral vine was in Brownwood on Granny Miller's chain link fence. Granny Miller never grew a flowering plant that was difficult to care for and coral vine worked wonderfully on her fence. If you are looking for an easy-to-grow flowering perennial vine that will thrive where hardy in Texas, take a look at this vine. It puts out a sufficient amount of leaves to make nice shade in the summertime on a trellis or other structure. Try it on a gazebo or other upright structure where you wish to have a great blooming plant. In Zones 8 and 9, it comes back year after year, but it is "iffy" in Zone 7. Heavy mulching may ensure its reemergence in succeeding years. A. leptopus 'Album' is a white flowering variety.

Other Common Name
Queen's Wreath

Bloom Period and Seasonal Color
Summer to fall blooms in pink and white.

Mature Length
Vining to 10 to 15 ft.

When, Where, and How to Plant
Plant coral vine in early spring after all danger of frost has passed, in improved, well-drained soil. Incorporate 3 in. of organic matter into the top 3 in. of native soil. Remove transplant from its container and insert into the soil at soilball depth. Firm the soil, water thoroughly, apply root stimulator according to label directions, and mulch. When planting seeds, make sure the soil temperature is above 70 degrees Fahrenheit. With the bed improved, plant in a sunny spot according to seed package directions.

Growing Tips
While coral vine is quite drought tolerant, it will appreciate an occasional long, deep drink of water. Water as necessary to prevent soil dryness. Maintain a layer of 3 to 4 in. of bark mulch to aid in soil moisture retention. Coral vine will benefit from applications of fertilizer throughout the growing season. Use granular rose, water-soluble, or liquid fertilizers. Apply first in spring as new growth begins. Follow with an additional application approximately twelve weeks later, and one early in the fall.

Care
Prune if necessary to train and direct its growth. Usually, placing the plants or seeds at the base of support structures (including fences) is sufficient. Coral vine may freeze to ground level, to return in the spring from its tuber-like roots. It therefore may be necessary to prune away winter kill. Coral vine is considered pest-free.

Companion Planting and Design
This beauty may be utilized in any type of garden setting where a tough blooming vine is desired. Try planting in large containers and training the vine to grow on various shapes of structures or lattice. It looks great as a backdrop for beds of perennials including marigolds and salvias. Coral vines create a delicate, lacey effect and offer blooms in late summer and fall. Coral vine usually is not overpowering.

I Suggest
For apartment dwellers or others with limited gardening space, try one or more of these vines on a heavy lattice in a 16 in. container filled with a quality potting soil. During our long growing season, you will be treated to great color in your small spaces.

Dusty Miller

Centaurea cineraria

When, Where, and How to Plant

Plant dusty miller in the spring in well-drained soil, after all danger of frost has passed. Do not plant in damp soil or in shady locations. Improve the soil by incorporating 3 to 4 in. of organic matter. Remove your transplant from its container, insert into the prepared soil no deeper than originally grown, and firm the soil. Water thoroughly, apply root stimulator, and mulch with 3 in. of bark mulch to bare soil.

Growing Tips

Water as necessary to prevent soil dryness. While this is considered a relatively tough plant, do not allow the soil to become dry for a prolonged period of time. Fertilize dusty miller in the springtime as new growth begins. Specialty granular, water-soluble or liquid fertilizers work equally well. Be sure to read and follow label directions.

Care

Remove blooms and prune throughout the growing season to maintain a more compact and uniform habit. Dusty miller is considered virtually insect and disease free.

Companion Planting and Design

The shorter varieties may be used in masses to create a groundcover effect. Taller varieties are excellent background plants and help to accentuate the color of shorter plants growing in front. We are currently growing dusty miller in front of broadleaf evergreens, and the combination is outstanding. When planting in borders, use a dwarf variety such as 'Frosty' or 'Silver Queen'. The neutral, yet vibrant, silver foliage brings out the mixed colors of other flowering annuals and perennials.

I Suggest

For you Dallas Cowboys fans, try plantings of dusty miller with mealy blue sage to show your support. They may also be grown in containers for those with limited space. Use a quality potting soil and containers 14 in. and larger.

My young gardener and eighteen-year-old baby girl Ashley likes the looks of dusty miller in a landscape bed with colors. The name dusty miller is a common name applied to more than one group of plants. The Artemisia genus is often called dusty miller in Texas. While it does produce some flowers, dusty miller is grown for its striking foliage. It's excellent in sunny locations and works wonderfully when combined with blue. Whether your soil is sandy or a clay-type soil, dusty miller requires a well-drained location. Be sure to check with local nurseries to determine the hardiness of your selection. Varieties include 'Diamond', 'Silver Queen', and 'Frosty'. Zones for dusty miller are 7 to 9 but may vary with varieties selected.

Bloom Period and Seasonal Color
Foliage in white to silver.

Mature Height × Spread
8 to 18 in. × 12 to 18 in.

Four-O'-Clocks
Mirabilis jalapa

Though many gardeners don't think of them as perennials, four-o'-clocks are truly old-fashioned Texas perennials. Loaded with beautiful, scented flowers that begin opening in the afternoon and remain open through the evening and into the nighttime, four-o'-clocks add a wonderful fragrance to our gardens no matter what the time. Tough and durable, they can grow in full sun in all parts of Texas, though they prefer a bit of shade from the hot afternoon sun. Four-o'-clocks are seen in areas where old, abandoned homesteads have been—just another indication of how tough and durable these plants really are. Four-o'-clocks come in seed mixtures. Pigmy mixture includes the twenty-inch height. A taller-growing mixture is 'Four-o'-clock Special'. Four-o'-clocks are hardy in all zones in Texas except Zone 6.

Bloom Period and Seasonal Color
Summer blooms in white, pink, salmon, lavender, yellow, magenta, and blends.

Mature Height × Spread
3 to 4 ft. × 3 ft.

When, Where, and How to Plant
Plant seeds or transplants in spring after the soil warms. Four-o'-clocks grow in sandy or heavy clay soils if given sufficient light and moisture. Four-o'-clocks will grow in many different types of soil conditions, but they prefer moist, loamy soils. For best results, make sure your soil is improved. With a tiller, spading fork, or shovel incorporate 3 to 4 in. of organic matter into the top 4 in. of the existing soil. Remove transplants from the containers, and insert into the prepared seedbed at the same level they were growing in the containers. Firm the soil around the rootball, water thoroughly, add root stimulator, and mulch bare soil with 3 in. of bark mulch. When planting seeds, plant them approximately 1/2 in. deep in a well-prepared bed.

Growing Tips
Water as necessary to maintain a moist soil. Maintaining a thick 3 to 4 in. mulch layer will maintain soil moisture and reduce the frequency of watering. Fertilize four-o'-clocks in the spring as growth emerges, using a granular rose fertilizer or any other form of fertilizer.

Care
Prune as necessary through the summer season. With careful selection of your plant's location, the need for future pruning will be reduced. Give these plants ample room to grow and multiply. Four-o'-clocks can become invasive with their tough and extensive root systems. Thin the plants out as they come up in the spring to keep them within bounds. Four-o'-clocks are virtually insect and disease free.

Companion Planting and Design
Use as four-o'-clocks as tall background plants. They look great in a container with solid white annual vinca trailing over the edges. Use four-o'-clocks as filler plants, border plants, or in mass plantings. They may be used in an out-of-the-way garden area, as they are virtually maintenance free and will form large plantings.

I Suggest
I suggest four-o'-clocks for first time gardeners because there is almost always success. In limited space, use the dwarf varieties that reach only 20 in. high. Plant dwarf selections in large containers of 16 in. or larger for lots of blooms and fragrance with easy care.

Garden Mum

Dendranthema × grandiflorum

When, Where, and How to Plant

Plant garden mums in the fall in full bud/full bloom or plant in the spring when all danger of frost has passed. Don't plant in heavily shaded locations, areas that are difficult to water, or in poorly drained soil. Plant garden mums from container-grown stock in well-prepared beds. Improve the soil by incorporating 4 in. of organic matter (including brown Canadian sphagnum peat moss and compost), into the top 4 in. of the existing native soil. Plant mums no deeper than originally grown in the container. Firm the soil around each individual plant, water thoroughly, apply root stimulator, and mulch bare soil with 3 in. of bark mulch. When planting in containers, use lightweight potting soil and plant at the same depth as with ground plantings.

Growing Tips

Water as necessary to maintain a moist soil, and do not allow chrysanthemums to become totally dry. Fertilize as new growth begins in the spring with a long-lasting, slow-release, granular rose fertilizer or a water-soluble, liquid, or encapsulated fertilizer of your choice. Apply approximately every eight weeks throughout the growing season.

Care

Pinching is important to have a good show of blooms in the fall. Begin pinching back to 4 in. in the springtime after growth reaches 6 in. Continue pinching back until mid-July. By selecting the best locally adapted varieties, I have had virtually no problems with insects or diseases. Staking may be required on tall-growing varieties with heavy blooms.

Companion Planting and Design

Use in many different locations in your landscape. Plant along walkways and around garden structures such as decks, gazebos, benches, ornamental pools or water fountains. They also work well in large containers. Garden mums may be utilized in beds with autumn clematis, American beautyberry, bouncing bet, and a host of other perennials, annuals, and shrubs.

I Suggest

I highly recommend trips to public gardens to view the garden mum displays in the fall. This allows the potential Texas grower to view, up close and personal, what may be created with mass plantings of mums in full bloom.

Garden mums belong to a family that includes florist's chrysanthemums, football mums, and feverfew. Because of the variations in height and form, use as border plants, mass plantings, or as a single planting. They may be grown in cascade form, from a hanging basket, or even as miniature trees. Garden mums are easy to grow but prefer a deep, rich, well-drained soil with adequate moisture. They require a sunny location that receives approximately six hours of full sun, but shade from the hot afternoon sun. Visit botanical gardens in the fall throughout the state to see magnificent sweeps of color created by chrysanthemums. There are many different types, including pompom, singles, cushion, spoon (with anemone-type blossoms), and buttons. Garden mums are hardy statewide.

Other Common Name

Mums

Bloom Period and Seasonal Color

Fall blooms in all colors except blue.

Mature Height × Spread

12 to 18 in. or more.

Lantana

Lantana montevidensis

The trailing forms of lantana are excellent for use in containers, in beds for a groundcover effect, or weeping over walls. Lantana lends itself to excellent season-long color in Texas, including July and August. I live in Zone 7b and have grown the same lantana for years—making it a true perennial in my beds. Try the varieties 'Lavender Swirl' and 'White Lightnin'. Also look for L. camara (yellow, pink, red, orange, and white), and L. horrida, a native Texas species (bicolor mixture of yellow and pink). These are super. Lantana is hardy in Zone 7b and southward. In Zones 6b and 7a mulch heavily for winter.

Other Common Name
Trailing Lantana

Bloom Period and Seasonal Color
Spring, summer, and fall blooms in lavender and white.

Mature Height × Spread
12 to 30 in. × 30 to 48 in.

When, Where, and How to Plant

Plant lantana in early spring to summer. Lantana may be planted in the fall but must be well established to avoid possible freezing. In Texas, use lantana for durable color the entire season with minimum maintenance. Lantana is a tough and heat-tolerant plant for hot spots in the landscape. It needs a location where the soil drains well and it receives a minimum of six hours of full sun. It will grow in heavy clay or light, sandy soils. To obtain maximum growth and benefit, plant in well-prepared beds. Incorporate 3 in. of organic matter into the top 3 in. or more of the existing soil. Set transplants in individual planting holes no deeper than originally grown in the containers. Firm the soil well and water thoroughly, apply root stimulator, and mulch bare soil with 3 to 4 in. of bark mulch. Be sure to use premium-quality lightweight potting soils with containers.

Growing Tips

Water as necessary to prevent soil dryness. Fertilize in the spring with a long-lasting, slow-release granular rose fertilizer, or a water-soluble, liquid, or encapsulated season-long fertilizer. Re-apply every ten to twelve weeks throughout the growing season.

Care

Prune to maintain the shape desired. Pruning will encourage new growth and more blooms. Removing flowers will prevent fruiting or berries, which are said to be poisonous. I've never had any pest problems with lantana, but it is subject to white fly, lace bugs, and red spider mites. If pests become a problem, visit your local garden center for controls.

Companion Planting and Design

Lantana may be used in large nursery containers. The trailing forms are useful in hanging baskets. Lantana adds great color to areas such as decks, gazebos, or swimming pools. The trailing forms are excellent in rock gardens and to fringe sunny walks and paths, adding an informal feeling.

I Suggest

I recommend lantana to the first time gardener because of its high success rate. For Texans with zero-lot lines, town homes, condos and/or apartments with sunny balconies, decks, porches, or patios, plant one or more planters of lantana.

Mexican Petunia
Ruellia brittoniana

When, Where, and How to Plant

Plant ruellia any time of the year in areas where it is hardy. A native of Mexico, Mexican petunia is more adaptable to lower Texas—Zone 8b and lower. It will grow well into Zones 8a and 7b, but an unusually cold winter may damage it. The preferred planting season is early spring, giving the plant time to put on foliage and produce blooms during its first season. Planting in early fall is also acceptable. Plant in a spot with at least six hours of sun. Do not plant ruellia in heavily shaded areas. For good results, plant in well-prepared beds. Blend 3 to 4 in. of high-quality organic matter into the native soil. Install ruellia in the soil no deeper than it was originally grown in the containers. Firm the soil well around the plant's rootball, water thoroughly, apply root stimulator, and mulch bare soil with 3 in. of bark mulch. Ruellia may also be planted in large nursery containers with lightweight potting soil. Plant at same depth described above.

Growing Tips

Water as necessary to prevent soil dryness and to encourage growth, vigor, and bloom. Maintaining mulch through the entire growing season will reduce the frequency of watering and conserve soil moisture. Fertilizing is not necessary.

Care

Pruning is rarely needed unless to remove spent bloom stalks. Ruellia has no insect or disease problems.

Companion Planting and Design

If you have an area in your landscape where other perennials have not survived, plant some ruellia and enjoy its color throughout the season. The taller variety of ruellia may be used in and among other perennials—including Texas native *R. nudiflora* (see page 133 for additional ruellias). Its color is accentuated when planted with some dusty miller.

I Suggest

Try ruellia in a small spot in your landscape. Ours is planted in Zone 7b, where the beauty of sweet clematis sets off the blooms of ruellia in the late summer/early fall. Beautiful!

Mexican petunia is an extremely tough, durable, carefree perennial. Very easy to propagate from divisions or seeds, standard varieties R. brittoniana (a tall purple variety), 'Chi Chi' (pink), and R. malacosperma (purple and white), may reach as tall as three feet. The dwarf variety, 'Katie', generally grows around eight to ten inches. Ruellia will grow in light, sandy soil as well as heavy clay, tolerating both damp and dry conditions. I dug some ruellia, placed them in a zip lock bag and mailed them to my friend Larry Burns outside of San Antonio. He planted them and had blooms the first season. Now that's tough! Mexican petunia is hardy in Zones 7 to 9.

Other Common Name
Summer Petunia

Bloom Period and Seasonal Color
Spring and summer blooms in lavender to purple.

Mature Height × Spread
10 to 36 in. × 12 to 18 in.

Pinks

Dianthus spp.

An old-time favorite of Texas gardeners, pinks are excellent when used in areas where you wish to create a mass effect for early-season bloom. The taller varieties make nice background plantings. The varieties and colors available today are vast when compared with those available in past decades. While dianthus in Texas is commonly called pinks, dianthus is in many colors, with single and double flowers. When selecting dianthus, look for dark-green foliage on compact plants loaded with buds in four- or six-inch containers. Pinks are available in clumping types, as well as low-growing groundcover selections. A few varieties include 'Queen of Hearts', 'Magic Charms', 'Snowfire', and 'Snowflake'. Pinks are hardy in all Texas zones.

Other Common Names
Garden Pinks, Sweet William

Bloom Period and Seasonal Color
Fall, winter, and spring blooms in rose, salmon, pink, lavender, magenta, bi-colors and white.

Mature Height × Spread
4 to 15 in. × spread.

When, Where, and How to Plant
Plant dianthus in early fall or in spring after all danger of frost has passed. Plant in areas where it will receive plenty of morning sun, but most varieties should be shaded from hot afternoon sun. Dianthus bloom best under cooler conditions. If you wish to grow dianthus in the sun, look and ask for sun-tolerant varieties. Do not plant in areas that are difficult to water or are poorly drained. According to *Hortus III*, there are over 300 species of dianthus, so seek additional information at local nurseries on where to use specific varieties for your landscape. Plant dianthus in well-prepared beds. Improve the soil by blending 3 to 4 in. of brown Canadian sphagnum peat moss or compost into the native soil. Set selections in individual planting holes dug no deeper than the depth of the plant soilball. Backfill, water thoroughly, apply root stimulator, and mulch bare soil with 3 to 4 in. of bark mulch.

Growing Tips
Water as needed to maintain a moist soil, but do not overwater. Maintaining a thick layer of 3 to 4 in. of mulch around your plantings will greatly conserve soil moisture and reduce the frequency of watering. Use rose fertilizer in the spring as new growth begins. Reapply fertilizer as needed through the entire growing season.

Care
Remove spent blooms to encourage additional blooming and to tidy up the overall look of your plantings. Leaf spot may visit your planting during cloudy, humid, muggy days. This is corrected when the sun comes out, humidity decreases, and good air movement occurs. If leaf spot becomes a concern, visit local garden centers for appropriate controls.

Companion Planting and Design
Dianthus looks great in mass, stand-alone plantings. Due to its various colors, entire drifts with shades of color may be created. Pinks are super in country cottage garden themes.

I Suggest
Plant in areas you visit daily. The individual flowers are lovely and the fragrance is pleasant. I suggest it be planted in large containers and in limited space areas, such as decks or porches.

Shasta Daisy
Leucanthemum × superbum

When, Where, and How to Plant

Plant Shastas in the early fall or very early spring. Do not plant them in areas that are difficult to water or where the soil tends to remain wet the entire year. They will not thrive in areas that are heavily shaded, or in unimproved heavy clay. Shasta daisies do best in soils that have been improved with organic matter. Dig individual planting holes no deeper than the depth of the plant's soilball. Firm the soil, water thoroughly, apply root stimulator, and mulch bare soil with 3 to 4 in. of bark mulch. I normally use pine bark mulch.

Growing Tips

Water as needed—especially during the blooming and growing season—to maintain a moist soil. Do not allow the soil to become dry, and never overwater. Maintain a thick layer of bark mulch year-round to aid in moisture retention and moderating soil temperatures. Fertilize in the spring as new growth begins, using granular, premium-quality, long-lasting, slow-release rose fertilizer, or a water-soluble or liquid fertilizer of your choice.

Care

Prune out spent blossoms to encourage additional blossoms and to help dress up plantings. Shasta daisies benefit from annual or biannual digging, dividing, and planting in the fall. Leaf spot may visit Shasta daisies in areas that are too wet or poorly drained. Root rot may also be a problem. To prevent root rot, plant in areas where the soil drains thoroughly, and never overwater. If root rot or other diseases become a problem, visit local garden centers to get information on controls. Generally these problems will self-correct once growing conditions improve. If spider mites or other "critter" pests visit your plantings, visit the garden centers for help with these undesirables too.

Companion Planting and Design

Use Shasta daisies along walkways, around garden structures, and even in large nursery containers. Shasta is a versatile perennial plant whose simple white blooms with yellow centers blend well in many locations. Use these beauties with daylilies, salvia, summer phlox, and rose plantings.

I Suggest

My wife Judy is a fan of Shasta daisies for their use in the landscape and as wonderful cut flowers.

Texans have successfully grown Shasta daisies for many years. This plant is relatively easy to grow, but it does have some care needs. Use in areas where it receives approximately six hours of full sun with some shade from the hot afternoon sun. If your Shasta daisies look a little bit ragged toward the end of the summer, don't despair. As the fall's cooling rains and temperatures arrive, they will be rejuvenated. Some varieties to look for at your local garden center are 'Little Miss Muffet', 'Alaska', 'Aglaia', 'Snow Lady', 'Marconi', and 'Cobham Gold'. Single petal flower-forms tend to do better. Shasta daisy is hardy in all Texas zones.

Bloom Period and Seasonal Color
Spring, summer to fall blooms usually in white with yellow centers.

Mature Height × Spread
12 to 30 in. × 24 in.

Southernwood

Artemisia abrotanum

Southernwood is an unusual type of artemisia that is used in the home landscape for its appearance as well as for its fragrance, which may be pungently aromatic. The finely divided, green, feathery foliage is wonderfully fragrant. Some varieties smell like tangerine, lemon, or even camphor. A relatively compact grower that requires good drainage, it is popular for its many uses when cut and dried. Potpourris, table arrangements, bouquets, and wreaths extend its value. Additional species include A. absinthium, common wormwood; A. dracunculus, French tarragon; A. ludoviciana, common artemisia; A. schmidtiana 'Nana', and A. vulgaris, known as mugwort. Give one or all a try.

Bloom Period and Seasonal Color
Summer blooms in yellow.

Mature Height × Spread
12 to 24 in. × 36 in.

When, Where, and How to Plant
Plant southernwood in early spring or early fall. Well-drained soil is essential to growing southernwood in Texas. If you have heavy clay, improve it thoroughly before attempting to grow any variety of artemisia. It needs a sunny location with a minimum of six hours of full sun, and sandy, deep, well-drained soil. If planting in heavy clay soil, add 2 in. of coarse, washed sand, 1 in. of perlite, and 2 in. of pine bark mulch to the top 4 to 5 in. of existing soil. In sandy soil, the incorporation of ground bark mulch, approximately 2 in. deep, blended with the top 4 in. of existing soil, will be sufficient. Make sure all soil drains well. Dig individual planting holes the depth of the soilballs. Plant no deeper than they were in the original container. Firm the soil around the rootball, water thoroughly, apply root stimulator, and mulch bare soil with 2 in. of bark mulch.

Growing Tips
Water only when soil becomes dry. Do not allow prolonged or extended periods of drought, but do not overwater. Overwatering may cause root rot and a decline. Fertilization is minimal; perhaps apply one time in the spring with a long-lasting, slow-release, granular rose fertilizer.

Care
Prune to maintain more compact growth, and remove spent blooms as necessary. Southernwood has no serious insect pests.

Companion Planting and Design
You may wish to pair southernwood with other easy-to-grow plants such as lantana or Mexican bush sage. Its soft, silver-green foliage blends beautifully with seasonal, colorful annuals and perennials. Good accent plant for rock gardens and in the Japanese garden.

I Suggest
Southernwood works well planted in large containers around the edges of tall-growing copper plants. This plant looks outstanding with the copper-colored plants in the center and fine-textured green-leaved southernwood around the outside edges.

When, Where, and How to Plant

Plant yarrow in the early spring after all danger of frost has passed. If not familiar with the average killing frost date in your area, contact your local county agent or nursery. Plant in any landscape location that receives at least six hours of sunlight and the soil drains well. Don't plant in poorly drained locations, damp areas, or areas with heavy shade. If your soil is heavy and poorly drained, blend in 2 in. or more of coarse washed sand and perlite. Next add 2 in. of ground bark into the top 4 in. of your existing soil. Remove the yarrow from its container and place no deeper than it was growing in the container. Firm the soil well around the root system, water thoroughly, apply root stimulator, and mulch bare soil with 2 in. of bark mulch.

Growing Tips

Water as needed to prevent soil dryness, but never over water. Fertilizing is normally not needed.

Care

Prune as necessary to maintain desired shape, usually by removing old flowers. No insects cause serious problems for yarrow.

Companion Planting and Design

The taller-growing varieties make excellent background plants. Smaller plantings can be used in mass plantings or in borders. Achillea also grows well in containers. These plants work well with other easy plants such as Mexican bush sage and salvias.

I Suggest

Yarrow with its fern-like foliage could be utilized both in the landscape and as a cut flower in your favorite arrangements. I suggest a planting with easy access from your home. When cutting for dried flowers, be sure to make the cut before blooms open.

Let this be the year for you to plant yarrow. With many different sizes and types to choose from, it is so easy to grow, and provides great color all season long—especially in the hot times in Texas. Once yarrow is established, it is relatively drought tolerant and will thrive in difficult-to-water areas, though it should be free of competition from shrubs and trees for growing space, nutrients, and water. A minimum of six hours of full sun per day is needed. Never plant in heavily shaded areas. Try some of these varieties: 'Coronation Gold', 'Moonshine', 'Gold Plate', 'Cerise Queen', 'Paprika', 'Summer Pastels', and 'Parker's Variety'. Yarrow is hardy in all Texas zones.

Other Common Name
Achillea

Bloom Period and Seasonal Color
Late Spring to early fall blooms in white, yellow and pink, with light-green or grayish fern-like foliage.

Mature Height × Spread
6 in. to 3 ft. × 8 in. to 3 ft.

Roses *for Texas*

There is nothing that speaks to a Texan's heart the way roses do. We Texans take great pride in our roses, and there are many selections from which to choose.

Many of our nation's rosebushes are produced in the area of northeast Texas around Tyler—often rightly considered the "Rose Capital of the World." Texas roses are available to us in a rainbow of colors, forms, types, and growth habits. They come packaged or container grown. The American Rose Society (ARS) lists over fifty categories of roses. This can be a bit confusing, even intimidating. While many rose aficionados are very serious about classification, I think growing roses should be much like other gardening activities—fun! With this in mind, I have supplied information to assist you when selecting roses to enjoy in your home landscape. In this chapter I've simplified classification into eight groups: climbers or runners (which includes ramblers), floribundas, grandifloras, hybrid teas, miniatures, heirloom, polyanthas, and species.

Making Your Selections

Be sure to take advantage of the opportunity to visit our fine public rose gardens around the state. Carry a camera, paper, and something to write with. You may find just the variety you want, and if you record its name, you will be able to ask for it at your local garden center. Examples include the Dallas Arboretum and the Fort Worth Botanic Garden. Both have a planting of roses. Don't forget to visit the free City of Tyler Rose Garden, where there are fourteen acres with thousands of roses all available for viewing by the general public. And just east of Texas, right off I-20 (in the direction of Shreveport), is the national headquarters for the American Rose Society (ARS). This is also a great place for rose growers to visit—even if it isn't in Texas.

I hope you enjoy your rose plantings as much as we do ours. Don't be intimidated by growing roses. Eldon Lyle, PhD, world-renowned plant pathologist, retired executive director of the Texas Rose Research Foundation, ARS judge, and all-around encyclopedia of rose information, once told me: "Roses don't need a lot of care, just a little care on a regular basis." If you tend to your roses on a regular basis, the results will be most satisfying.

'Double Delight'

Purchase and plant only top-grade healthy specimens. An under-sized or diseased bargain plant that has shrunken canes or dead limbs is truly not a good buy. You'll receive much more value for your investment by purchasing top-quality plants. I prefer two gallon or larger container-grown plants. Select the best locally adapted varieties for your area. The varieties I've selected for each of the nine categories are some of the best for Texas gardens. Many new rose varieties are introduced each year. From those introduced, the top All-America Rose Selections are made, honoring top quality and performance. When selecting new varieties for the garden, All-America Rose Selections are winners.

Climbing Rose

Protecting Your Investment

Rose hardiness varies with variety, but roses generally are hardy statewide. Consult your local retailer for specific information. Plant your roses in well prepared soil that drains well and receives a minimum of six hours of full sun. Professional producers grow their roses in full sun, and most successful home gardeners do too. Some shade from our hot afternoon sun is acceptable in the landscape. In sandy soils, use a planting mixture of 50 percent native soil and 50 percent organic matter. A 25 percent native soil to 75 percent organic matter mixture is advised for heavy clay soils. Raising beds twelve inches or more above heavy clay soils is also advised to ensure surface drainage. It's not uncommon to have eighteen inch raised beds built on top of heavy clay soils.

Disease control is essential in rose culture, and those who grow roses know that diseases are better prevented than controlled. More than one rose producer has told me that he or she could out-produce competitors with disease-controlling products despite having no insect-controlling products. The following are suggestions for a program to help prevent diseases. Remember: Don't do just one of these activities; combining them is most effective in preventing rose diseases.

1. Purchase disease-resistant varieties.
2. Plant in sunny locations with good air movement.
3. Don't water the foliage. Water at ground level. Drip irrigation works well.
4. Apply recommended fungicides according to label directions.

Garden Display of Roses

During the spring and fall when humidity is higher, there are usually more cloudy, rainy days. At these times, a weekly disease and insect preventive application is recommended. In summer, application every fourteen days is usually sufficient. Many successful rose gardeners begin applying fungicides shortly after initial spring pruning and cleanup of debris. Possible diseases are powdery mildew, leaf spot, and rust. Examples of pests that may visit roses include mites, thrips, aphids, and grasshoppers. Check with your local retail nurseries, American Rose Society consulting rosarians, or your county agent's office for the best fungicides and insecticides to prevent rose diseases and pests.

What Roses Need

Roses are considered relatively heavy feeders. Fertilize them, but don't overfertilize. Always read and follow label directions, and water thoroughly after each application. Long-lasting, slow-release, granular rose fertilizers work well. Begin fertilizing monthly as new leaves emerge, and discontinue about six weeks before the first average killing frost/freeze date in your area.

Roses derive great benefit from a three- to four-inch layer of organic mulch covering their

Miniature Roses

entire root system year-round. Pine bark, clean hay, hardwood bark, cypress bark, pecan shells, peanut hulls, aged wood shavings, shredded tree trimmings, pine needles, and other plant parts and products are often used as organic mulches in Texas.

Water sufficiently to maintain a moist soil. It is said that during the growing season roses usually need 1 to $1^1/2$ inches of rain or irrigation per week. Do not allow the root system to become dry any time of the year, even in winter. Roses like a moist soil, especially during their growing and blooming times, but will not tolerate prolonged wet soil. "Moist" is the key word. Poorly drained or wet soils are detrimental to rose health and vigor. If such a problem is not corrected, roses will decline and terminate. Do not set a watering system to apply water by the clock. Instead, be observant, check the soil moisture, and water as needed. When irrigating, water deeply and thoroughly. Drip irrigation systems are great for watering roses, and they will save 50 percent or more on your water bill.

Initial pruning is best done in late winter or early spring, three to five weeks before the last average killing frost date. Prune to shape and train, and remove spent blooms and dead branches during the growing and blooming season. Spent bloom removal is often referred to as "deadheading." A rather severe pruning is recommended, depending on the type of rose, to induce new canes and blooms. The exception would be late summer, when light pruning may be performed to promote fall blooms. Climbing roses are pruned to keep them in bounds, immediately following their peak of bloom.

Climbing Rose

Rosa spp. and hybrids

Climber is really a misnomer for this plant. The climbing rose doesn't climb—it leans and arches, or must be tied to structures. It tends to have long, stiff branches that grow ten to fifteen feet tall or more. Its blooms are carried in clusters and usually bloom twice during the year, though some may rightly be named continuous bloomers. Pillar is a sub-group that reaches about only ten feet and has strong stems that can be leaned against or tied to pillars or posts—hence the name pillar roses. Another sub-group is ramblers. Ramblers have very long and slender canes with a height of ten to twenty feet. Blooms are thick and small (about two inches across), extremely hardy, and bloom only once a year.

Other Common Name
Running Rose

Bloom Period and Seasonal Color
Spring, summer, or fall blooms in white, pink, yellow, and red.

Mature Height × Spread
Climbing to 10 to 20 ft.

When, Where, and How to Plant
Plant in January and February, and very early spring. Full sun locations that provide at least six hours of sunlight per day are best, in soils that have been prepared with organic matter. Plant bare root selections during the dormant season in prepared locations no deeper than their growth in the nursery row. Plant container-grown selections no deeper than the top of the plant's soilball. Choose varieties that are known to do well in your area. Nursery container roses may be planted into early summer. Gardeners often select them while they are in bloom. The later the rose is planted, the less it will be established for summer heat, and the more maintainance it will require.

Growing Tips
Usually during the growing/blooming season 1 to 1 1/2 in. of water is needed each week. Fertilizing with a long-lasting, granular rose fertilizer is a good choice. Maintain 3 to 4 in. of mulch year-round.

Care
Climbing roses require only minimal trimming and this should be done after it finishes blooming. Train your climbers to grow horizontally, and you will see an increase in blooming. (When trained horizontally, they send up more vertical laterals, which flower.) Visit retail garden centers for control possibilities, and prevent diseases and control pests as needed.

Companion Planting and Design
Climbing roses (including pillar, large-flowered climbers, and ramblers) may be the answer if you are looking for a tall, blooming plant to help camouflage or to break some areas in your landscape. I like to see climbers on some sort of structure, such as a garden entryway or a gazebo. Climbing roses are often grown on fences, though fences often do not provide the height that is usually required. Tall walls work well. Various types of climbers are often used to frame entrances to homes.

I Suggest
Try these varieties in your landscape: 'Don Juan' (velvet red, strong fragrance),'America' (red blend with white centers), 'Improved Blaze' (Bright scarlet, slight fragrance), and 'Golden ShoweBlaze' (daffodil yellow, moderate fragrance).

Floribunda Rose
Rosa hybrids

When, Where, and How to Plant

Plant bareroot in January and February. Nursery container grown plants may be planted into early summer and in the fall. These roses will grow in a minimum of six hours full sun, but full sun all day long is best. Plant in soil that has been prepared well. (See introduction for planting instructions) Choose varieties that are known to do well in your area.

Growing Tips

Maintain a moist soil throughout the growing season. Roses usually need 1 to 1^1/$_2$ in. of water per week during the growing/blooming season. Long-lasting, slow-release rose fertilizer should be applied according to label directions. Water thoroughly after any fertilizer application. Maintain a 3- to 4-in. layer of mulch, covering the root systems all year.

Care

Pruning is done in late winter, just before early spring growth. Prevent or control diseases and pests as necessary using products acquired at your local garden center.

Companion Planting and Design

The floribunda is excellent for use in landscaping, works wonderfully when used in beds, and may be planted in masses for an outstanding effect. Use floribundas to edge walkways or borders, surround garden structures, or create a low hedge. Try planting floribundas in groups of the same variety to create a drift of color throughout your landscape. Don't plant in squares or rectangles; plant them in free-form masses. They work well in large tubs on sunny decks, balconies, patios, or other areas where you have limited space. They serve as excellent background plantings for annual and perennial borders.

I Suggest

Try some of these varieties as color landscape plants: 'Angel Face', 'Europeana', 'Ivory Fashion', and 'Hot 'n Spicy'.

Hybrid tea and polyantha roses were crossed to create the floribunda. Floribunda's blooms are reminiscent of hybrid teas, while its foliage resembles that of polyantha—resulting in a plant that is often more robust than the hybrid tea. The flowers come in clusters, and growers say, "I can cut an instant bouquet from my floribunda." They have a delightful fragrance and are among the easiest roses to grow. Varieties include 'Angel Face' (deep lavender, strong, spicy fragrance, All-America Rose Selection 1996), 'Apricot Nectar' (apricot pink, with touch of gold), 'Cherish' (medium pink, fragrant), 'Europeana' (crimson, slight fragrance, All-America Rose Selection, 1968), 'Evening Star' (white), 'First Edition' (orange blend), 'Iceberg' (white with a hint of pink, strong fragrance), 'Little Darling' (pink and yellow blend, moderate fragrance), and 'Orangeade' (orange-red).

Bloom Period and Seasonal Color

Spring through autumn blooms in red, orange, yellow, pink, white, and mixtures.

Mature Height × Spread

2 to 3 ft. × 3 ft. or more.

Grandiflora Rose
Rosa hybrids

The grandiflora rose is a cross between hybrid tea and floribunda. It exhibits positive characteristics of both, but grows taller than either one. The flower form and the long stems are reminiscent of the hybrid tea parent, while the increased vigor and continuous, abundant blooming come from the floribunda parent. Bloom sizes are between those of the two parents, and the flower may be single or multiple, though most are double. Fragrance, when present, is relatively mild. Varieties of grandiflora include 'Aquarius' (light pink with gold), 'Carrousel' (deep red with moderate fragrance), 'Montezuma' (orange-red, slight fragrance), All-America Rose Selection, l955), 'Mount Shasta' (white, moderate fragrance), and 'Pink Parfait' (blend of light pinks, slight fragrance).

Bloom Period and Seasonal Color
Spring through autumn blooms in white, pink, orange, red, yellow, bi-colors, and blends.

Mature Height × Spread
5 to 7 ft. × 6 ft.

When, Where, and How to Plant
Plant bare-root plants in January and February, and in very early spring. Nursery container plants may be planted into early summer and in the fall. Plant in prepared soil that receives at least six hours of full sun per day. Daylong full sun is best. When planting container-grown grandifloras, plant no deeper than the top of the soilball. Bare root roses should be planted no deeper than they were grown in a nursery row. Choose varieties that are known to do well in your area.

Growing Tips
Maintain a moist soil, especially during the growing and blooming season. Roses need 1 to $1^1/_2$ in. of water per week in the growing/blooming season. Fertilize as needed. Long-lasting, slow-release rose fertilizers work well. Follow label directions and water thoroughly after applying any fertilizer. Maintain a 3- to 4-in. layer of mulch, covering root systems.

Care
If long bloom stems are desired, prune severely in late winter just before new spring growth. Prevent diseases and control insects if they become a problem. Visit local retail garden centers for prevention and control possibilities.

Companion Planting and Design
Because of their continuous bloom, the amount of bloom, and the size of the plants, majestic grandifloras work best as background plants. Grandiflora makes a nice, tall screen for hiding certain areas. For an absolutely breathtaking planting, try tall grandifloras with a shorter rose group in front, and another even shorter rose group in front of that. Grandifloras, hybrid teas, floribundas, and miniatures are all good for use in such a planting. Be sure to select the best varieties for quality and performance in your area, and pay attention to proper spacing, planting, and overall care.

I Suggest
Try one or more of these beauties in your landscape: 'Queen Elizabeth' (medium to light pink, moderate fragrance), 'San Antonio' (medium to deep red), 'Shreveport', and 'Gold Medal'.

Heirloom Rose
Rosa spp. and hybrids

When, Where, and How to Plant

Very early spring is the best time to plant from containers. Fall is also a good time for planting these. Bare-root selections should be planted during the dormant season in January and February. Plant in a location with full sun for best results, making sure it receives a minimum of six hours of sun per day. Heirloom roses need room to grow and spread, so take that into consideration when selecting your planting sites. They will perform best if planted in improved soils, but will survive in almost any Texas soil as long as it is well drained. Plant container-grown selections no deeper than soilball depth. Bare root selections should be planted no deeper than they were grown at the nursery. Choose varieties that are known to do well in your area.

Growing Tips

Water as needed to prevent soil dryness. During the growing/blooming season, roses need 1 to $1^{1}/_{2}$ in. of water per week. Apply rose fertilizer according to label directions. Maintain 3 to 4 in. of mulch.

Care

Unlike some of the modern roses, most heirloom roses will do well without regular pruning. If you have running or rambling-type old garden/antique roses, prune after bloom as necessary. Bush-type roses require no special pruning unless you wish to shape them. If you do, prune in late winter and early spring just before new growth. These tend to be relatively low-maintenance roses. Old garden roses usually require a minimum of pest and disease control and prevention.

Companion Planting and Design

Heirloom roses are often used as stand-alone plantings in Texas. They may be used as focal points in the landscape, and in beds with perennials or evergreen landscape plants. Use caution when placing near high traffic areas because many of them are very thorny, and many grow rather large.

I Suggest

Try some of these "oldies" in your landscape: Lady Banks (soft-yellow and white, fragrant, thornless), 'Baroness Rothschild' (light pink, exceptional fragrance), 'Marie van Houtte' (lemon yellow, washed with lilac), and 'Old Blush' (light pink shaded into darker pink, slight fragrance).

The definition and classification of roses is subjective—it depends on who is providing the information. Some believe that any roses found or introduced after 1867 cannot be considered heirloom roses. Others feel that roses close to eighty years old and exhibiting the characteristics of heirloom roses should be classified as such. One of those old garden characteristics is petal color—it tends to be less intense than that of many modern roses. Yet the outstanding fragrance is indisputable, and many of these roses have large hips that can be harvested to make tea and even jellies. Heirloom roses are vigorous, relatively care-free members of the rose family.

Other Common Names
Antique Rose, Old Garden Rose

Bloom Period and Seasonal Color
Spring blooms, or continuous blooms in soft white, pink, and red.

Mature Height × Spread
2 to 6 ft. × 8 ft. or more.

Hybrid Tea Rose
Rosa hybrids

Because they have long, sturdy stems with one relatively large, fragrant bloom, these popular roses are often sold in flower shops and on street corners. Hybrid tea is parented by the hybrid perpetual and the tea rose. This hybrid was created through lots of dedicated effort and decades of crossbreeding. Hybrid tea gains its fragrance and delicate look from the tea roses and its vigor from hybrid perpetuals. Most blooms are fragrant. Generally blooming throughout the growing season, hybrid tea roses are the rose group of choice for rose show enthusiasts. If you would like to have a show-type rose for your own personal use, try one or more hybrid teas.

Bloom Period and Seasonal Color
Spring through autumn blooms in red, orange, yellow, white, pinks, mixtures, and blends.

Mature Height × Spread
3 to 6 ft. × 4 ft.

When, Where, and How to Plant
Plant bare-root selections in January and February or late winter/very early spring before they break dormancy. Plant container-grown plants in spring, summer, or fall, though early spring is best. Locations with daylong sun are desirable, though you may plant in any moist, well-drained, fertile location with at least six hours of sun. Plant bare root selections no deeper than they were growing in the nursery row. Container-grown roses should not be planted any deeper than the top of the individual plant's soil-ball. Perpare the soil before planting. Choose varieties that are hardy in your area.

Growing Tips
Water as needed to maintain a moist soil, especially during the growing and blooming season. Usually 1 to $1^{1}/_{2}$ in. of water per week is needed during that time. Fertilize according to label directions with your favorite rose fertilizer, maintaining a 3- to 4-in. mulch layer.

Care
Prune severely in late winter just before new growth begins. Experience has shown a mid-February date to be a good timeframe for pruning these beauties. Control insects when needed, and prevent diseases. Visit your local garden center for prevention and control.

Companion Planting and Design
Hybrid tea roses are usually utilized as stand-alone plantings. They may be incorporated into color plantings including annuals, perennials, and other roses. I do not recommend them as foundation plants, as they have their show in bloom in their season but then are not very attractive through the dormant season.

I Suggest
Try these varieties of hybrid tea roses in a spot in your landscape: 'Tropicana' (coral-orange, strong fragrance, All-America Rose Selection, 1963), 'Broadway', 'Double Delight' (red-blend), 'Mister Lincoln' (dark red, strong fragrance), and 'Perfume Delight' (medium pink, fragrant).

Miniature Rose

Rosa spp. and hybrids

When, Where, and How to Plant

Plant miniatures in spring or fall from containers, and during the dormant season for bare-rooted selections. Plant in full sun or in areas that receive a minimum of six hours of full sun. Miniatures may be planted in the ground or grown in containers outdoors. Never plant in heavily shaded locations. When temperatures drop below 20 degrees Fahrenheit, be sure to provide container-grown selections some protection, especially if temperatures are expected to be in the mid-twenties or lower for an extended period. This added winter protection normally is not needed for selections planted in the landscape. Remember, all plants lose several degrees of winter hardiness when grown in containers and allowed to remain above the ground through the winter. Plant container-grown selections at soilball depth. Plant bare-root plants at the same depth they were growing in the nursery. Choose varieties that are hardy in your area.

Growing Tips

Maintain a moist soil, especially during the growing and bloom season. During this time roses normally need 1 to 1^1/$_2$ in. of water per week. Fertilize with a premium-quality rose fertilizer. Always maintain a 3- to 4-in. layer of mulch, covering the root systems.

Care

Prune rather severely as new spring growth begins on all except the running forms. If desired, prune the running forms after the bloom cycle is complete. Visit your local retail garden center for pest control and prevention methods.

Companion Planting and Design

Miniature roses are excellent when used as borders around landscape shrubs, in front of perennials, or in front of taller rose cousins. You may create a complete miniaturized rose garden using the various types available today. Try some of these little beauties anywhere a spot of color is desired, including on decks, patios, and balconies. The gardener who has a zero-lot line or a townhouse with limited space may happily plant an entire bed of the many mini-roses.

I Suggest

Try the varieties 'Merry Marshall', 'Golden Song', 'Red Cascade', 'Acey Deucy' and 'Minnie Pearl'.

Miniatures are the smallest roses, yet have the characteristics of many larger roses. Scale of bloom, leaf size, and stem size are reduced. Bloom sizes generally range from ^{1}/$_2$ to 1^1/$_2$ in. across. Because of its small size, some gardeners attempt to grow these beauties indoors. This is possible if you have a very sunny location and high humidity. Because of these two important elements, it is better to grow miniatures outside where they will be as hardy as their larger cousins. Many Texas gardeners mistakenly believe miniature roses are delicate because of their small leaf, stem, and flower size. In fact, miniature roses are as easy—if not easier—to grow than many of their larger cousins.

Other Common Name
Mini-Rose

Bloom Period and Seasonal Color
Continuous blooms in many colors and blends.

Mature Height × Spread
2 to 3 ft. × 1 to 2 ft.

Polyantha Rose
Rosa spp. and hybrids

Polyanthas are usually low-growing roses, and have been in existence for many years. Its parentage is a combination of multiflora rosa and hybrid teas. Polyantha means "many flowers." Polyantha produces many small flowers in great quantities, from spring until the first hard freeze. It has more vigor than its hybrid tea parent. It has very small, narrow leaves that are delicate-looking and finely textured; the leaves come from its multiflora parentage. Polyanthas have perfectly formed buds. Its blooms are single, double, or semi-double, and come in less intense colors than those of its parent hybrid tea. Sometimes it's scented, sometimes not. Not all garden centers will carry certain selections of polyantha. Ask your garden retailer to order them for you.

Bloom Period and Seasonal Color
Spring through autumn blooms in orange, pink, yellow, white, and red.

Mature Height × Spread
24 in. × 3 ft.

When, Where, and How to Plant
Plant polyantha from containers in early spring for best results. They also do well when planted from containers in the fall. Install bare-root selections during the dormant season in January and February. Plant in well-prepared soil in locations with a minimum of six hours of full sun. Plant container-grown varieties at soilball depth. Bare-root selections should be planted no deeper than grown at the nursery. Choose varieties that are known to do well in your area.

Growing Tips
Water as needed to maintain a moist soil, especially during the growing and blooming periods, and fertilize throughout this time. Roses need 1 to 1^1/$_2$ in. of water per week during growning and blooming season. Long-lasting, slow-release rose fertilizer works well. Maintain a 3- to 4-in. mulch layer around root system.

Care
Prune severely just before new spring growth if desired. Prevent disease and control insects as needed. Visit local nurseries for control and prevention possibilities.

Companion Planting and Design
Polyantha roses are spectacular when planted where space is limited yet a profusion of bloom is desired through the entire season. When planted in masses of single colors, this rose is a show-stopper. Because of its low growth, it's an ideal candidate for hedges and borders, though some varieties such as 'La Marne' may reach 4 to 6 ft. in height. The plants tend to be dwarf or compact, a quality that makes them good for container growing.

I Suggest
Try some of these interesting yet lesser known rose types: 'Cecile Brunner' (pink and yellow blend, delicate fragrance), 'China Doll' (medium pink), 'Mother's Day' (deep red), 'Margo Koster', 'Pearl d'Or', 'The Fairy', 'Climbing Cecil Brunner', 'La Marne, 'Jean Mermoz', 'Garnette', and Marie Pavie'.

Species Rose

Rosa spp.

When, Where, and How to Plant

Early spring is a great planting time for container-grown selections. Container-grown selections also do well when planted in the fall. All bare-root plants should be installed during the late winter, dormant season. Plant in locations with full sun for best results or where they will receive a minimum of six hours of full sun. While species rose will grow in virtually any native Texas soil, they benefit from improved soil preparation. Plant container-grown selections at soilball depth. Plant bare-root plants at the same depth they were growing while being produced. Choose varieties that are hardy in your area.

Growing Tips

Species roses benefit from watering, mulching (3 to 4 in. deep), and fertilizing as other roses do. These actions enhance the overall vigor and blooming period of species roses. By maintaining a moist soil through the growing season—and fertilizing with a rose fertilizer—better bloom and growth is usually achieved. During the growth/bloom season, these roses will benefit from 1 to 1 1/2 in. of water per week.

Care

Minimal care is usually necessary for species roses. Normally no pruning is needed. However, pruning may be performed if desired. Pruning is best done by mid-February or earlier. Insects and diseases are usually not a problem for species roses.

Companion Planting and Design

Species roses such as Lady Banks' work well as specimens due to their size. They are especially good in old styles of landscapes, including country cottage garden themes. Species roses may be successfully used in combination with any other rose type, evergreen plants, annuals or perennials.

I Suggest

For something different in your Texas landscape try, 'Seven Sisters' (small blooms in shades of pink, mauve, and purple), 'Austrian Copper', 'Cherokee' (five petals, white, large, fragrant), or Lady Banks (soft yellow to white, single or double blooms, slightly fragrant).

There are over 100 different species of roses all over the world. Some species are shrubs, others are climbing or trailing. Species roses grow naturally in the wild, or are indigenous to particular areas. It is the oldest type/classification of roses we grow. Be sure to allow plenty of room for maximum growth. Most species roses are very fragrant and thorny. The species rose most commonly used in Texas home landscapes may be Rosa banksiae 'Lutea', commonly known as the yellow Lady Banks' rose. Roses can hybridize while being grown in the wild. Species roses may be grown by specialized growers, and most of these reputable growers will also make sure that you are purchasing a true species rose.

Bloom Period and Seasonal Color

Varying bloom periods in many colors.

Mature Height × Spread

4 to 20 ft. × 6 to 8 ft. or more.

Shrubs *for Texas*

Shrubs can be thought of as the furniture in our home landscapes. Ranging from a dwarf height of only twelve inches up to shrubs that grow to twenty feet or more, we can move them around, arrange them, and use them to dress up our foundations.

It is strongly recommended that when in search of shrubs, you ask the following questions when visiting your local garden center or nursery.

* How tall and wide does this shrub grow in my area?
* What specific sun/shade conditions are best? (Morning sun/afternoon shade, daylong dappled sun/shade)?
* Does it have blooms, and if so, what are the bloom colors?
* When does it bloom, and for how long?
* Does it have any special soil requirements (Acid or alkaline soil, well-drained soil, deep soil, or moist soil)?
* Does it require special bed preparation? (Azalea nearly always requires special beds in Texas gardens).
* If deciduous, ask these two additional questions:
* Does it have fall leaf color? If so, what are the colors?

Pyracantha

Hibiscus

- Are there any special conditions necessary to obtain these colors? (Special conditions might be a gradually cooling fall season, sun/shade, relatively mild or harsh summers, or overall care.)

This information will help you decide whether or not to purchase a particular shrub and where to place it in your landscape. If you are seeking more maintenance-free specimens, be sure to select shrubs that will grow to a desired height and width without requiring pruning.

When laying out your foundation landscape beds at home, be sure to make them at least five feet wide, or in many cases, wider. Improve the soil thoroughly before planting.

Mapping Out a Plan

Once your bed is laid out and the soil prepared, determine where you wish to plant your shrubs by using researched information and your own personal taste. You may find it helpful to draw a diagram of your home on ¹/4 inch grid drafting paper (one-quarter inch on paper equals one foot of property). Draw your house on the paper, marking the windows, doors, and any existing plants and structures. You will be able to see the places that are suitable for planting new shrubs. If you are uncomfortable putting together a plan, pay a visit to a landscape designer or landscape architect.

If purchasing a home with an existing landscape, remember that it doesn't have to remain the same. We remodel our homes—repaint, recarpet, rearrange furniture, add rooms, and move walls. You can do the same thing with the home landscape. If you don't like the looks, change it!

Nandina

Some blooming shrubs bloom in the spring, some in the fall, and others bloom almost continuously. Two of the best blooming shrubs in Texas are abelia, *Abelia × grandiflora*, and crape myrtle, *Lagerstroemia indica*. If you are unsure how to determine a high-quality shrub or don't know a lot about shrub varieties, be sure to deal with a reputable local garden center.

I have included thirty-six shrubs in this chapter, and there's something for every Texas gardener.

Abelia

Abelia × grandiflora

This is a flowering shrub that adds to landscapes with its interesting foliage and blooms. Abelias are tough and are often found in former homesites. This is what my granny called a "thrifty" plant; it goes a long way on a little water. Thrifty also meant tough, requiring minimal care. This was especially important to Granny because she had to carry all the water she applied to her Indian Creek garden. 'Frances Mason' is a variegated cultivar. 'Edward Goucher' is semi-evergreen in some areas, has small clear-pink blooms, and grows three to five feet tall. White-flowered 'Prostrata' is the lowest, with a height and width of three feet. 'Sunrise' has cream and pink variegated foliage. Abelia is hardy in all Texas zones.

Other Common Name
Glossy Abelia

Bloom Period and Seasonal Color
Summer to fall blooms in white to pink with bronze, fall foliage.

Mature Height × Spread
3 to 8 ft. × 3 to 8 ft.

When, Where, and How to Plant
Abelia grows in Zones 6 to 9 and can be planted plant any time of the year. In Zones 6a and 6b, plant early spring through early fall. Abelias grow in light sandy soils or heavy clay when located in full sun. Do not plant in wet, poorly drained, or shady locations. For foundation plantings, install in beds 5 ft. wide tilled with 4 to 6 in. of organic matter. Individual planting holes may be dug as wide as desired, but no deeper than the soilball. Backfill, water thoroughly, apply a root stimulator, and cover bare soil with 3 to 4 in. of organic mulch.

Growing Tips
Water as needed to maintain soil moisture; deep and infrequent irrigation is preferred. Drip irrigation works very well. I fertilize with slow-release rose or lawn granular fertilizers. If you live along the Gulf Coast, first apply around March 15; in central Texas, March 21; and in north Texas (including the High Plains) April 1. Reapply twice during the growing season, and once again in the fall. For a less aggressive fertilizer plan, apply only in spring and early fall. Maintain a 3- to 4-in. layer of mulch.

Care
Prune as desired to maintain the shape wanted, but please don't make a boxed hedge out of this shrub. Abelias will take rather severe pruning and come back with more blooms on the new growth. Early spring is best for radical pruning. Do selective pruning throughout the growing season. Don't prune after September. This plant has no serious pests. Disease is not a problem in full-sun locations that have good air movement.

Companion Planting and Design
Abelia is a great tall, wide blooming shrub. Do not plant in front of porches, low windows, narrow beds, or in limited spaces, because it will soon outgrow these areas. It is best used as a stand-alone planting without any companion plants. Annuals may be planted outside its spread if desired.

I Suggest
Abelia grandiflora (or glossy abelia) is the tallest-growing and oldest abelia commonly used. 'Compacta' is a favorite of ours.

Althea

Hibiscus syriacus

When, Where, and How to Plant

Althea is hardy in Zones 6a-9b. In the Panhandle, plant it in very early spring. In the rest of Texas, plant any time (fall is best) in a location with a minimum of six hours of full sun, though it does best in daylong, full-sun locations. Do not plant in full shade locations or where soil drainage is poor. Althea grows in all types of soil that drains well. To plant in a well-prepared bed, measure the area in length, and calculate at least one plant for every 6 ft. Make sure your bed is at least 5 ft. wide. Remove any rocks, sticks, or weeds, and till the area. Add 4 to 6 in. of organic matter and till again. Plant in the center of the bed, and dig the planting holes as deep as the plant's soilball but no deeper. Backfill and water thoroughly. Apply a root stimulator and 3 to 4 in. of organic mulch covering all bare soil at the planting site.

Growing Tips

I prefer a slow-release granular rose food. In Zone 9, make the first application around March 1; Zone 8, mid-March to April 1; Zone 7, April 1; and Zone 6, April 1 to mid-April. Reapply approximately every six to eight weeks through early fall. For a less aggressive program, fertilize only in spring and fall. Remember to water plants thoroughly after fertilizers are applied. Maintain a 3- to 4-in. mulch layer.

Care

Aphids may occasionally visit tender new leaf growth. During July and August, when the humidity is very low, spider mites may be present, themselves. Consult your local retailer for controls.

Companion Planting and Design

Use althea as a summer blooming screen planting. Tropical hibiscus, *Hibiscus rosa-sinensis*, is often used for summer color. Altheas trained as tree forms may be used in large containers. Groundcovers, perennials, and annuals may all be planted in a bed of althea.

I Suggest

'Diana', my favorite, is a beautiful, single variety that has large, pure white blooms. Try one in your garden with solid white annual vinca/periwinkle in its bed—outstanding and classy—just like Diana, the people's princess.

Althea is another old-fashioned landscape plant that has been around as long as I can remember. Altheas are great summer color plants that can be used as tree forms, accomplished by selective pruning. In this form they are an excellent patio tree. Unpruned, althea tends to grow into a tall, upright, bushy shrub. The United States National Arboretum's (U.S.N.A.) selected releases are 'Aphrodite' (deep rose-pink with a showy deep-red center), 'Hélène' (pure white with a deep reddish purple center), and 'Minerva' (lavender-pink with a reddish purple center). Non-U.S.N.A. releases include 'Blushing Bride' (double pink), 'Collie Mullens' (double purple-lavender), 'Blue Bird' (single blue), 'Admiral Dewey' (single pure white), 'Rubis' (single red), and 'Hamabo' (pale pink single with red stripes). Althea is hardy in all Texas zones.

Other Common Name

Rose of Sharon

Bloom Period and Seasonal Color

Summer blooms in white, pink, red, purple, and blends.

Mature Height × Spread

8 to 12 ft. × 3 to 6 ft. or more.

Aralia

Fatsia japonica

Texas gardeners love shade, but if an entire property is shaded, the selection of landscape planting possibilities becomes limited. When I suggest, even in jest, to a caller on my radio show that he or she should cut down trees in order to get more light, I usually hear a moan or sigh that lets me know that the suggestion is unacceptable. Lucky for us, aralia is an outstanding shrub that grows best in shady areas. Aralia, or fatsia, is known by several names in catalogs, books, and nurseries. The scientific names are usually Fatsia japonica, Aralia sieboldii, *or* Aralia japonica. *All of these names will lead you to the same plant.* 'Moseri' *is a more compact form, and* 'Variegata' *has creamy white leaf margins.* × Fatshedera—*a similarly used plant—is a hybrid of* Hedera helix *and* Fatsia japonica. *It is more of a leaner than a shrub or vine but takes its traits from both. Aralia is hardy in Zones 8a to 9b.*

Other Common Name
Japanese Aralia

Bloom Period and Seasonal Color
Evergreen foliage.

Mature Height × Spread
5 to 7 ft. × 4 to 5 ft.

When, Where, and How to Plant
In Zone 8a, plant in early spring through early fall. In Zones 8b, 9a, and 9b, plant anytime. Aralia will not grow well in hot, dry, windy locations. An eastern exposure with sun until 10 a.m. (or daylong dappled sun) should be fine—though daylong shade is best. Aralia will tolerate a poorly drained clay or sandy soil. To maximize growth, improve soil before planting. Add organic materials to the native soil. If you develop beds around trees, just blend organic matter with the native soil between the roots. To protect roots, handwork (not a tiller) is best. Plant no deeper than the plant's rootball, backfill with loose soil, and apply root stimulator. Water thoroughly and cover bare soil with 3 to 4 in. of bark mulch.

Growing Tips
Keep moist but not wet. Aralia responds with vigor to a good fertilization program. Use a 3:1:2 ratio, long-lasting lawn fertilizer (such as 15-5-10 or 18-6-12). Note: Don't use agricultural-grade fertilizers or those containing herbicides. In Zones 9a and 9b, make your first application around mid-March; in Zones 8a and 8b, around April 1. Apply approximately every six to eight weeks through early fall. For a less aggressive fertilization program, fertilize in spring and early fall only. Remember to water thoroughly after fertilizing. Maintain a 3- to 4-in. layer of mulch.

Care
This plant has no serious pests.

Companion Planting and Design
Use as a mass background planting in shady bed locations with ferns to create a pleasing effect under trees. It works well with ferns and aucuba to create interesting tropical effects. You may also use aralia as a stand-alone or in mass plantings in large containers. Aralia also works well as a corner foundation planting.

I Suggest
Aralia is one of my most often recommended plants in Texas for heavily shaded areas. It may not be as widely available as other shrubs, but if you have deep shade, it's worth the hunt.

Arborvitae
Thuja occidentalis

When, Where, and How to Plant
Plant any time of the year. It grows in all Texas soils including loose blow sand and compact clay. The Eastern arborvitaes do better when protected from southwestern summer winds. Chinese arborvitaes will take any exposure, including drying winds. Both types prefer rich, moist, fertile soils. When planting in beds, till 4 to 6 in. of organic matter into the soil. For the larger-growing specimens or tall screen plantings, plant individually in the loosened native soil. Dig the plant's hole no deeper than the soilball, but loosen the soil as wide as desired. Set the plants, backfill, water thoroughly, apply root stimulator, and cover the bare soil with 3 to 4 in. of bark mulch. I use pine bark mulch. For best overall growth, I suggest full sun locations.

Growing Tips
Water as needed to maintain sufficient moisture for growth. For maximum growth and water usage, install a drip water system. Maintain a 3- to 4-in. layer of bark mulch year round. Fertilize in early spring: in Zones 9a and 9b around March 1; Zones 8a and 8b in mid-March; Zones 7a and 7b on April 1; and Zones 6a and 6b in mid-April. Use slow-release lawn fertilizer that has the 3:1:2 ratio (such as 21-7-14 or 15-5-10). After a spring application of fertilizer, reapply in mid-growing season, and in the fall. Make sure there are no herbicides in the fertilizer you use.

Care
Arborvitae may be sheared into all sorts of shapes—including animals. So, if you are interested in some formal style, or unusual style clippings, try arborvitae! Juniper blight, spider mites, and bagworms are more of a problem on oriental than on eastern varieties. The gardening aid industry has products to help control these.

Companion Planting and Design
Use arborvitae as tall screening, windbreak, or specimen plantings. I would not use them as foundation plantings and do not recommend the use of companion plantings with this group.

I Suggest
If you like a cedar look but don't want the prickly feel or plants as large as our typical cedar, try arborvitae.

Oriental arborvitae, Chinese arborvitae, and Eastern arborvitae are all common names for different types of this plant. If you have seen arborvitae in abandoned homesites, it is most likely Chinese arborvitae. The Eastern arborvitae grows best from Wichita County along the Red River, south-southeast to Blanco County in central Texas, and northeast to Sabine County along the border. T. occidentalis, 'Golden Globe' is four feet tall and wide. 'Holmstrup' is five to seven feet tall. 'Little Giant' is six feet high. T. orientalis, 'Aurea Nana' is four to six feet high. 'Blue Cone' is eight feet high. 'Westmont' is three feet high and 'Minima Glauca' is three to four feet high. Arborvitae is hardy in all Texas zones.

Bloom Period and Seasonal Color
Evergreen foliage.

Mature Height × Spread
3 to 40 ft. × 3 to 15 ft.

Aucuba

Aucuba japonica

I have two 20-gallon containers of aucuba that I use for seasonal shady color. Diversity is easily accomplished by using different colors in containers each season or anytime you want a change. Aucuba cannot build up the ability to take direct sun, and it sunburns badly. The color drains out of the leaves, and they eventually turn black. If your aucubas get sunburned, do not try to nurse them through the problem. Move them! Either relocate them or construct a shade. 'Mr. Goldstrike' has dark-green leaves splashed with gold. 'Picturata' has lots of bright, gold-yellow centers on its leaves. 'Sulphurea' has wide golden leaf edges. 'Variegata' is dark glossy green with specks of gold and is compact. 'Serratifolia' has serrated solid-green leaves with showy red fall berries. Aucuba is hardy in Zone 7b and borderline in Zone 7a.

Other Common Name
Gold Dust Plant

Bloom Period and Seasonal Color
Evergreen foliage in green with yellow-gold.

Mature Height × Spread
4 to 8 ft. × 4 to 6 ft.

When, Where, and How to Plant
Plant any time of the year (fall is a great time) when you are in the mood for some color in shady situations. Shade is the key! Aucubas will grow in heavy clay or sandy soils. They prefer moist growing conditions but will not tolerate constantly wet soil. Do not plant in a poorly drained area. Thoroughly improve the soil. Remove rocks, sticks, and weeds before adding any organic matter. Till the area to be planted, add 4 to 6 in. of high-quality organic matter such as compost, ground bark, brown sphagnum or peat moss, and till again. Make beds at least 5 ft. wide. Planting holes should be no deeper than the plant's soilball. Set the plants, backfill, water thoroughly, apply a root stimulator, and mulch the bare soil with 3 to 4 in. of bark.

Growing Tips
Throughout the growing season, maintain a moist, but not wet soil. Aucuba responds to light applications of a 15-5-10 or 21-7-14 slow-release lawn fertilizer. In Zones 9a and 9b, fertilize around March 1; in Zones 8a and 8b, mid-March; in Zone 7a, April 1. Be sure to water thoroughly after each fertilizer application. Maintain a 3- to 4-in. layer of bark mulch year-round.

Care
Prune selectively because pruning scars remain visible longer on aucuba than on most landscape plants. This plant has no serious pests.

Companion Planting and Design
Aucuba makes a wonderfully tall foundation plantings. Don't place in front of a low window, porch, or entry unless you want it covered up. Try planting on the inside of a protected courtyard, atrium, or solarium. It also lends itself well to a containerized culture and does well in beds of shade-loving ferns.

I Suggest
This is another of the few plants I often recommend to Texans with deep shade on their property. It's available at most nurseries in various sizes from 1 gallon to 5 gallons. Remember no direct sun, or it will cook and sunburn like my redheaded, fair-skinned wife, Judy.

Azalea

Rhododendron spp.

When, Where, and How to Plant

Plant in early spring through fall in Zones 6a, 6b, and 7a. In Zones 7b, 8a, 8b, 9a, and 9b, plant anytime. The kurumes and satsukis benefit from shade. Southern indicas will grow well in full sun. Azaleas need an acid soil that drains well. Don't plant in heavy clay soils, poorly drained soils, or those with a high alkaline pH. These beauties perform best in naturally occurring, sandy acid soils amended with organic matter. In heavy clay soils, remove 12 in. of soil, backfill with a 50/50 mixture of brown peat moss and pine bark mulch, and raise the bed an additional 6 in. above the grade. Azaleas are shallow, fibrous-rooted plants that require moist soil but will not tolerate wet feet or poorly drained soils. Plant azaleas in thoroughly prepared, raised, 5-ft.-wide beds. Dig planting holes the depth of the plant's soilball and install. Backfill with planting mix, apply root stimulator, water thoroughly, and cover bare soil with 3 to 4 in. of pine bark mulch.

Growing Tips

Keep soil moist but not wet. Fertilize after bloom drop, mid-season, and early fall with granular azalea fertilizer according to label directions, and water thoroughly. Maintain 3 to 4 in. of mulch. Prune as needed to desired heights or shapes after bloom drop. Do not prune during the fall because you may be removing buds for next season's blooms.

Care

Mites, lace bugs, and scale are potential pests. Leaf gall, leaf spots, and flower or petal blight are potential diseases. Chlorosis is also possible. Keeping plants in a healthy state will prevent most pests and diseases. If any of these do become a problem, contact your local nursery or county agent's office to identify problems and obtain recommendations for treatments.

Companion Planting and Design

Depending on the type, azaleas may be planted under low windows or used as tall specimens. Often utilized in mass effect with outstanding results, camellias and gardenias also grow well with azaleas.

I Suggest

Visit areas known for azaleas including shows and trails in areas of Houston, Dallas, and East Texas to see their beauty firsthand.

For spring color, these beauties are hard to beat. Requiring more effort than many shrubs, the rewards often exceed the requirements. Azaleas are members of the rhododendron genus and have some of the rhododendron's typical characteristics. There are several types of azalea that do well in Texas. The kurume hybrid, which include 'Coral Bells', 'Hino-Crimson', and 'Flame', are hardy into the Panhandle's Zone 6b. They will also grow in all other Texas zones. Meanwhile, the southern hybrids are hardy in Zones 8a, 8b, 9a, and 9b. These include 'George L. Tabor', 'Fielder's White', and 'Formosa'. The satsuki hybrids are hardy in Texas Zones 7a, 7b, 8a, 8b, 9a, and 9b and include 'Higasa', 'Macrantha', and 'Gumpo Pink'. Depending on the species, azaleas are hardy in all Texas zones except Zone 6a.

Bloom Period and Seasonal Color

Evergreen with spring blooms in red, coral, salmon, pink, white, and lavender.

Mature Height × Spread

3 to 10 ft. × 3 to 8 ft.

Barberry
Berberis thunbergii

Most barberry shrubs are in the B. thunbergii group. The ones I am most familiar with are all deciduous. However, there are some interesting evergreen varieties. These are tough, durable, low-care plants that add interesting spots of color to the landscape. They can take both Texas heat and cold (what a deal!) though they will not do well in prolonged dry spells. Barberry does best in moist, fertile beds that are neither too wet nor poorly drained. It is especially useful in color accent beds. You may wish to try B. × mentorensis, or mentor barberry, which is semi-evergreen. 'Atropurpurea', 'Aurea', 'Monomb', 'Crimson Pygmy', 'Kobold', 'Rose Glow', and 'Sparkle' are cultivars worth trying. Barberry is hardy in all Texas zones.

Other Common Name
Japanese Barberry

Bloom Period and Seasonal Color
Fall foliage in red, amber, and crimson.

Mature Height × Spread
1 to 6 ft. × 2 to 7 ft.

When, Where, and How to Plant
Plant any time you like. All species and cultivars do best in full sun for growth and color. Don't plant in locations that are poorly drained or receive less than 6 hours of full sun. Remove sticks, rocks, weeds, and turfgrass from a sunny location. Till the area to be planted, add 6 in. of organic matter, and blend thoroughly by tilling again with the native soil. Make beds a minimum of 5 ft. wide—larger if possible. Dig planting holes as deep as the plant's soilball (no deeper), and set the plants into the ground. Backfill, water thoroughly, apply root stimulator, and mulch bare soil 3 to 4 in. deep with bark mulch or similar material.

Growing Tips
A drip irrigation system is ideal for maintaining a moist, but not wet, soil. Fertilize during the spring approximately 2 weeks after the last killing frost. Fertilize twice more during the growing season and once in the fall. Any 3:1:2 ratio, slow-release lawn fertilizer (such as 21-7-14 or 15-5-10) should work well.

Care
Prune as needed during the growing season. Aphids may visit new growth, but usually aren't much of a problem. In the event of a problem, your local garden retailer will have a wide assortment of products available to help. Root rot may also be an issue in wet locations. The best solution is to simply not plant in those areas. Maintain a 3- to 4-in. mulch layer.

Companion Planting and Design
Use barberry as a special planting in color beds. A few good varieties to be used as foundation plantings are *B. buxifolia* 'Nana' ($1^{1}/_2$ × 2 ft. evergreen) and *B. × gladwynensis* 'William Penn' (4 × 4 to 5 ft. evergreen). For the best effect, mass planting is recommended. Multiple offset rows also work well in specific applications. Barberry's colors are often enhanced in landscape plantings by white blooms of periwinkle or other white bloomers.

I Suggest
If space is limited, and you like the color, try a 'Crimson Pygmy' in your plantings.

Boxwood

Buxus microphylla

When, Where, and How to Plant

Fall is a good time for planting boxwood, but it may be planted any time of the year. Do not plant in poorly drained soils, in full sun areas, or where the shrubs will receive reflected heat from a driveway. Boxwoods are good choices for shady locations; most prefer shade from the hot western sun. For bed plantings, remove all sticks, rocks, weeds, and turfgrass from the area to be planted and till the area. After the initial tilling, add 2 in. each of brown sphagnum peat moss, compost, and ground pine bark. Thoroughly till these materials into the native soil, and you are ready to plant. Make all your foundation beds a minimum of 5 ft. wide, and dig planting holes no deeper than the plant's soilball. Set plants, backfill, water thoroughly, apply root stimulator, and cover bare soil with 2 to 3 in. of bark mulch.

Growing Tips

Keep soil moist but not wet. Boxwood must drain well or root rot may occur. Fertilize two weeks after your last killing frost, twice more during the growing season, and once again in the fall. I use a slow-release 15-5-10, 21-7-14, or similar 3:1:2 ratio lawn fertilizer. Water thoroughly after each application. Maintain a 3- to 4-in. layer of bark mulch.

Care

If your soil has root knot nematodes, do not plant boxwood; dwarf yaupon holly is a better choice. Have your soil tested for these pests by the Texas Agricultural Extension Service. Leaf miners and spider mites may visit, but they usually don't cause problems for healthy plants. Control products are available at your local garden retailer.

Companion Planting and Design

The versatile boxwood may be used as foundation plantings, screens, or specimens. 'Green Velvet', 'Winter Gem', Japanese, and 'Green Mountain' are the better selections for shady locations. They work well with the holly family in Texas landscapes.

I Suggest

For year-round green beauty from boxwood, the variety 'Winter Gem' is hard to beat in Texas.

Boxwood is the shrub of choice for training into formal clipped hedges. B. microphylla is the largest shrub group and contains the popular bright-green Japanese boxwood, which is hardy in both Zones 7a and 7b, but does better in Zones 8a, 8b, 9a, and 9b. The other varieties of B. microphylla are hardy anywhere in our state. Some boxwoods such as B. microphylla var. koreana, are great dwarf shrubs, while others are relatively tall. B. sempervirens 'Arborescens', may reach ten to twelve feet in height. B. microphylla 'Winter Gem' has dark-green foliage year-round with small, oval-shaped leaves. B. harlandii is Harland boxwood; B. sempervirens is English boxwood, the boxwood of old England and France. Depending on the variety, boxwoods are hardy statewide.

Other Common Name
Japanese Boxwood

Bloom Period and Seasonal Color
Evergreen foliage.

Mature Height × Spread
1 to 20 ft. × 1 to 6 ft.

Burning Bush
Euonymus alata

Burning bush is a show stopper. If you want fall color in your landscape this tough, durable, and easy-to-grow shrub is for you. With a growth rate that is moderate to slow, these shrubs require minimal pruning. Try it as a background planting in that color bed you have been thinking about developing near your mailbox. It also works well as plantings in sunny locations for viewing from inside your home. You won't find a more winter hardy or colorful shrub for Texas landscapes. E. alata 'Compacta', sometimes called dwarf, is slow growing and compact. Occasionally this dwarf may grow five to six feet tall. Burning bush is hardy in all Texas zones.

Other Common Name
Winged Euonymus

Bloom Period and Seasonal Color
Fall color in red with red-orange fall fruit.

Mature Height × Spread
8 to 10 ft. × 8 to 12 ft.

When, Where, and How to Plant
Burning bush is hardy even in Zone 3, which is along the Canadian border. It is easily Texas-hardy. It may be planted anytime (fall is best) and will grow in almost any soil condition, including moderately moist to moderately dry. It does best in moist, well-drained, fertile soils and full sun locations. For best growth and fall color, don't plant in areas with less than six hours of full sun. Remove any turfgrass, weeds, or debris from the area and till the native soil. Add 4 to 6 in. of organic matter and till again. If you plan to use burning bush as a foundation planting, background planting, hedge, or in front of other landscape shrubs, make the beds at least 5 ft. wide. A spacing of 3 to 4 ft. should work well in most bed applications. After digging the hole no deeper than the soilball, plant and backfill. Water thoroughly, apply a root stimulator, and cover bare soil with 3 to 4 in. of bark mulch.

Growing Tips
Water as needed to prevent dry soil. Fertilize with a 15-5-10 or similar 3:1:2 ratio slow-release lawn fertilizer. Administer spring applications 2 weeks after the last killing frost date, twice more during the growing season, and once in the fall. Water thoroughly after each application. Maintain 3 to 4 in. of bark mulch.

Care
Prune as desired, though spring is best for radical pruning. Burning bush has no serious pests or diseases. While euonymus scale visits evergreen varieties, it usually does not cause problems with this species. For powdery mildew controls, seek help from your local nursery.

Companion Planting and Design
Burning bush is suitable for use as a screening hedge. For a super look, plant it in front of dark-green, broadleaf, evergreen shrubs such as tall-growing hollies. It works well in large tubs or containers. Burning bush may be trained into a multiple-stemmed small tree suitable for sunny patios and other limited-space applications.

I Suggest
Because of burning bush's normal height and width (8 × 10 ft. tall by 8 × 12 ft. wide), you may prefer the smaller variety 'Compacta' (average height and width of 5 × 6 ft. tall and wide).

Butterfly Bush
Buddleia davidii

When, Where, and How to Plant

Buddleia is hardy even in Zone 5, so it is definitely Texas-hardy. Plant anytime, though I find early spring to be the best. Select a full sun, well-drained, and fertile location. Don't plant in areas that are poorly drained or receive less than six hours of full sun. Remove any weeds, turfgrass, rocks, or sticks. Till the area and add 4 to 6 in. of organic matter such as compost, brown peat moss, or ground pine bark, then till again. Make your bed a minimum of 5 ft. wide, larger if possible. Dig planting holes no deeper than the soilball, but as wide as desired. Plug in plant, backfill, and water thoroughly. Apply root stimulator and cover bare soil with 3 to 4 in. of your favorite bark mulch. I usually use pine.

Growing Tips

Water as needed to keep the soil from drying out. More frequent watering is needed during the first year, less in the following years. Never allow the plant's rootball to dry out. A slow-release granular rose fertilizer is the ideal choice to nourish buddleia. Apply according to label directions when new growth begins in the spring, twice during the growing season, and once again in the fall. Water thoroughly after each fertilizer application. Maintain 3 to 4 in. of bark mulch.

Care

Prune to shape during the growing season, and it may be radically pruned just before new spring growth if desired. Butterfly bush has no serious disease or insect problems.

Companion Planting and Design

I do not endorse the use of butterfly bush as a foundation planting. I highly recommend it in mass bed plantings and in combination with perennials or relatively large blooming specimens.

I Suggest

Plant butterfly bush for fragrance, color, long bloom period and its ability to attract butterflies. Plant where your family can view it—both indoors and out.

As the name implies, butterflies like this shrub. If you are looking for a shrub that has wonderful color, fragrance, and attracts Mother Nature's flying living color, buddleia is for you! For a perennial bed, large border plantings, or use in masses, you'd have a hard time finding a better choice. No matter where you live in our great state, you owe yourself the treat of growing buddleia. At least give one a trial for a couple of years. Any of the following varieties of B. davidii are worth trying: 'Black Knight', 'Ile De France', 'Pink Delight', 'Royal Red', 'White Bouquet', 'White Profusion', and 'Harlequin'. For more buddleias check out woolly butterfly bush on page 115. Butterfly bush is hardy in all Texas zones.

Bloom Period and Seasonal Color
Summer blooms in white, pink, yellow, and purple.

Mature Height × Spread
3 to 8 ft. × 4 to 6 ft.

Camellia

Camellia japonica

Camellias are to Texas gardeners as rhododendrons are to other areas of the country—outstanding landscape color shrubs. These great bloomers thrive from Texarkana to Presidio and points southeast. With proper care, camellias are very long lived, so not only are you planting for enjoyment today, but perhaps for generations to come. Bloom shapes are labeled as single, semi-double, formal double, peony form, anemone form, and rose form. Bloom sizes range from 2¹/₂ to over five inches across. Varieties of C. japonica include 'Kramer's Supreme', 'Professor Sargent', 'Snow Queen', and 'Anita'. The C. sasanqua species boasts 'Hana Jiman', 'Yuletide', 'Shishi Gashira', and 'Setsugekka', among others. C. oleifera is a great fall bloomer. Hardy in Zones 7a to 9b, depending on variety.

Bloom Period and Seasonal Color
Fall through spring blooms in red, pink, white, rose, and blends.

Mature Height × Spread
6 to 8 ft. × 6 to 8 ft., up to 25 ft. × 20 ft.

When, Where, and How to Plant

For most of us, spring and fall are the best planting times. In Texas, camellias may not grow or bloom well in full sun. Heavy shade is not recommended either. Dappled sun throughout the day is ideal. Camellias require a soil that has an acid pH and drains well but is moist and fertile. In alkaline soil areas of Texas it may be best to grow in totally raised beds. An option is to remove the existing soil approximately 12 in. deep, fill with a 50/50 mixture of ground bark mulch and brown sphagnum peat moss, and then raise 6 in. above the existing grade. In sandy soils add 6 in. of high-quality organic matter and till after removing rocks, sticks, weeds, and turfgrass. Dig the planting hole no deeper than the plant soilball. Cover the plant's soilball when you backfill. Water thoroughly, apply a root stimulator, and cover bare soil with 4 in. of pine bark mulch.

Growing Tips

Fertilize with a granular azalea/camellia fertilizer after bloom, two weeks after the last killing frost in spring, once in mid-season, and once again in the fall. Water thoroughly after each application. Irrigate your planting(s) as needed to maintain a moist but not wet soil. Maintain 3 to 4 inches of bark mulch.

Care

Tea scale is usually the camellia's only pest problem, and a once-a-year application of dormant oil will take care of it. Some diseases such as leaf spot may create a problem. Camellias in good health usually don't have pest or insect problems.

Companion Planting and Design

The most spectacular camellias are found in beds underneath the canopies of large shade trees. *Camellia sasanqua* lends itself better to foundation plantings. Camellias are great when used in large containers or trained into patio trees, screens, hedges, or color beds.

I Suggest

My wife, Judy, and I live in Zone 7b and really enjoy the variety 'Yuletide'. It has the traditional Christmas red for its bloom color and is in bloom throughout the holiday season. Judy enjoys using the blooms and branches in various indoor holiday arrangements.

Cherry Laurel
Prunus laurocerasus

When, Where, and How to Plant

Plant cherry laurel anytime where it is hardy. I prefer fall planting, though early spring also works well. Cherry laurel tolerates a range of soils, including light sandy soil and heavy clay. It prefers well-drained locations in moist, fertile soils. Do not plant in wet areas. When using individual plants as specimen plantings, do not add any soil amendments—simply loosen the native soil thoroughly to the soilball's depth and as wide as desired. When planting in beds, add 4 to 6 in. of organic matter, and till. After the plants are set, backfill, water thoroughly, apply a root stimulator, and cover bare soil with 3 to 4 in. of your favorite mulch.

Growing Tips

Water as needed to prevent dry soil. Fertilize in the spring two weeks after your last killing frost. Use premium-quality, slow-release 3:1:2 lawn fertilizers (such as 21-7-14 and 15-5-10). Apply according to label directions, twice during the growing season and once again during the fall. Water thoroughly after each fertilizer application. Prune during growing season if needed to shape plants and/or direct growth. Maintain 3 to 4 in. of bark mulch.

Care

Grasshoppers may visit during the summer, and leaf spots may be seen where air movement is poor and humidity is very high. Planting in sunny locations with good air movement will usually prevent this problem. There are control possibilities available at your local garden center.

Companion Planting and Design

Use the tall-growing *P. laurocerasus* as individual specimens, screen plantings, or trained into patio trees. Don't plant as foundation plantings near walkways or driveways or in front of entrances or windows as they will quickly outgrow these areas. The variety 'Nana' makes an excellent 4 to 6 ft. high and wide hedge or tall foundation planting. For a 4 to 6 ft. tall and 6 to 8 ft. wide hedge, 'Schipkaensis' fills the bill.

I Suggest

Cherry laurel is one of the old-fashioned landscape shrubs in Texas. Because of its popularity, this excellent shrub may not be available at every nursery in Texas.

Due to its many varieties, cherry laurel may be a low foundation planting, a large specimen, or many applications in between. 'Mount Vernon' reaches eighteen to twenty inches in height but spreads seven to eight feet, making it an interesting choice for wide, low shrub plantings or a tall groundcover effect. Other cherry laurels reach twelve feet or more in height, with a width of eight feet or more, making excellent screens when placed in rows. Because of its ability to grow in almost any type of Texas soil, partial shade or full sun, this shrub should find spots in many Texas landscapes. Varieties of P. laurocerasus include 'Mount Vernon', 'Nana', 'Schipkaensis', 'Otto Luyken', and 'Zabeliana'. Cherry laurel is hardy in Zones 7b to 9b.

Other Common Name
English Laurel

Bloom Period and Seasonal Color
Spring and summer blooms in white.

Mature Height × Spread
18 in. to 25 ft. × 3 to 16 ft.

Cleyera

Ternstroemia japonica

I first became familiar with cleyera in 1969 while pursuing a horticulture degree at Stephen F. Austin State University in Nacogdoches, Texas. My wife Judy and I lived in married housing on campus where I kept noticing this interesting looking plant. Since then I've seen it in many landscape applications. I also propagated thousands of them as a nursery production manager. You might say I've had the opportunity to know these shrubs from the seed up. Cleyera is a candidate for areas that do not receive the hot direct western sun. The T. japonica 'Variegata' and 'Burnished Gold' varieties have colorful creamy-to-yellow to yellow-gold foliage in various patterns. Cleyera is hardy in Zones 7a-9b.

Bloom Period and Seasonal Color
Summer blooms in yellow, red to purple fruits in late summer to early fall, and winter foliage in bronze.

Mature Height × Spread
6 to 8 ft. × 4 to 8 ft. up to 6 to 20 ft. × 4 to 8 ft.

When, Where, and How to Plant
In the zone where cleyera is hardy, plant at any time. Fall is best with early spring a close second. Don't plant in daylong full-sun locations, western exposures, or where radiant heat is received. Cleyera prefers daylong dappled shade. While it has some tolerance to various soil conditions, don't expect great results if it is planted in poor locations. Hard, compact soils or poorly drained areas are not desirable. For plantings around the foundation or out in the landscape, make beds at least 5 ft. wide. Remove any turfgrass, weeds, or debris from the area, till, and add 6 in. of high-quality organic matter. Then till the area again. Dig the individual planting hole no deeper than the plant's soilball, install, and backfill. Water thoroughly, apply a root stimulator, and cover bare soil with 4 in. of pine bark or your favorite mulch.

Growing Tips
Water as necessary to maintain a moist soil during the growing season, and to prevent soil from drying in the winter. Fertilize in the spring two weeks after the last killing frost, twice during the growing season, and once again in the fall. Light applications of a 3:1:2 ratio slow-release lawn fertilizer should work well. Maintain 3 to 4 in. of bark mulch.

Care
Cleyera has no serious pests or diseases. Pruning is normally not needed due to its growth habit. Should you need to prune, do so through the growing season. Spring and early summer are the best times.

Companion Planting and Design
Cleyera is great when planted in groups, corners, or alcoves. I would not use it as a hedge or screen. Its rate of growth is slow-to-moderate under average conditions. If you are patient, cleyera will grow to make interesting specimens in shady areas. They also make interesting plantings in beds under tall trees. Cleyera is a good companion for dwarf hollies.

I Suggest
Because there are variations in appearance when trying to grow some of these plants from seeds, if propagation is an activity you wish to undertake do so from cuttings. I have enjoyed the japonica species for several decades.

Cotoneaster
Cotoneaster spp.

When, Where, and How to Plant

Plant at any time, but fall is best. Install in locations with good air movement and well-prepared soils that are moist and fertile. Do not plant in a location that receives more than six hours of full sunlight, next to a solid fence, or in an area where there is reflected heat. Make the beds a minimum of 5 ft. wide. Remove debris, weeds, and turfgrass, then till. Add 4 to 6 in. of organic matter and till a second time. The same preparations should be made when planting in rock gardens and ground-cover beds, but it's not necessary to make these areas 5 ft. wide. For all applications, dig the planting holes no deeper than the plant's soilball, install, and backfill. Water thoroughly, apply a root stimulator, and mulch bare soil 3 to 4 in. deep with your favorite bark.

Growing Tips

Water to prevent dry soil. Apply spring fertilizer two weeks after the last killing frost. Reapply one time during the growing season, and once in the fall. Use a slow-release granular rose fertilizer, and water thoroughly after each application. Prune late spring to early summer if needed.

Care

Cotoneaster is susceptible to a bacterial disease known as fire blight. Planting in ideal locations and keeping plants healthy is the best prevention measure, though there are products available at your local garden center for control.

Companion Planting and Design

For rock gardens, I suggest *C. horizontalis* 'Perpusilla', *C. dammeri* 'Eichholz', *C. salicifolius* 'Repens', *C. dammeri* 'Coral Beauty' or 'Royal Beauty', and *C. dammeri* 'Moner'. All 6 to 18 in. tall, they may be used as a groundcovers. *C. apiculatus*, or cranberry cotoneaster, which reaches 3 ft. tall and 3 to 6 ft. wide, makes interesting foundation plantings. The larger-growing varieties may be trained into interesting tree forms. Cotoneaster is compatible with holly, nandina, Indian hawthorne, and others.

I Suggest

Become familiar with fire blight. Information fact/tip sheets are available at your county agent's office. By learning more you will have a better understanding of the disease and how to prevent it.

With a selection of plant sizes to choose from, this member of the rose family will add interest and variety to any number of landscape applications. I would recommend a visit to your local nursery to see its selection of cotoneaster before planting a substantial quantity. Try a bed or a grouping first to see how you like it. There are many species and even more cultivars. Here are a few: C. actifolius, Peking cotoneaster; C. adpressus var. praecox and 'Tom Thumb'; C. congestus, Pyrenees cotoneaster; C. divaricatus spreading cotoneaster; C. glaucophyllus, gray-leaved cotoneaster; and C. horizontalis 'Variegatus' and 'Robusta'. Cotoneaster is hardy statewide.

Bloom Period and Seasonal Color

Spring blooms in white and pink with red fruit.

Mature Height × Spread

1 to 8 ft. × 3 to 10 ft.

Crape Myrtle
Lagerstroemia indica

Crape myrtle may be found in old homesites and road-ways where it thrives and blooms with ease. It is as tough as any other imported blooming shrub and as durable as many natives. Crape myrtles are, without a doubt, my favorite blooming landscape shrubs. They are easy to grow, come in a wide range of sizes, and provide out-standing summer color. You owe it to yourself, your family, and your area to select the varieties and bloom colors that work best in your landscape. Plant them this year! They will yield rewards for a long time to come. Varieties include 'Natchez', 'Tightwad Red'®, 'Near East', 'Pink Lace', 'Potomac', 'Raspberry Sundae', 'Sioux', 'Miami', 'Pink Velour', 'Firebird', 'Red Rocket'®, 'Catawba', 'Victor', 'Dynamite', 'Peppermint Lace', 'Baton Rouge', and many more. Crape myrtle is hardy in Zones 7 to 9.

Bloom Period and Seasonal Color
Summer blooms in white, pink, red, lavender, purple, and magenta, with fall foliage in red, red-orange, and yellow.

Mature Height × Spread
18 in. to 25 ft. or more × 3 to 25 ft.

When, Where, and How to Plant
Plant any time of the year in most Texas zones, although I prefer fall planting. Do not plant in shady areas! In order for crape myrtles to perform in growth and bloom, they must be in full-sun locations receiving at least eight hours of full sun-light. Plant where they can be easily watered. Don't plant in a poorly drained location. Crape myrtles will grow in sandy or heavy clay soils, yet they prefers a moist, but not wet, fertile loam soil. Remove sticks, weeds, turfgrass, and rocks from the planting area and till. Add 4 to 6 in. of high-quality organic matter. Till again. Dig the planting hole no deeper than the rootball and set in plant. Backfill, water thoroughly, apply a root stimulator, and mulch bare soil with 3 to 4 in. of your favorite bark mulch.

Growing Tips
Water as needed to maintain moist soil. These plants will tolerate dry conditions, but don't like them. The best bloom occurs on new growth that is stimulated by moist, fertile growing conditions and fertilizer. Apply 21-7-14, 15-5-10, or a similar 3:1:2 ratio slow-release lawn fertilizer in the spring 2 weeks after your last killing frost. Reapply twice more during the growing season and once again in the fall. Water thoroughly after each application. Maintain a 3- to 4-in. bark mulch.

Care
Prune to shape in late winter. Do not make a flat top out of your plants. Powdery mildew may visit your crape myrtle under very humid conditions with poor air movement. Aphids may visit as well. Your local retailer can offer you several controls.

Companion Planting and Design
Crape myrtle works well as a specimen, in mass plantings, in large containers, in extended founda-tion beds, and in stand-alone beds developed in sunny locations. Because it is deciduous, I do not recommend crape myrtle as your primary founda-tion plant.

I Suggest
One of our *favorite* plantings in our landscape is a row of tall growing 'Natchez' with its beautiful white blooms and the rose-red blooms of the dwarf variety 'Baton Rouge' below them in a wide bed.

Elaeagnus
Elaeagnus pungens

When, Where, and How to Plant
Plant any time you wish, but fall is best. While *E. pungens* will tolerate relatively undesirable conditions, it prefers a moist, loamy, fertile soil. Remove any weeds, rocks, turfgrass, or sticks from the area to be planted. Till the area and add 4 in. of organic matter such as brown sphagnum peat moss, ground pine bark mulch, or compost (homemade or commercial). Till again. Because of its wide spread, plant *E. pungens* on 8 ft. centers. For quicker impact, plant on 6 ft. centers. Install and backfill. Water thoroughly, apply a root stimulator, and cover bare soil with 3 to 4 in. of your favorite bark mulch. I usually use pine bark mulch.

Growing Tips
Water as needed to prevent soil from drying out. Fertilize with a slow-release product once in the spring, two weeks after the last killing frost, and once during the fall. Fertilizer ratios of 3:1:2 (including 21-7-14, 18-6-12, and 15-5-10) all work well. Apply according to label directions and water thoroughly after each application. Maintain 3 to 4 in. of bark mulch.

Care
Pruning the elaeagnus can be a frequent chore if it's maintained relatively short and narrow. Instead, allow it to grow to its natural shape/size, and little additional pruning will be necessary. Spider mites may occasionally visit elaeagnus plantings. Visit your local retailer for control solutions. There are no other pest problems.

Companion Planting and Design
A large specimen in sunny locations, this is an excellent plant for large screening. Because of its large size, elaeagnus is not recommended for a home foundation planting. Various annuals may be planted at the outside edges of elaeagnus plants if desired.

I Suggest
Due to its size, let me again emphasize not to use elaeagnus as a foundation plant. Do, however, use as a screen and provide ample room so little to no pruning is needed. Try one of its ripe fruits and see if it's tasty to you.

This moderate-to-rapid growing shrub makes excellent screens, natural hedges, and windbreaks. Large and dense, it needs plenty of room to grow, and re-growth from pruning is rapid. Both old and new growth has sharp spurs, so be sure to wear protective gloves when pruning. Elaeagnus is tough and grows rather well in difficult locations. High heat, drought, and a wide range of soil conditions are tolerated. If you are looking for a large-growing plant that requires minimal maintenance and will add a silvery and green color combination to your landscape, try elaeagnus. E. × ebbengei has larger leaves, no spines, and flowers in the fall. Elaeagnus is hardy in Zones 7a to 9b.

Other Common Name
Silverberry

Bloom Period and Seasonal Color
Evergreen foliage, non-showy flowers, red fruit.

Mature Height × Spread
8 to 12 ft. × 8 to 10 ft.

Euonymus
Euonymus japonica

Euonymus is a durable, easy-to-grow shrub that will thrive in nearly all Texas conditions. If you have a little one who wants to select and care for some colorful shrubs, E. japonica is a good place to start. The same is true for you first-time gardeners. There are many cultivars, and here are a few to choose from: 'Aureo-marginata', 'Aureo-variegata', 'Microphylla', 'Microphylla Variegata', 'Silver King', 'Grandifolia', and 'Silver Princess'. Additional species are E. alata, E. fortunei, and E. kiautschovica. Euonymus is hardy in all Texas zones.

Other Common Name
Evergreen Euonymus

Bloom Period and Seasonal Color
Evergreen foliage in green with white, silver, and yellow to yellow-gold.

Mature Height × Spread
1 to 10 ft. × 1 to 6 ft.

When, Where, and How to Plant
Plant anytime, though fall is best. *E. japonica* has the desirable ability to grow in shade or full sun. Six to eight hours of full sun, along with shade from the hot west afternoon sun, is most desirable. It will tolerate difficult and dry soils, but prefers moist, fertile soils. Don't plant in poorly drained locations. Remove turfgrass, rocks, sticks, and weeds from the area and till or hand dig. Add compost, brown sphagnum peat moss, and ground bark. Till again. I prefer beds at least 5 ft. wide or wider. Install plants no deeper than the soilball. Backfill, water thoroughly, apply root stimulator, and cover bare soil with 3 in. of bark.

Growing Tips
Water as needed to prevent the soil from drying. Maintaining heavy mulch year-round will aid in moisture conservation. Fertilize two weeks after the last killing frost in your area, two times during the growing season, and once in the fall. The same 3:1:2 ratio fertilizers often recommended for use on our lawns will work well. Use only slow-release fertilizers and water thoroughly after each application. Maintain 3 to 4 in. of bark mulch.

Care
Pruning isn't required if a natural shape is desired. Euonymus lends itself well to shearing and training into various shapes. *E. japonica* may be invaded by scale. An application of dormant oil once a year—I recommend applying it in December or January—will usually control scale. In areas where air movement is poor, powdery mildew may also visit. New growth is more prone to such a problem. If this occurs, there are several controls available at your local nurseries.

Companion Planting and Design
Because of its leaf colors and ability to re-grow, euonymus is a good candidate for screens, hedges (formal and natural), foundation plantings, mass plantings, and specimens. Use in large pots, planters, and other containers.

I Suggest
Make one application of dormant oil (according to label directions) annually. Think of it as plant maintenance as you would pruning, mulching, and/or fertilizing. For a very small-leafed and fine-textured plant, try the variety 'Microphyllus'.

Flowering Quince
Chaenomeles japonica

When, Where, and How to Plant

Plant flowering quince anytime but fall is ideal. Plant in full-sun locations where there is adequate moisture and fertile soil. Prepare the soil thoroughly. Remove any debris, weeds, and turfgrass from the planting area. Till or hand dig the area, and add 4 to 6 in. of your favorite organic matter. Till or dig again until the materials are evenly blended. Make beds at least 5 ft. wide. Dig planting holes no deeper that the plant's soilball, install, and backfill. Water thoroughly, apply a root stimulator, and cover bare soil with 3 to 4 in. of bark mulch.

Growing Tips

Water as needed to prevent soil dryness. Fertilize in the spring (two weeks after the last killing frost), in mid-growing season, and in the fall, with a slow-release, granular rose fertilizer. Water thoroughly after each application. Maintain 3 to 4 in. of bark mulch.

Care

Prune as desired, although it's not required. Do severe pruning in the spring, just after blooming is complete. Aphids may visit new top growth, but they usually aren't a long-term problem. There are several ways to control aphids, and your local retailer will have several selections.

Companion Planting and Design

I like the striking effect of quince in mass plantings. In sunny areas where azaleas are very difficult to grow, flowering quince works well. It may be clipped if desired to form an interesting hedge or other arrangement. Flowering quince also works well in color beds. Its blooms are a standout when used in wide beds in front of tall-growing broadleaf evergreens like holly. Flowering quince may also be used in extended foundation planting beds, though I wouldn't use them as primary foundation plantings. They may be planted in containers or directly in the ground.

I Suggest

Judy and I have some of these durable shrubs growing among rocks in a bed on the west side of our property. Minimum care and no pruning is needed. For very early spring blooms when Carolina jasmine, redbud, and other bloomers are out, flowering quince adds the red-orange color we also enjoy. Try some yourself.

If you are speaking of flowering quince and another Texas gardener mentions his beautiful japonica, chances are you are probably talking about the same plant. Japonica actually denotes the plant's original home of Japan. However, Texans have been using flowering quince in our homes and commercial landscapes for decades. Flowering quince grows in almost any soil type in Texas, and it is sometimes found in old homesites and abandoned areas. There are several varieties: 'Cameo' is a soft, apricot-pink double flower; 'Super Red' or 'Monred' has extra-bright large blooms; 'Texas Scarlet' has fiery-scarlet blooms; and 'Jet Trails', a C. speciosa hybrid, has white blooms. The named variety of flowering quince that is easiest to find is C. japonica 'Texas Scarlet'. Understandably so in Texas! Flowering quince is hardy in all Texas zones.

Other Common Name
Japonica

Bloom Period and Seasonal Color
Early spring blooms in white, red, pink, and coral.

Mature Height × Spread
3 × 4 ft. to 5 ft.

Forsythia
Forsythia × intermedia

Forsythia originally came from Japan, but it adapts well to Texas landscapes. It is a spring-blooming shrub that has been used for generations in Texas gardens—both in home and commercial applications. Where adapted, this is one easy plant to transplant, propagate, grow, and enjoy. It is one of the earliest bloomers in the landscape and is very dependable about putting on its show. The sunny bloom colors are a welcome harbinger of spring. It will grow in almost any soil as long as that soil is not dry. 'Lynwood Gold', with yellow-gold blooms, is the variety that is easiest to find. 'Beatrix Farrand' has golden-yellow blooms. 'Spring Glory' flowers are primrose yellow. Forsythia is hardy in all Texas zones.

Bloom Period and Seasonal Color
Early spring blooms in gold and yellow.

Mature Height × Spread
6 to 8 ft. × 6 to 10 ft.

When, Where, and How to Plant
Fall is best for planting forsythia but it may be planted in early spring or midwinter. Sun is essential for forsythia to put on its best show. After six hours of sun, it may be shaded for the rest of the day. Never plant in totally shaded locations. Don't plant in low, wet, or poorly drained locations—or in areas where the soil tends to dry rapidly and is difficult to irrigate. After removing all debris, weeds, and turfgrass, and tilling the soil, add 4 to 6 in. of organic matter. Till again. Don't dig the planting hole any deeper than the plant's soilball. Set the plant in its planting hole, backfill, water thoroughly, apply root stimulator, and mulch bare soil with 4 in. of mulch.

Growing Tips
Though it is winter hardy, forsythia isn't fond of dry conditions at any time. Soil moisture is important even during our winters. A heavy mulch applied 3 to 4 in. deep is beneficial year-round and it will help to conserve soil moisture. Fertilize three times a year with your favorite brand of slow-release, granular rose fertilizer. Follow label directions and water thoroughly after each application. Make the first application two weeks after the last killing frost in your area or when new leaves are appearing (whichever comes first). Make the second application approximately ten weeks later, and the last one in the fall.

Care
Prune to shape in the spring after blooming is complete. To prevent cutting off future blooms, don't prune in late summer, fall, or winter. There are no serious pests or diseases that bother forsythia.

Companion Planting and Design
Forsythia makes a wonderful show of color in large beds with early spring blooming bulbs planted outside the drip line. Because of forsythia's size, the plants may be trained into specimens or hedges.

I Suggest
Try the 'Lynwood Gold' variety for good-looking, early spring, yellow-gold blooms in your landscape.

Gardenia
Gardenia jasminoides

When, Where, and How to Plant

Plant gardenias in the very early spring or early fall. Plant in a location that has early morning sun and shade from the direct hot afternoon sun. The best light is dappled daylong sun/shade. Don't plant in locations that receive reflected heat or in soils that tend to be dry or poorly drained. Gardenias do best in moist, sandy, acidic soils. If the soil is heavy clay, you will have to do some serious soil preparation. The planting area should be a minimum of 5 ft. wide. Remove at least 6 in. of the soil—1 ft. if possible. Blend brown sphagnum peat moss and pine bark mulch 50/50 with the removed soil, and backfill the excavated area to 6 in. above the natural grade. Water thoroughly and allow to drain overnight before planting. Install the plants no deeper than its soilballs, firm the mix, water thoroughly, and apply a root stimulator. Add 4 in. of pine bark mulch to the finished planting area. Pine bark mulch will help to maintain an acidic soil pH.

Growing Tips

Drip irrigation is good for keeping the soil moist and will save 50 percent on your water bill. For overall health, growth, and bloom it is important to maintain a moist soil for gardenias—not wet or dry. Fertilize with a granular azalea fertilizer after the spring bloom flush, once in mid-season, and again in the fall according to label directions. Water thoroughly after each application. Maintain 3 to 4 in. of mulch year-round.

Care

Aphids, white flies, nematodes, mites, scale, sooty mold, and leaf spots can all hit gardenias. There is a wide assortment of aids and methods available at your local retailer to help.

Companion Planting and Design

For small spaces, try one of the smaller varieties such as 'Radicans' as an indoor/outdoor container planting. The taller-growing varieties make interesting foundation plantings. Other varieties are good as mass plantings, specimens, hedges, groundcovers, and container plants. Gardenias also work well in beds of azaleas and camellias since all have the same management/care.

I Suggest

Give soil, light, and moisture requirements special attention.

According to Hortus III, gardenias are among 200 species of shrubs and small trees native to the tropical and subtropical regions of the world. In our slice of the world, an old-time Texas and Southern favorite, Cape jasmine, is a member of Gardenia jasminoides. At times, there is friendly debate in the horticulture world about which variety of gardenia is the true cape jasmine. Some say the variety 'Mystery' is the true cape jasmine, while others believe it is 'August Beauty'. If you want an extremely fragrant bloomer, both are hard to beat. If you can grow roses, you can grow gardenias. Try these cultivars: 'August Beauty', 'Candle Light', 'Variegated', 'Mystery', 'Veitchii', 'Radicans', 'Radicans Variegata', and 'First Love' or 'Aimee'. Gardenia is hardy in Texas Zones 8b to 9b.

Other Common Name
Cape Jasmine

Bloom Period and Seasonal Color
Summer blooms in white and creamy white.

Mature Height × Spread
6 in. to 6 ft. × 3 to 6 ft.

Hardy Hibiscus
Hibiscus moscheutos

If you like the beauty of tropical hibiscus blooms but want a hibiscus that doesn't freeze, you're in luck: hardy hibiscus is great for adding color to any landscape. Texas gardeners who have seen cotton grow and bloom may believe that hardy hibiscus looks as if it is in the same family—and it is! Some classify hardy hibiscus as a perennial. However you wish to classify it, hardy hibiscus is a wonderful large-leaved, large-bloomed plant that adds color to beds, nooks and corner plantings, mass plantings, or planters. It works in several kinds of locations and is easy to plant and maintain. Parents who help a little gardener plant hardy hibiscus will be doubly rewarded when they see the excitement in the children's eyes during the spring. Kids love these easy-to-grow color sources. Hardy hibiscus is hardy in all Texas zones.

Other Common Name
Rose Mallow

Bloom Period and Seasonal Color
Spring to autumn blooms in white, pink, purple, and red.

Mature Height × Spread
2 to 6 ft. or more × 3 to 6 ft.

When, Where, and How to Plant
Plant early spring to early summer. Try locations that receive morning to midday full sun with afternoon shade, or dappled sun/shade all day long. These plants perform better away from reflected heat sources such as bright walls and concrete. Good air movement is advised. Don't plant in difficult-to-water areas, as it does best in moist soils. Be sure adequate organic matter is incorporated into the planting area. Remove any debris, weeds, and turfgrass, and till the planting area. Add 4 in. of peat and 2 in. of compost, or 6 in. of peat only, and till again. After digging the planting hole soilball deep, insert the plant, backfill, water thoroughly, apply a root stimulator, and mulch the bed with 4 in. of pine bark mulch. When developing hardy hibiscus beds, make them at least 5 ft. wide unless you're spot planting where it's not necessary.

Growing Tips
Water as needed to maintain a moist soil. Fertilize in early spring two weeks after the last killing frost, or when you see new buds arising from the ground. Apply slow-release premium-quality granular rose fertilizer. Apply again approximately ten weeks later, then once in the fall. Water thoroughly after each fertilizer application. Maintain 3 to 4 in. of mulch to retain moisture and control weeds.

Care
Prune very low or to the ground by the end of the winter. I usually prune to approximately 1 ft. after hard fall freezes, then to the ground just as new buds emerge. Pests and diseases are usually not problems for this plant. If any pest problems arise, visit your local nursery for assistance in identifying and controlling the pest.

Companion Planting and Design
Don't use these plants indoors where they will go dormant and drop leaves. I do not recommend them for primary foundation plantings. They work well in front of broadleaf evergreen foundation plantings, in extended beds, and almost any color bed.

I Suggest
Being a native Texan, I must recommend the variety 'Texas Star'. However, all varieties are worth growing in our Texas landscapes.

Holly

Ilex spp.

When, Where, and How to Plant

Plant any time, though fall is best. Be sure to match the plant's sun and soil requirements with your desired location. Some varieties produce a denser and more robust planting in full sun than when grown in the shade. Others varieties prefer some protection from the hot afternoon sun. Holly likes a moist soil; don't plant in hard, compact, or poorly drained soils. All varieties will grow in acidic soils; several grow well in alkaline soils. Remove all debris, weeds, and turfgrass, and till the native soil. Add 4 to 6 in. of organic matter to the planting area. Till again. Construct prepared landscape beds at least 5 ft. wide, dig planting holes no deeper than the plant's soilball, set the plants, backfill, water thoroughly, apply a root stimulator, and cover any bare soil with 3 to 4 in. of bark mulch.

Growing Tips

Irrigate as needed to prevent drying of the soil, and maintain a 3- to 4-in. mulch blanket year-round to aid in soil moisture conservation. Holly responds well to a good seasonal fertilizer program. Make your first application two weeks after the last spring frost in your area, reapply 2 times during the growing season, and once in the fall. Premium-quality, slow-release, 3:1:2-ratio lawn fertilizers work well (such as 19-5-9, 15-5-10, and 21-7-14). Water thoroughly after each application.

Care

For severe pruning, early spring is best. Hollies that produce fruit/berries usually do so on second-year wood. Tea scale may become a problem on some varieties in relatively shady areas; this is usually not a problem in sunny locations. Grasshoppers may visit some varieties in rural areas.

Companion Planting and Design

Dwarf varieties work well in front of low windows and porches and along walkways. Hollies may be utilized with any other landscape shrub listed in this publication and can have annuals and perennials planted in front of them.

I Suggest

For the past twenty-three years, we have been growing 'Nellie R. Stevens', dwarf yaupon, yaupon, 'Willowleaf', 'Dwarf Bufordii' and 'Carissa' hollies in our landscape and enjoy them all.

The holly family is without a doubt my favorite landscape shrub group. These shrubs are versatile, available in many varieties, easy to grow, reliable, and found at nearly all retailers statewide. You will find these tough, durable shrubs growing at old homes, schools, churches, and other buildings. Many different types of holly are available to Texas gardeners, in sizes ranging from 1 gallon to large ready-to-plant specimens. Visit several retailers and ask to see the holly selections. Several species and many varieties include I. cornuta 'Bufordii', 'Dwarf Bufordii', 'Carissa', 'Nellie R. Stevens', 'Rotunda', 'Needle Point', and 'Dazzler'; I. × 'Nellie R. Stevens'; I. vomitoria 'Nana', 'Stoke's Dwarf', 'Pendula', 'Pride of Houston', and 'Will Fleming'; I. crenata 'Compacta', 'Green Lustre', 'Helleri', and 'Hetzi'. Holly is hardy in all Texas zones.

Bloom Period and Seasonal Color

Evergreen foliage, fall to winter red berries.

Mature Height × Spread

3 to 50 ft. × 3 to 20 ft.

Hydrangea

Hydrangea macrophylla

Many Moms in Texas received their first hydrangea as a gift on Mother's Day. This has been a tradition for generations. The first blue-flowered hydrangea I remember seeing was in Nacogdoches, Texas, when my wife and I were attending Stephen F. Austin State University—it was an outstanding blue color. The naturally acidic soils of the area lend themselves to producing blue colors in hydrangeas, and the shrub I saw was a beaut. These are colorful, low-maintenance, showy plants, and they should be used more often. Try one or more of the following in your landscape: H. macrophylla 'Kuhnert', 'Mariesii Variegata', 'Merritt's Pride', 'Nikko Blue', 'Sister Teresa', 'Monred', 'Lanarth White', and 'Bluebird'; H. paniculata 'Grandiflora', or peegee hydrangea; H. quercifolia, or oakleaf hydrangea. Hydrangea is hardy statewide.

Other Common Name
Garden Hydrangea

Bloom Period and Seasonal Color
Spring, summer and fall blooms in white, red, pink, and blue—some varieties with multi-colored foliage.

Mature Height × Spread
5 to 7 ft. × 6 to 8 ft.

When, Where, and How to Plant
Plant very early spring or early fall. Hydrangeas do best in fertile, deep, moist soils that drain well. Eastern or northern locations are preferred. Dappled daylong sun/shade also works well. Remove any weeds, turfgrass, and debris from the area, and till. Blend in 6 in. of organic matter, and till again. Dig the planting holes no deeper than the plant's soilball, set the plant(s), backfill, water thoroughly, apply a root stimulator, and add 4 in. of mulch to cover all bare soil in the bed.

Growing Tips
Maintain a moist soil throughout the growing season, especially during bud-forming and blooming periods. Maintain a moist soil year-round with bark mulch. Water sufficiently to prevent the soil from drying out during the dormant season. To create pink blooms, the soil needs to be alkaline, above 7 pH. Growing plants in an acid soil below 7 pH forms blue blooms. Fertilize with granular rose fertilizer for pink blooms, and granular azalea fertilizer for blue. Supplement these fertilizers to enhance bloom color. Apply in spring just as new growth begins, 10 weeks later, and once in the fall. Water thoroughly after each application.

Care
Prune if needed to shape after peak bloom, but before September. This plant has no serious pests.

Companion Planting and Design
Many hydrangeas do very well as understory plantings, beneath shade trees with tall canopies. I don't recommend its use as foundation plantings because it is deciduous. It's a standout with holly growing behind it. Grow hydrangea in large containers on a shady deck—in masses or as a single specimen. Annuals including wax leaf begonias, coleus, and hardy perennial ferns work well around hydrangeas.

I Suggest
Hydrangeas are another of the old-fashioned landscape plants. I'll bet your mom, grandmother, or great-grandmother grew these beauties at one time in their landscapes or gardens. Not only will they add interesting color to your landscape, but their blooms and stems may be dried for long term indoor use as well.

Indian Hawthorne

Raphiolepsis indica

When, Where, and How to Plant

Plant Indian hawthorne in fall or very early spring in almost any place except in total shade, poorly drained soils, or with reflected heat. I suggest a minimum of six to eight hours of full sun without reflected heat. Indian hawthornes do best in deep, fertile, moist, well-drained soils. Remove weeds, turfgrass, and debris from the planting area, till it, then add 4 to 6 in. of compost, brown peat moss, and/or ground bark. Till a second time. Dig the planting holes soilball deep, install plants, backfill, water thoroughly, apply root stimulator, and cover the bare soil with 3 to 4 in. of bark mulch. Beds should be at least 5 ft. wide. Give Indian hawthornes plenty of room to grow for best results.

Growing Tips

Maintain a moist soil and a 3 to 4 in. thick mulch year-round. Drip irrigation works very well. First fertilize in the spring two weeks after the last killing frost, again ten weeks later, and once again in the fall. A premium-quality, slow-release granular rose fertilizer works well.

Care

Perform any severe pruning during the spring after bloom is finished, and selective pruning as needed. Don't prune mid- to late fall. This plant has no serious pests. Leaf spot may appear. In full-sun locations it is usually not a problem.

Companion Planting and Design

Some of the taller varieties make top-notch foundation plantings against relatively tall walls. Other varieties work equally well in mass plantings or under low windows or other structures. Indian hawthorne usually looks best when allowed to grow into natural forms, but it can be trained as hedges. The taller varieties may be trained into tree forms. Salvia, lantana, and other plants used in Xeriscapes are companions for Indian hawthorne.

I Suggest

Judy and I have a double row of Indian hawthorne along the south side of our garden room and a single row along our south wall. Both of these plantings are in full sun. The double- planted row is in a bed 8 ft. wide, while the single row bed is 5 ft. wide. Try some Indian hawthorne as a spring blooming evergreen shrub for a Xeriscape.

Indian hawthorne is a very showy evergreen shrub that does well in a large portion of our state. It is a good shrub to try if you want spring-blooming, broadleaf evergreen shrubs. With good soil preparation, Indian hawthorne should provide you with a good show year after year. I've grown Indian hawthornes for years and continue to enjoy them. Ask your local retailers for suggestions on some of the best varieties available. Try one or more of these: R. indica 'Moness', 'Monto', 'Monrey', 'Monte', 'Monant', 'Pink Dancer', 'Clara', 'Harbinger of Spring', 'Pinkie', 'Ponto's Pink Clara', 'Majestic Beauty', 'Ballerina, 'Dwarf Pink', 'Pink Lady', and 'Snow White'; and R. umbellata 'Minor'. Indian hawthorne is hardy in Zones 7b-9b, and will grow but may have winter burn or damage in Zone 7a.

Bloom Period and Seasonal Color
Spring blooms in white, pink and rose-red.

Mature Height × Spread
3 to 8 ft. × 3 to 6 ft.

Japanese Yew

Podocarpus macrophyllus

Japanese yew makes striking specimens in the landscape. These shrubs may be clipped into interesting shapes using proper pruning techniques. The Oriental horticultural art of bonsai works well when applied to Japanese yew. If you planting Japanese yew in Zone 7b, be aware that it may suffer freeze damage and will suffer freeze damage in Zone 7a. A word of caution: don't get the true yew or Taxus fruits or seeds confused with Podocarpus or Japanese yew. Taxus plant parts are poisonous. Unlike most shrubs in this book, there are only limited choices of Japanese yew. The parent is P. macrophyllus, and there is one variety, 'Maki', which is hardy in Zone 7b. Plants are grown from seeds, so variation may occur. Japanese Yew is hardy in Zones 7a to 9b.

Other Common Name
Podocarpus

Bloom Period and Seasonal Color
Evergreen foliage

Mature Height × Spread
8 to 12 ft. or more × 3 to 10 ft.

When, Where, and How to Plant
Plant anytime where hardy, though fall is best and very early spring is good. Podocarpus will grow in most soils unless they are wet or poorly drained. It does best in deep, loose, moist soils where at least six to eight hours of full sun is available daily. It tolerates considerable shade but the density of the foliage decreases in heavy shade. Japanese yew does not tolerate wet feet—a term meaning a root system in wet soils—for prolonged periods of time. Remove debris, weeds, and turfgrass, and till. Blend in 4 to 6 in of brown sphagnum peat moss, compost, or ground bark mulch. Till again. Dig individual planting holes no deeper than the plants' soilballs, set the plants, backfill, water thoroughly, apply root stimulator, and cover all bare soil with 3 to 4 in. of bark mulch.

Growing Tips
Irrigate as needed to maintain a moist soil. Maintain a 3 to 4 in. layer of bark mulch year-round. Fertilize in the spring 2 weeks after the last killing frost, two times during the spring/summer growing season, and once in the fall. A granular 3:1:2 ratio (such as 21-7-14, 19-5-9, and 15-5-10) or similar slow-release, granular lawn fertilizer works well. Follow label directions and water thoroughly after each application.

Care
Japanese yew lends itself to shearing almost anytime, although if needed, early spring is best for severe pruning. This plant has no serious pests. In poorly drained areas, root rot is a possibility, so make sure soil is not kept wet.

Companion Planting and Design
Plant any place tall, dense, upright shrubs desired. When planted relatively close together, these shrubs will make very tall screens and/or hedges. Podocarpus is not recommended as a foundation planting but is great for use as a specimen or an accent. Make sure there is room for the plants to grow to its usual height.

I Suggest
I have grown these dark-green, narrow-leafed plants for thirty years. Take a look at one or more in a nursery and/or public garden to decide if you want to include it in your landscape.

Juniper
Juniperus chinensis

When, Where, and How to Plant

Plant early fall and very early spring. Chinese junipers will grow on most well drained soils and prefer full-sun locations or no more than four hours of shade. Chinese junipers prefer a relatively moist, well-drained, fertile soil but will tolerate relative dry soils. Most junipers will not tolerate the relatively dry soil indefinitely. Remove any debris, weeds, and turfgrass from the area to be planted, then till. Add 4 to 6 in. of organic matter such as compost, brown sphagnum peat moss, and ground bark, then till a second time. Dig the holes no deeper than the plants' rootballs, install the plants, backfill with the soil mix, water thoroughly, apply root stimulator, and cover all bare soil with 3 in. of your favorite bark.

Growing Tips

Plant in areas where they will not receive reflected heat, and irrigate as needed to prevent dry soil. Drip irrigation is great for growing junipers. Two weeks after the last spring frost in your area, fertilize with your favorite 3:1:2 ratio slow-release lawn fertilizer. Reapply ten weeks later and again in the fall (21-7-14 and 15-5-10 are 3:1:2 ratio lawn fertilizers). Maintain 3 in. of bark mulch year-round.

Care

Do not perform radical pruning on older stems without foliage or they may not regrow. Prune lightly to shape as new spring growth appears. Spider mites could be a problem in hot, dry locations with poor air movement. If they appear, your local retailer will have possible solutions for control. Follow label directions when using any garden aid.

Companion Planting and Design

Junipers may be used as hedges, around foundations, as corner plantings, groundcovers, and screens, and in formal or natural arrangements. Junipers also work well in manipulated forms such as bonsai, twists, spirals, and pompoms. They work well in confined planter areas and large containers. Companion color include any bloomers suitable in Xeriscapes, including lantana and Mexican bush sage.

I Suggest

Northern gardeners wishing to use familiar plants should try some of the varieties listed.

Junipers offer many possibilities for our landscapes. They range from low-spreading groundcover applications to tall, upright shrubs. They will grow in sunny locations but will not do well in shady areas. As a group, Chinese junipers offer nice colors and forms. Among them are light green; deep, rich, blue-green; golden-yellow; bright green, frosty blue, bluish green, mint green, gray-green, silvery-blue; brilliant green; sage green; and emerald green. Some varieties you may wish to try: 'Torulosa' 'Kaizuka', 'Wintergreen', 'Spartan', and 'Blue Point'. Other species are J. conferta, J. horizontalis, J. procumbens, J. sabina, J. scopulorum, J. squamata, and J. virginiana, the native Texas or Eastern red cedar. For more information review the cedar entry on page 96. Juniper is hardy in all Texas zones.

Other Common Name
Chinese Juniper

Bloom Period and Seasonal Color
Evergreen foliage in golden-yellow, frosty blue, silvery-blue, and various shades of green. Some varieties have green berries.

Mature Height × Spread
1 to 20 ft. × 3 to 15 ft.

Loquat
Eriobotrya japonica

I've seen this plant grown in Zone 7b, but it sometimes suffers from "winter burn (parts including leaves and stems freeze). I have been growing loquat in Zone 7b for a decade with great results so far. In very severe winters the entire plant may freeze. Because of its unusually large leaves, loquat tends to impart a tropical effect wherever it is used. This is a very coarse-textured plant. The fruit is small, edible, and has an interesting taste, but I still prefer a peach. In Zones 7b and the upper parts of Zone 8a, its ultimate height and width potential will not be reached due to winter burn. In Zones 8b, 9a, and 9b, expect full growth. The only loquat variety I'm familiar with is the hybrid 'Coppertone', which is more leathery in appearance and has smaller leaves. Loquat is hardy in Zones 8b to 9b.

Bloom Period and Seasonal Color
Fall blooms in white and light yellow.

Mature Height × Spread
20 to 25 ft. × 20 to 25 ft.

When, Where, and How to Plant
Plant in spring. Loquat will grow in sandy clay soils, or poorly drained locations, but prefers relatively moist, well-drained and fertile soils. Select a location where the soil drains well and is easily irrigated. Remove debris, turfgrass, and weeds from the planting area. Dig the hole soilball deep but twice the width of the ball. Install the plant, backfill, water thoroughly, apply root stimulator, and cover all bare soil with 3 to 4 in. of bark mulch. For bed plantings, first till the area, then add 4 to 6 in. of organic matter such as brown sphagnum peat moss, compost, or ground bark. Till a second time, and plant. Mulch as for single plantings.

Growing Tips
Water as needed to maintain a moist soil. Fertilize twice a year with a long-lasting, slow-release granular rose food according to label directions. Apply two weeks after the last killing frost in your area and again in the middle of the growing season. Water thoroughly after each fertilizer application. Maintain 3 to 4 in. of bark mulch year-round.

Care
Prune as needed to shape the plant's natural form in the spring, but limit this activity. Loquat has no serious insect problems, but the bacterial disease fire blight may appear. Don't over-fertilize or place in areas with poor air movement, because fire blight has a better chance of invading under these circumstances. Products for fire blight control are available from your local retailers. You may wish to secure a fact/tip sheet on fire blight from your county agent's office.

Companion Planting and Design
In Zones 8a, 9a, and 9b large containers of loquat work well in locations such as pools, decks, and other outdoor entertainment areas. A loquat will complement banana trees, tropical hibiscus, mandevilla, and other tropical or tropical-looking plants in these areas. Loquats make interesting specimens or accent plants because of their leaf size, color, and umbrella-like crowns. Don't use as foundation plantings. Loquats may be used in very tall, full-sun screen plantings or as specimen plants.

I Suggest
If you don't mind "gardening on the edge," try one of these plants in Zone 7b.

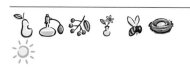

Mahonia

Mahonia bealei

When, Where, and How to Plant

Due to its winter hardiness, plant any time of the year. Fall and spring are best. Leatherleaf mahonia will grow in light to heavy Texas soils as long as the soil isn't wet or poorly drained. It does best in moist, improved, fertile locations. Improve your planting area with 4 to 6 in. of organic matter. Remove turfgrass, weeds, and debris, and till. Spread the organic matter, and till again. Be careful about damaging the root systems if you are planting near trees. Dig planting holes as deep as the plant's soilball and no deeper. Install plants, backfill, water thoroughly, apply a root stimulator, and cover all bare soil with 3 to 4 in. of bark mulch.

Growing Tips

Water as needed to maintain a moist soil. A 3 to 4 in. layer of bark mulch will greatly aid in soil moisture retention. Leatherleaf mahonia will respond with vigor to a fertile soil. Apply 15-5-10, 21-7-14, 19-5-9, or a similar 3:1:2 ratio long-lasting, slow-release lawn fertilizer four times a year according to label directions. Apply 2 weeks after the last spring frost in your area, twice more during the growing season, and once during the fall. Remember to water thoroughly after each fertilizer application.

Care

For a great look, prune back one or more stems of each plant at different levels in very early spring. Leatherleaf mahonia has no serious pests.

Companion Planting and Design

Mahonia may be used as foundation plantings in two or more rows, in masses under trees, or in containers. When used as multiple-row foundation plantings, alternate in a checkerboard pattern for a very interesting planting. Use the same technique when planting in masses, adding as many rows as needed to fill your designed area. It works well in shaded areas along with aucuba, aralia, English ivy, and ferns.

I Suggest

This is one "stiff" or ridged-leaf plant but a good selection for shaded areas where a limited selection of plants will grow. Look at them in nurseries. Do plant in locations away from foot traffic, such as by walks, because they are a little prickly.

Mahonia bealei, *or leatherleaf mahonia, grows in relatively heavy shade and the black clay soil typically found from the Red River to the Gulf. Mahonia does prefer shady locations, and does not do well in daylong full sun or reflected heat. Eastern sun till midmorning is acceptable, but mahonia prefers shade for the remainder of the day. Dappled daylong conditions are also acceptable.* Mahonia bealei *has no known cultivars, but it does have some relatives:* M. aquifolium *or Oregon grape holly, with a dwarf cultivar 'Compacta';* M. fortunei, *or Chinese mahonia; and* M. repens, *or creeping mahonia. Mahonia is hardy in all Texas zones.*

Other Common Name
Leatherleaf Mahonia

Bloom Period and Seasonal Color
Winter blooms in yellow.

Mature Height × Spread
4 to 6 ft. × 3 to 5 ft.

Nandina

Nandina domestica

Nandina is an extremely easy-to-grow, multi-trunk or stemmed shrub. With a medium-to-dark or metallic green hue during the growing season, it has outstanding fall and winter foliage color when grown in full sun. My first experience in relocating N. domestica was when we purchased our first home 2¹/₂ miles south of downtown Canton on Texas State Highway 19. We were certainly proud of that place. The nandinas were scattered throughout the landscape. I dug them up in early winter and mass planted them on the northwest side of our home. The planting turned out great and some thirty years later still thrives. Try these varieties: 'Compacta', 'Harbor Dwarf', 'Moon Bay', 'Nana', 'Gulf Stream', 'Ori-Hime', 'Wood's Dwarf', and 'Firepower'. Nandina is hardy in all Texas zones.

Other Common Name
Heavenly Bamboo

Bloom Period and Seasonal Color
Summer blooms in white with fall foliage in red, bronze, and purple with red berries on some varieties.

Mature Height × Spread
5 to 7 ft. × 3 to 6 ft.

When, Where, and How to Plant
Early spring and early fall are the best planting times. To relocate existing plantings, wait until after a hard freeze in the fall, then dig and relocate any time during the dormant season. Plant in sunny locations without reflected heat. Nandina will grow in dense shade, but much of its winter color is often lost, and the plants will not be full. My ideal sun/shade location would be eight hours of full sun without reflected heat along with shade from the hot afternoon sun. *N. domestica* is a durable shrub tolerant of most Texas soil conditions, but it responds with vigor to deep, fertile, moist soils. Remove weeds, turfgrass, rocks, and sticks from the planting area and till. Blend 4 to 6 in. of organic matter such as compost, ground bark, and/or brown sphagnum peat moss into the native soil. Dig the planting holes soilball deep, set the plants in the holes, backfill, water thoroughly, apply root stimulator, and cover all bare soil with 3 to 4 in. of bark.

Growing Tips
Water to prevent soil dryness. Maintain 3 to 4 in. of mulch. Fertilize with long-lasting slow-release 3:1:2 ratio lawn fertilizer (such as 19-5-9, 21-7-14, or 15-5-10). Apply in the spring two weeks after the last killing frost in your area, eight weeks later, again eight weeks later during the growing season, and once in the fall. Water thoroughly after each application.

Care
Prune each spring. If the long shoots of the tall-growing types become too leggy, cut approximately half of the stems back to the points where new branching is desired. After the stems have produced new foliage, cut back the remaining half of the stems to the desired height. Nandina has no pests or diseases.

Companion Planting and Design
Nandina may be used in masses as foundation plantings, stand-alone yard beds, backgrounds, and in confined areas such as planters. This tough plant may be used in beds around trees with annuals, bulbs, and perennials.

I Suggest
One of my favorite varieties is 'Firepower' because of its fullness, dwarf habit, and year-round colors.

Oleander

Nerium oleander

When, Where, and How to Plant

Plant in early spring after all danger of frost or freeze has passed and almost anytime throughout the growing season. Avoid late fall or winter. Oleander will tolerate almost any Texas soil, but it prefers a deep, moist, fertile, loose soil. The plant needs a well-prepared soil. Remove any debris, weeds, and grass, and till the area. Blend in 4 to 6 in. of organic matter. Till again. After digging planting holes soilball deep, install the individual plants, backfill with the soil mix, water thoroughly, apply a root stimulator, and cover all bare soil with 3 to 4 in. of your favorite bark mulch.

Growing Tips

Water sufficiently to prevent soil dryness; maintaining a 3- to 4-in. mulch will greatly aid in moisture retention. Fertilize in the spring two weeks after your last killing frost, again eight weeks later, and once in early fall according to label directions. Use a slow-release, granular rose fertilizer and water thoroughly after each application.

Care

The plants are much more attractive when allowed to grow into their natural shape and size. Remove any dead stems by pruning in early spring. Caterpillars may visit but are easily controlled by several possibilities available at your area retailer.

Companion Planting and Design

Oleander makes great natural screens 8 to 15 ft. high and wide for the standard varieties, 5 to 7 ft. high and wide for dwarfs, and 4 to 6 ft. tall and wide for the petites. It also works well as a natural hedge. Train tall-growing standards into tree forms. Use as patio plantings or in containers around pools, on decks, or other locations where relatively tall, upright, blooming tree-form plants are desired. It may be used in any Xeriscape type of landscape design too.

I Suggest

I'm currently growing and enjoying 'Little Red' inside a sunny enclosed area in Zone 7b. I suggest you look no farther than the tough oleander if you are interested in heat-tolerant, evergreen, blooming shrubs that are winter hardy and low maintenance.

Oleander is a blooming shrub that's so tough it's used in some highway medians like the I-35 median from the Austin area southward. Oleander withstands intense heat, salt, and neglect. This is a very adaptable blooming shrub where it is winter hardy and when it is planted in sunny locations. The dwarf varieties may be used as foundation plantings, but they are often more showy as specimens. They are also good in large color beds. CAUTION: All parts of oleander are poisonous, whether green or dry. 'Hardy Red', 'General Pershing', and 'Sugarland'™ are all considered hardy in Zone 7b. Varieties hardy in Zones 8 and 9 include 'Hardy Pink', 'Hardy White', 'Mrs. Roeding', and 'Cherry Ripe'. Oleander is hardy in Zones 8a-9b with a few varieties hardy in Zone 7.

Bloom Period and Seasonal Color

Spring to fall Blooms in white, pink, red, coral, and yellow.

Mature Height × Spread

4 to 15 ft. × 5 to 12 ft.

Photinia

Photinia × fraseri

Fraser's photinia, or Photinia × fraseri, is planted as a screen on the northwest side of our landscaped area. This is a full-sun location with excellent air movement in a rural setting. My soil is deep, loose, doodle bug sand (as we call it locally). When given the needed room, Fraser's photinia screening tendency is excellent for reducing unwanted noise and good for all types of screens including wind and privacy screens. Unless you have very wide beds and extra-tall walls, I would not recommend using red tips as a foundation planting. Photinia fraseri is a hybrid cross between P. serrulata and P. glabra. Photinia is hardy in all Texas zones except Zone 6.

Other Common Name
Red Tips

Bloom Period and Seasonal Color
Spring blooms in white. New leaf growth is red.

Mature Height × Spread
10 to 15 ft. × 8 to 10 ft.

When, Where, and How to Plant

Plant in early fall and early spring in full-sun locations with ample room, well-drained soils, and good air movement. Do not plant as foundation plants, or in confined or limited space where constant pruning would be need. Do not plant in poorly drained, wet soils, or shady locations. Remove weeds, turfgrass, and debris from the planting area which should be at least 5 ft. wide (and wider if possible). Till the area, then add 4 to 6 in. of organic matter. Till again. Dig the individual planting holes no deeper than soilball depth, set the plants in the holes, backfill with the mix, water thoroughly, apply a root stimulator, and cover all bare soil with 3 to 4 in. of bark mulch.

Growing Tips

Water as needed to prevent soil dryness, applying water at the soil line. Fertilize spring, mid-season, and fall with a long-lasting, slow-release 3:1:2 ratio lawn fertilizer. Maintain 3 to 4 in. of mulch year-round.

Care

Minimal pruning is needed when growing into its natural form; pruning at least every week is needed when growing as short-clipped or sheared hedges. To prevent leaf spot disease, place the plants in full-sun locations with good air movement, don't over-fertilize and water at the soil line. There are several products available for leaf spot control.

Companion Planting and Design

These are top-notch plants when properly located and can be grown as tall screens, hedges, or specimens. Photinia may be trained into tree form and works well as a patio tree, specimen, or container plant. Because red tips will quickly outgrow areas, do not plant in front of standard windows, porches, walks, or as foundation plants.

I Suggest

I also enjoy *P. serrulata*, or Chinese photinia, especially in tree form. It is usually more difficult to locate than red tips, but it is an interesting old-time plant. Again, I recommend red tips as stand-alone plants in full sun locations with great air movement around them and minimum-to-no pruning. My planting is 60 ft. long, 12 ft. tall, and 10 ft. wide and has never had one leaf spot in over a decade.

Pyracantha
Pyracantha coccinea

When, Where, and How to Plant
Early fall and very early spring are both good planting times. Pyracantha will grow in most Texas soils unless they are poorly drained or very wet, but it prefers fertile, moist, well-drained locations. Improve the soil before planting. Remove any weeds, turfgrass, and debris from the planting area then till. Add 4 to 6 in. of organic matter such as brown sphagnum peat moss, compost, or ground bark then till. Dig the planting holes soilball deep, insert the plants, backfill, water thoroughly, apply a root stimulator, and cover bare soil with 3 to 4 in. of bark. Make beds a minimum of 5 ft. wide.

Growing Tips
Maintain a moist, but not wet, soil during the growing season. Fertilize three times a year, using a granular, long-lasting, slow-release, rose fertilizer according to label directions. Apply two weeks after the last killing spring frost, again ten weeks later, and once in early fall. Maintain 3 to 4 in. of mulch year-round.

Care
Firethorn requires minimal pruning; espaliers may require several prunings during the growing season to train and maintain their form. Lace bugs or spider mites may visit. Plantings in sunny locations with good air movement are much less likely to have any pest problems. If pests or diseases do visit, your local retailer will have several controls.

Companion Planting and Design
Some very low-growing varieties work as groundcovers. Other varieties work as screens, accents, bank plantings, specimens, and espaliers. Pyracantha is usually not recommended for foundation plantings due to its size and growth pattern. Espaliers of pyracantha may be used on walls, fences, and landscape structures in formal patterns. Prolonged pruning is necessary to keep a firethorn espalier looking good. Various low-growing annuals may be planted in front of pyracantha.

I Suggest
Visit parks and public gardens and be observant of pyracantha applications before deciding to utilize it in your landscape. I suggest if room is not a problem letting your planting grow to a natural shape.

One of the most striking ornamental features of pyracantha is the large clusters of berries that often give color into the fall and winter. The bloom clusters are nice, but the berries are much more colorful. With compact branching and a spreading habit, this is an interesting shrub when allowed to grow in its natural form. Be sure to watch out for the plant's thorns when pruning. The thorns actually make firethorn more desirable in plantings designed to curtail passage. Pyracantha may be clipped into a relatively formal hedge but it is best in its natural form when used for hedges or screens. Our feathered friends enjoy pyracantha berries during the winter. Cold hardiness varies with pyracantha's species and cultivars.

Other Common Name
Firethorn

Bloom Period and Seasonal Color
Spring blooms in white, red berries in the fall and winter.

Mature Height × Spread
2 to 10 ft. × 2 fto 10 ft.

Spirea

Spiraea japonica

If you live in the colder regions of Texas and are looking for an early spring- through midsummer-blooming shrub that will not be lost due to winter cold, take a look at Japanese spirea and other spireas. They will dependably grow and bloom in all areas of Texas. They may be used in beds near your foundation or as hedges, screens, and specimens—depending on the varieties or species selected. One name often used by gardeners when discussing spirea is Bridal wreath, but that common name actually applies to S. prunifolia. Spirea is hardy in all Texas zones.

Other Common Name
Japanese Spirea

Bloom Period and Seasonal Color
Spring through mid-summer blooms in pink, rose-pink, purplish-pink, white, and red.

Mature Height × Spread
1 to 6 ft. × 3 to 5 ft.

When, Where, and How to Plant
Plant anytime, though fall and very early spring are best. Best bloom and growth are achieved in full-sun locations with moist, well-drained, fertile soils. This plant will tolerate some shade and almost any Texas soil. To obtain best results, improve the soil. Remove any debris, weeds, and turfgrass, and till the planting area, which should be at least 5 ft. wide. Next add 4 to 6 in. of organic matter such as compost, brown sphagnum peat moss, and ground bark. Till again. Dig the planting holes no deeper than soilball deep (being sure not to crowd), install plants, backfill, and water thoroughly. Apply a root stimulator and cover bare soil with 3 to 4 in. of bark.

Growing Tips
Water sufficiently to maintain a moist soil, especially during growth and bloom periods. Prevent soil dryness during the remainder of the year. A 3 to 4 in. layer of mulch maintained year-round will greatly aid in soil moisture conservation. Fertilize in the spring 2 weeks after the last killing frost, ten weeks after that, and once again in the fall. Use long-lasting, slow-release granular rose fertilizer applied according to label directions.

Care
After blooming is completed, minimal pruning may be necessary to aid in natural shaping. This plant has no serious pests.

Companion Planting and Design
The lower-growing varieties will add color and interest to extra-wide foundation plantings. The blooms stand out when planted in front of taller-growing broadleaf evergreens such as holly. Use taller varieties as informal hedges or screens. Spirea specimens are often standouts in the landscape.

I Suggest
Like many senior Texas gardeners, I suggest you become familiar with this shrub. It is a dependable bloomer, easily grown, drought tolerant, and requires minimal maintenance. What more could you ask for in a Texas landscape shrub?

Viburnum

Viburnum spp.

When, Where, and How to Plant

Plant in fall or in very early spring. In Texas, viburnums may be planted anytime. Most do best in sun with shade from the hot afternoon sun. *V. rhytidophyllum* and *V. opulus* prefer partial shade to dense shade or dappled daylong sun and shade. Some viburnums will grow in a wide range of Texas soils, but they all prefer a deep, fertile, moist, well-drained soil. Do not plant on wet or poorly drained soils of any type. Remove any debris, turf-grass, and weeds, then till the planting area at least 5 ft. wide. Add 4 to 6 in. of brown sphagnum peat moss, compost, ground bark, or other organic matter. Level and till again. Dig the planting holes rootball deep, place the viburnums in individual holes, backfill, water thoroughly, apply a root stimulator, and cover bare soil with 3 to 4 in. of bark.

Growing Tips

Soil moisture is needed, but don't overwater. Fertilize three times a year with a long-lasting slow-release granular rose fertilizer. Apply two weeks after the last spring killing frost, again ten weeks later, and once in the fall. Remember to water thoroughly after each application. Maintain 3 to 4 in. of bark mulch.

Care

Prune as needed to shape. I prefer spring pruning for removing wild shoots, branches, and dead or damaged parts. Do major pruning after the main bloom flush and just as new growth begins. Do not prune in late summer or the fall because blooms may be reduced for the following spring. Viburnum has no serious pests.

Companion Planting and Design

V. davidii, or David viburnum's, usual height is 2 to 3 ft. tall by 3 to 4 ft. wide—making it a candidate for a low, wide foundation planting or hedge. Japanese viburnum, or *V. japonicum*, may reach 18 ft. tall and 16 ft. wide. It would make an outstanding specimen or very tall, wide screen. Choose your planting site according to the variety. Annual or perennial color may be utilized in front of the evergreen types if the beds are wide enough.

I Suggest

Viburnum is often an overlooked group of interesting blooming shrubs for Texas landscapes. They will add interesting form, texture, and color.

A popular common name in Texas for viburnum is snowball bush, usually referring to V. opulus 'Sterile', but there are many other noteworthy viburnums. There are selections that may be used as foundation plantings, tall or short hedges, screens, specimens, or mass plantings. If you want to know more about these plants, visit arboretums such as the Stephen F. Austin State University Mast Arboretum in Nacogdoches and other public gardens. Give one or more of these a try: V. opulus 'Sterile'; V. plicatum; V. rhytidophyllum; V. suspensum; V. tinus; V. plicatum tomentosum 'Mariesi'; V. lantana 'Mohican'; V. japonicum macrophyllus, 'Atrosanguinea', and 'Rosea'; V. dentatum; V. nudum; V. rufidulum; and V. awabukii 'Chindo'. Deciduous varieties are hardy state wide. Evergreen varieties are hardy in Zones 7-9, depending on variety.

Other Common Name
Snowball Bush

Bloom Period and Seasonal Color
Spring blooms in white, cream, pink, pinkish-white, and rose-tinted white.

Mature Height × Spread
3 to 18 ft. × 3 to 16 ft.

Wax Leaf Ligustrum

Ligustrum japonicum

L. japonicum—*also known as* L. texanum, *is a tall, wide shrub ideal for a natural screen. Wax leaf is available just about everywhere in Texas and has been used for many years—though sometimes not in the best locations. Don't even think of planting wax leaf in front of windows, porches, or other areas best left unobscured. And, unless you have a very tall, solid wall, don't use wax leaf as a foundation plant. Just make sure to anticipate its ultimate size and the pruning frequency it will require. Wax leaf is a type of privet. You may want to try members of its immediate or expanded family. Wax leaf ligustrum is normally hardy in Zones 7b-9b though it has frozen in Zones 7b and 8a.*

Other Common Name
Wax Leaf

Bloom Period and Seasonal Color
Spring and summer blooms in white.

Mature Height × Spread
10 to 14 ft. × 8 to 12 ft.

When, Where, and How to Plant

Plant anytime in hardy zones, though early fall or early spring is best. Wax leaf is a tough, rapid-growing shrub that will grow in almost any soil type. It plants and transplants easily, tolerates drought, and will grow in sun or shade. Minimal soil preparation is needed, but if you want it to start off strong, soil improvement should be on your agenda. After removing any debris, weeds, and turfgrass, and tilling the planting area, add 4 to 6 in. of compost, brown sphagnum peat moss, or ground bark. Till again. Install individual plants in holes no deeper than the soilball, backfill, water thoroughly, apply a root stimulator, and cover bare soil with 3 to 4 in. of pine bark or your favorite mulch.

Growing Tips

Water as needed to prevent soil dryness. To aid wax leaf's color and growth, fertilize 4 times a year with a slow-release 3:1:2 ratio lawn fertilizer (such as 15-5-10, 19-5-9, and 21-7-14) according to label directions. Apply in the spring two weeks after the last frost, two times during the growing season approximately ten weeks apart, and once in the fall. Maintain 3 to 4 in. of mulch year-round.

Care

When training wax leaf as a hedge, prune weekly during the growing season. Don't prune in late fall or winter. Early spring is best for radical pruning. This plant has no serious pests.

Companion Planting and Design

Wax leaf lends itself well to horticultural training in forms such as patio trees, pyramids, and pom poms. It may be used as an accent, specimen, or large container plant. Wax leaf is easily trained into various hedge shapes including square, round, and oval.

I Suggest

Make sure you understand the ultimate height and width plus the pruning needed if you decide to use wax leaf as a formal sheared hedge in your landscape. It's something I would not do. I suggest this large growing plant is best used as a specimen or natural-growing screen.

Winter Jasmine

Jasminum nudiflorum

When, Where, and How to Plant

Fall and spring plantings are best but winter jasmine may be planted anytime. Never plant in heavily shaded spots. Winter jasmine requires at least eight hours of full sun, and it prefers daylong full sun. Make planting beds at least 5 ft. wide. Remove any debris, weeds, and turfgrass, and till the area. Soil improvement is enhanced with the addition of 4 to 6 in. of organic matter. Add 4 to 6 in. of organic matter to the area and till. Never dig shrub planting holes deeper than soilball depth. After digging the holes, insert the shrubs, backfill with soil mix, water thoroughly, apply root stimulator, and cover bare soil with 3 to 4 in. of your favorite bark. I usually use pine bark.

Growing Tips

Water as needed to maintain a moist soil throughout the growing season and to prevent soil dryness. Fertilize in the spring after blooming is completed, twice more during the growing season, and once in the fall. Use a slow-release rose fertilizer. Maintain 3 to 4 in. of bark mulch to keep soil moisture.

Care

Winter jasmine may be sheared to shape in spring after bloom is complete. This is a minimum-care shrub that has no serious pests.

Companion Planting and Design

Plant on hillsides, in large wide beds with other colorful shrubs, or grouped together in masses. It is great for low shrub planting in the landscape. It works well cascading over walls, in masses, and on banks, and is good in spots where erosion may cause problems. When planted in very wide beds in front of tall-growing, dark-green, broadleaf evergreens, its early spring color really stands out. The contrasts between the greens and the leaf sizes of holly and winter jasmine are also interesting.

I Suggest

The jasmine group has a fragrance enjoyed by most Texans. Since *J. nudiflorum*, or winter jasmine, is easily grown, I suggest you include it in your landscape.

During late winter to very early spring—the time of the year when gardeners begin to think that spring may never arrive, J. nudiflorum comes to the rescue. With bright-yellow one-inch flowers on green stems, winter jasmine assures us that spring will arrive as usual. Winter jasmine is considered a fast grower, growing in areas of poor soil and full sun. J. nudiflorum or winter jasmine is a stand-alone plant and is hardy statewide. Family members you may wish to try include: J. sambac (hardy in Zones 8 and 9), J. primulinum (hardy in Zones 8 and 9), J. polyanthum (hardy in Zones 8 and 9), J. floridum (hardy in Zones 7 to 9), and J. nitidum (hardy in Zone 10). Hardiness of other species is dependent on the variety.

Bloom Period and Seasonal Color

Winter and early spring blooms in yellow.

Mature Height × Spread

3 to 4 ft. × 4 to 6 ft.

Trees *for Texas*

Trees should be considered mother nature's air conditioners. They actually do cool the air and climate for us. On a hot Texas summer day, you may find the temperature under a nice shade tree ten degrees Fahrenheit cooler than the temperature in the open sun.

We have more trouble with heat than we do with cold in Texas. Properly selected and placed, shade trees can help cool our homes. High-quality, long-lived shade trees planted on the west side of a home will help its inhabitants make it through the scorching Texas summers. Certain deciduous varieties will provide great fall color while allowing the sun to warm our homes during the relatively short, traditional winters.

Planning for Trees

It's a good idea to plant trees first in a home landscape. Many gardeners don't plant trees until they have finished the rest of their landscape plan, but trees generally take longer to grow and provide the framework for other landscape material. Draw a landscape plan or have one created for you. When the plan is completed, plant your trees before any other plants.

Trees are usually classified by height. Trees that grow less than thirty feet tall are considered small. Medium trees grow thirty to fifty feet, and large trees grow over fifty feet. Ask the staff at your local nursery or garden center how tall and wide a particular tree will grow in your area. It's disappointing to plant a tree that looks as if it will remain relatively small but later grows to a tremendous height and

Green Ash

width. If planted too close to your home, foundation, drive, pool, or other structure, such a tree can cause damage. Gather your information before purchasing.

The best time to plant trees is in the early fall. This allows for almost a full year of growth before the July and August heat. Trees may, however, be planted at any time during the year. This is especially true of container-grown selections.

Properly selected and placed trees can also help break the wind. Windbreaks have been successful in reducing energy usage, saving valuable topsoil, and helping to create a more enjoyable home-site environment. This is especially true in West Texas.

Trees are generally classified as deciduous or evergreen. Most shade trees we use are deciduous, and there are some great varieties that provide outstanding fall color. Among these are shumard red oak, *Quercus shumardii*, Chinese pistachio, *Pistacia chinensis*, and ginkgo, *Ginkgo biloba*.

It may be possible for you to grow palm trees. Depending on zones, palm trees can grow in approximately 40 percent of Texas.

I am often asked for recommendations for fast-growing shade trees for the home landscape. The most important thing to keep in mind is that most of these "fast-growing" shade trees are weak-wooded, problem-prone, and short-lived. Properly selected, planted, and cared for, high-quality, long-lived shade trees grow almost as rapidly as those we consider "fast-growing"—and they will be around for decades.

Tree Maintenance

Shade trees may need to be shaped and pruned. While you may not feel comfortable doing this yourself, here are some helpful tips and suggestions when hiring someone to prune your trees:

1. Make sure the person you hire is a professional arborist with proper insurance. Ask for references and check them out.
2. Put the agreement or contract for services in writing before work begins. Both you and the contractor will benefit from having a written record of exactly what services are to be performed. The contract should also indicate the total fees as well as when and how those fees are to be paid. No payment should be made before work is completed.
3. Don't hire someone who calls on you with a pickup, chain saw, and ladder, or who lacks references, insurance, and a business site.

We Texans have a wide selection of trees from which to choose. In this chapter I have included nineteen tree families in which you will find interesting, outstanding varieties.

Bald Cypress
Taxodium distichum

Bald cypress is a conifer, but unlike pine, fir, or other members of the conifer family, it is deciduous. I first noticed the bald cypress near the Stephen F. Austin State University library when my wife Judy and I were students there in 1970. I thought they looked great then and I still do today. They are often used in both home and commercial landscapes. In the South we associate the bald cypress with swamps. It's true bald cypress grows in these locations, but it also adapts well to urban landscape locations. Once established, bald cypress will tolerate drought. In the short term, bald cypress' fern-like foliage may change colors; in longer dry periods, leaf drop may occur. This rarely damages the tree. Bald cypress is hardy statewide.

Other Common Names
Swamp Cypress, Southern Cypress, Gulf Cypress

Bloom Period and Seasonal Color
Nonshowy spring bloom in the fall. Fall foliage in copper to bronze.

Mature Height × Spread
50 to 100 ft. × 20 to 50 ft.

When, Where, and How to Plant
Fall is the best planting time; early spring is second best. Bald cypress prefers moist, full sun areas but will grow in nearly any standard lawn areas. I would not plant them in areas that are dry, difficult to water, or shady. Loosen the soil in an area several times as wide and as deep as the rootball but no deeper. Dig the planting hole rootball deep. Install the tree and make sure it sits straight. Backfill with loosened soil, water thoroughly, and apply a root stimulator. Mulch bare soil with 3 to 4 in. of bark mulch. Temporary staking may be required.

Growing Tips
Bald cypress does best in deep, moist-to-damp soils and responds with vigor to fertilizer. Three times per season, apply a premium-quality, long-lasting, slow-release 3:1:2 ratio lawn fertilizer (such a 19-5-9, 21-7-14, or 15-5-10) according to label directions. Make the first application just as new spring growth begins, again ten weeks later, and again in the fall. Water thoroughly after each application.

Care
Requires little care. No pruning required. No serious pests.

Companion Planting and Design
The bald cypress needs room to grow—spacing of 25 to 50 ft. may be necessary to obtain an attractive result. If you want a tree in an area that is both sunny and a bit damp, bald cypress is a great choice. These tough and durable trees also work well in a Xeriscape or waterscape. Their durability makes them very adaptable and tolerant of growing conditions in street plantings and confined urban areas. Utilize them in any landscape theme where there is ample room, but do not crowd them.

I Suggest
Use bald cypress as a specimen plant, a single accent plant, or in informal, natural groupings. Its upright pyramidal form is well suited to limited spaces.

Chinese Pistachio

Pistacia chinensis

When, Where, and How to Plant

You can easily transplant container-grown stock in the fall or early spring. I prefer planting from 7-, 10-, or 15-gallon containers. Smaller and larger container-grown plants are available in Texas. Plant in any sunny location where you want a low-maintenance, small to medium shade tree that will also provide outstanding fall color. With your favorite shovel or digging fork, loosen the soil in the planting area. Dig the actual planting hole no deeper than the soilball, remove from the container and plant. Backfill with loosened soil, water thoroughly, and apply a root stimulator. After planting is completed, mulch bare soil with 3 to 4 in. of bark mulch.

Growing Tips

Water as needed. Chinese pistachio will grow quickly when fertilized and offered extra water, even during our typical July and August blast furnace conditions. Fertilize three to four times a year with a premium-quality, long-lasting, slow-release 3:1:2 ratio fertilizer (such as 19-5-9, 21-7-14, or 15-5-10) according to label directions. Make the first application just as new leaf growth begins in the spring, eight weeks later, again in eight more weeks, and once during the fall. Water after each application.

Care

Pruning may be desired when the tree is young in order to train its growth, but is usually unnecessary after this early stage. There will be no insects.

Companion Planting and Design

Chinese pistachio will grow in confined or hot areas. Due to its size and deep roots, you may plant it close to your home, but allow enough room for it to reach its normal form. It offers light shade that will allow you to grow other plants—like St. Augustinegrass—beneath it. Chinese pistachio is a great tree in a Xeriscape. Use as a single accent or in a line planting or informal natural grouping.

I Suggest

Add one or more of these trees to your landscape especially if your space is limited and you want a tough, trouble-free tree for fall color. Judy and I planted two in a rocky outcropping back in 1995 and think they are super.

Chinese pistachio is an excellent small- to medium-sized tree that is nearly perfect for Texas landscapes. It tolerates a wide range of locations and soil conditions. Once established, Chinese pistachio is deep-rooted and drought tolerant. The wood from Chinese pistachio is strong. Wind and ice usually do little, if any, damage. There are no known cultivars of Chinese pistachio. P. vera is the pistachio tree that produces nuts. It isn't hardy in Texas, except in the Zone 9 areas, which include the Gulf Coast and Rio Grande Valley areas. Two other family members are P. texana, the Texas pistachio, and P. atlantica, which exhibits excellent drought tolerance. Both are more difficult to secure than P. chinensis, common Chinese pistachio. This tree is hardy statewide.

Bloom Period and Seasonal Color

Non showy spring bloom. Fall foliage in yellow, red-orange, and red. Thick heads of small reddish-brown fruit or seed in the fall.

Mature Height × Spread

20 to 40 ft. × 20 to 30 ft.

Flowering Crabapple
Malus spp.

If you're looking for showy trees in the spring, flowering crabapples are hard to beat. They offer beautiful blooms, fruit, and foliage. They work well in small areas and are in scale with single story structures. If you have an eating area with an outside view and like birds, plant one or more flowering crabapples. You will then get to enjoy the colors from the blooms, fruits, and foliage as well as the birds. Nearly all flowering crabapples available at Texas nurseries are hybrids. The following are known to be disease-resistant: 'Sutyzam', 'Snowdrift', 'Jackii', 'Prairiefire', 'Robinson', and 'Centurion'. Flowering crabapple is hardy statewide.

Bloom Period and Seasonal Color
Spring blooms in white, pink, red, and blends. Small fruits are red to red-orange.

Mature Height × Spread
10 to 25 ft. × 15 to 30 ft.

When, Where, and How to Plant
Fall or early spring is the best planting time. You can plant container-grown nursery stock anytime. While tolerating most types of soil, crabapples grow best in deep, fertile, moist soils. Measure the width of the soilball and loosen the soil in the planting area to two or three times wider than the soilball. Dig a hole as deep as the soilball, remove the tree from the container, and place in the hole. Backfill with the loosened soil, water thoroughly, and apply root stimulator. Mulch bare soil with 3 to 4 in. of bark mulch. The tree may need temporary staking.

Growing Tips
Fertilize three times a year with a premium-quality, long-lasting, granular rose fertilizer. Follow label directions and water thoroughly after each application. Apply the first treatment after bloom drop, again approximately ten weeks later, then once again in the fall. Flowering crabapples may benefit from supplemental watering during our normally dry July and August months.

Care
Prune as needed for shape in the spring after bloom drop. There are usually no serious insect problems, although borers may attack unhealthy trees. Maintaining a healthy tree is the best prevention. Fire blight, powdery mildew, and apple scab are potential problems. Control by planting in sunny locations that have good air movement. Local retailers will have a wide selection of products to treat pest and/or disease problems. Follow label directions when using any aid. Your local county agent's office has a fact sheet covering fire blight on landscape plants. To help prevent problems, always plant disease-resistant plants.

Companion Planting and Design
Plant flowering crabapples in groups or groves, and in rows along drives or walkways. Groups of three or more trees, planted in triangular patterns, are great for sunny corners of the yard. These are outstanding additions to gardens with decks or gazebos. They may also be used in beds with plantings of annuals or perennials.

I Suggest
Use this spring-blooming beauty in areas of limited style. Flowering crabapples are welcome in Japanese gardens.

Flowering Pear
Pyrus calleryana

When, Where, and How to Plant

Plant flowering pear in the fall or early spring. Container-grown selections can be planted year-round. Flowering pears prefer sunny locations with deep, fertile, well-drained, moist soil. They will tolerate poor soils, heavy clay, restricted root space, wind, drought, and limited water. Do not plant in poorly drained or wet locations, in shady locations, or where they will be crowded. No special soil preparation is needed. Loosen the soil in the planting area wider than the soilball. Dig the hole only soilball deep. Place in the planting hole. Backfill, water thoroughly, and apply a root stimulator. Mulch bare soil with 3 to 4 in. of your favorite bark mulch.

Growing Tips

Water as needed to maintain a healthy tree, while the tree is establishing itself and during our July and August "oven times." My soil is deep "doodle-bug" sand (a highly technical description), so I fertilize four times per growing season. (In soils that hold nutrients better, two or three times a year is adequate). Use a premium-quality, long-lasting, slow-release 3:1:2 ratio lawn fertilizer (such as 15-5-10 or 18-6-12). Apply after bloom drop as new growth begins. Fertilize again in ten weeks, again in the next ten weeks, plus one fall application. No matter how often you fertilize, always make the first spring and fall applications. Water thoroughly after each application.

Care

Prune as needed to ensure strong branch/limb structure. Failure to do early corrective pruning on some varieties (including 'Bradford'), may result in a mature specimen splitting as a result of an ice storm. This plant has no serious pests.

Companion Planting and Design

Flowering pear is an adaptable tree for urban landscape uses. Flowering pears are used to line entrances to property, along driveways, and as street trees. They are acceptable in urban lots, estates and rural plantings in all types of themes and designs including Xeriscape. They may be utilized as a single specimen, as accent plants, in formal line plantings or groupings, and in Japanese gardens.

I Suggest

Take a drive to look at flowering pear trees during the spring and fall. I suggest the variety 'Aristocrat'.

Flowering pears originate from a tough and durable lineage: P. calleryana or callery pear. They grow well in all areas of Texas. Depending on the variety selected, some flowering pears are columnar in shape; they fit well in limited spaces, and can be used to frame structures or designate drives. Others have a more rounded shape and can be located near decks and gazebos, and in specialty gardens. In the spring, flowering pears are covered with masses of white spring blooms. Spring and summer foliage is shiny and dark green. Fall color is outstanding. Try some of these in your home landscape: 'Capital', 'Redspire', 'Whitehouse', 'Bradford', 'Aristocrat', and 'Glens Form'.

Other Common Name
Ornamental Pear

Bloom Period and Seasonal Color
Spring blooms in white with fall foliage in gold, orange, deep mahogany, purple, reddish purple, and crimson.

Mature Height × Spread
30 to 50 ft. × 20 to 40 ft.

Ginkgo

Ginkgo biloba

If you want to see a living fossil, look no farther than ginkgo. The maidenhair common name is taken from the similarity in the ginkgo's leaf to the leaflets of the maidenhair fern, Adiantum. Fossil records of ginkgo have been found in North America. Living plants were believed to be extinct until ginkgo was found growing in China in the late 1700s. Subsequent propagation has made ginkgo available throughout our country. One of the most spectacular gingko trees I've seen in Texas is on the lawn of Tyler City Hall in downtown Tyler. There are male and female ginkgoes. Due to their foul-smelling fruits, the female selections are not desirable. Quality male varieties include 'Autumn Gold', 'Fastigiata', and 'Pendula'. Gingko is hardy statewide.

Other Common Name
Maidenhair Tree

Bloom Period and Seasonal Color
Outstanding fall foliage in lemon and golden yellow.

Mature Height × Spread
50 to 70 ft. × 20 to 50 ft.

When, Where, and How to Plant

Fall and spring are the best planting times. Ginkgo will tolerate a wide range of urban conditions, including restricted root growth space and pollution. Ginkgo is a relatively slow grower unless it is provided ideal conditions. It prefers deep, fertile, moist soil and sunny locations. Given these conditions, ginkgo will grow substantially every year (after root establishment). Do not plant in areas of poor soil drainage, poor soils, shady locations, or spots that are difficult to water. Loosen the soil wider than the soilball, and dig the planting hole soilball deep. Remove from the container, and place in the planting hole. Backfill with loose soil, water thoroughly, and apply a root stimulator. After planting is complete, mulch bare soil with 3 to 4 in. of bark mulch.

Growing Tips

Water as necessary to maintain moist soil, especially during early establishment. During our typical July and August heat and other periods of light rainfall, ginkgo may benefit from a long, slow, deep drink. Beginning with the second year, fertilize ginkgo four times a year to obtain maximum yearly growth. Apply a premium-quality, long-lasting, slow-release 3:1:2 ratio lawn fertilizer (such as 15-5-10, 19-5-9, or 21-7-14) according to label directions. Make the first application as new buds break in the spring. Reapply in ten weeks, again in another ten weeks, and once during the fall. Always water thoroughly after each fertilizer application.

Care

Pruning is rarely needed. Ginkgo has no pests.

Companion Planting and Design

Ginkgo is an outstanding lawn tree and a knockout in the fall once sizable height and width are obtained. It has graceful branches near the ground. I believe gingko is best as a stand-alone specimen. When deciding on placement of a gingko tree make sure there is ample room. Plant one near the street so everyone passing by may enjoy it. Gingkos may be used in large planters and in Japanese gardens.

I Suggest

This fall, visit our horticultural parks that have sizeable gingkos and you will see their true fall beauty. Another interesting location is around some of the old plantations in the Natchitoches, LA, area.

Golden Rain Tree
Koelreuteria paniculata

When, Where, and How to Plant

Fall and spring are the best planting times. Don't plant in shade or semi-shady locations. Golden rain trees will grow in a wide range of Texas soils, but they prefer loose, moist, fertile soils. Don't plant in poorly drained areas or in spots that are difficult to water. I prefer to plant 7- or 10-gallon sizes. Loosen the soil wider than soilball width and dig the planting hole no deeper than soilball depth. Remove tree from the container and place in the hole. Backfill with loosened soil, water thoroughly, and apply a root stimulator. Mulch bare soil with 4 in. of your favorite bark (I usually use pine bark) after planting is completed. Stake temporarily if necessary.

Growing Tips

During initial establishment, water as needed to prevent dry soil; be especially attentive during our famous July and August hot and dry months. Use a premium-quality, long-lasting, slow-release 3:1:2 ratio lawn fertilizer (such as 21-7-14 or 15-5-10). In my loose sand, I fertilize four times a year. The first spring application should be two weeks after the last freeze or just as new buds break. Reapply in ten weeks, again in ten more weeks, and once during the fall. Water trees thoroughly after each fertilizer application.

Care

Prune when young to ensure strong branching. No additional pruning is usually required. Box elder bugs may appear in the fall. Local retailers offer several control possibilities. Follow label directions on any product you use.

Companion Planting and Design

Golden rain tree is wonderful in areas where space is limited. It works well along the sides of walkways and driveways of single story homes on small urban lots. Its compound, dark-green to blueish-green leaves (during the growing seasons) plus yellow blooms, interesting seed pods, and great fall foliage color make golden rain tree a standout. This tough tree works in a Xeriscape.

I Suggest

Try golden rain tree in a small space on the west side for shade, color in the spring and summer, and fall color and winter sun rays.

Our home is in a rural area, where we have loose, fine soil ("doodle-bug" sand). We also have outcroppings of rusty-red sandstone. People used to ask me, "What are you going to do around all these rocks?" My answer was, "Landscape around and with them." Today no one asks, "What are you going to do?" Instead the question is, "What are those?" In this area are golden rain trees. They are growing in the wide cracks of the large stones and doing well. Try one if you want an easy-to-care-for, small to medium tree that has bright-yellow fragrant blooms and attractive foliage during the growing season. The foliage turns golden yellow in fall, and, as a bonus, the tree has interesting seedpods. Golden rain tree is hardy statewide.

Bloom Period and Seasonal Color

Spring blooms in yellow, summer panicles of pink to mauve seed pods, and fall foliage in golden yellow.

Mature Height × Spread

20 to 40 ft. × 20 to 35 ft.

Green Ash
Fraxinus pennsylvanica

Green ash may be grown in most Texas soils, except for heavy clay. These trees grow naturally in soil with a high moisture content, but they adapt well to urban applications. When given reasonable care, they quickly provide excellent shade. Green ash will adapt to compressed growing areas and is relatively drought tolerant once established. F. pennsylvanica cultivars include 'Patmore', 'Summit', and 'Marshalls Seedless'. Another ash is Texas ash or F. texensis (growing up to forty-five feet tall and thirty to thirty-five feet wide). See page 108 for more on Texas ash. This tree is hardy statewide.

Bloom Period and Seasonal Color
Non showy spring blooms and seeds. Fall foliage in golden yellow.

Mature Height × Spread
40 to 70 ft. × 30 to 50 ft.

When, Where, and How to Plant
Space green ash approximately 20 ft. from the foundation of a structure. This will give it room to spread. If you have a septic system, plant it 20 ft. or more from your field lines to prevent the roots from plugging the lines. The best times to plant are fall and spring in deep, moist, non-heavy clay. Green ash prefers a soil pH of 6.5 to 7.5. If your soil is highly alkaline or heavy clay, I wouldn't recommend planting green ash. Dig the planting hole no deeper than the soilball, but as wide as desired. After loosening the soil and digging the planting hole, install the tree. Backfill with the loose soil, water thoroughly, and apply a root stimulator. Mulch bare soil with 3 to 4 in. of your favorite bark. I usually use pine bark nuggets. You may need to stake the tree temporarily.

Growing Tips
Supplemental irrigation may be needed in July and August. During the first year, applications of root stimulator are advisable. At the beginning of the second season, apply a premium-quality, long-lasting, slow-release, tree-and-shrub or 3:1:2 ratio lawn fertilizer (such as 21-7-14, 18-6-12, or 15-5-10) according to label directions. Make your first application about two weeks after the last killing frost or just as new spring growth begins. Apply again in ten weeks, and once more during the fall. Water thoroughly after each application.

Care
The best way to prevent borer damage is to keep your green ash healthy. Remove any dead branches and/or twigs yearly during very late winter. Borers may visit unhealthy trees.

Companion Planting and Design
For maximum cooling benefits, plant on the west side of your home. This is one of the better ash trees for Texas landscapes due to its availability, fast growth, medium size, and rounded form. It is best utilized as a stand-alone specimen.

I Suggest
I DO NOT suggest planting Arizona ash! Arizona ash, *F. velutina*, is a "trash tree," and I wouldn't plant it if the tree were given to me. It is weak-wooded, relatively short-lived, and problem prone. DON'T plant Arizona ash . . . please!

Japanese Maple
Acer palmatum

When, Where, and How to Plant

The best planting times are early fall or very early spring. Do not plant in midsummer. Smaller varieties may be planted in groups near your foundation if the soil pH is acidic. If the soil test indicates an alkaline pH (above 7) you will need to make extensive bed improvements and maintain an acidic pH (below 7). Loosen the soil several times wider than the soilball. Dig the planting hole no deeper than the soilball, remove the plant from the container, and install. Backfill with loosened soil, water thoroughly, and apply root stimulator. Mulch bare soil with 6 in. of pine bark mulch. In beds, plant in the same type of bed mix as used for azalea plantings.

Growing Tips

Keep the soil moist during the growing season. Fertilize three times a year with long-lasting, slow-release, granular azalea fertilizer according to label directions. Water thoroughly after each application. Make the first application just as new leaves begin to emerge during the spring, reapply in ten weeks, and again in the fall. Maintain mulch year-round.

Care

Prune only to remove dead or damaged branches. Aphids may visit new growth. Japanese maple may suffer freeze damage on tip growth when exposed to severe cold.

Companion Planting and Design

In most Texas locations where there are spring azalea and/or spring flower trails, Japanese maple adds extra excitement to the plantings. It's a real knock out interplanted with pink dogwood. Plant groups of Japanese maples under the canopy of tall shade trees for a stunning visual effect that will stop traffic. They also make outstanding accent plantings. The most spectacular Japanese maples I've ever seen were grown with beds around them. Japanese maples may be grown in containers, as bonsai, and in Japanese gardens.

I Suggest

In East Texas, the soils and climate are usually acceptable for individual plantings. If your space is limited or all you have is a deck, porch, patio, or balcony, a Japanese maple is one tree to try. It is very winter hardy.

Japanese maple is one super colorful, small landscape tree. The tall green varieties are also attractive. The dissectum group has fern-like or lacy foliage. While this is usually desirable, our July and August furnace temperatures and southwestern winds may burn the leaves. Don't plant in a western full sun location. Eastern to northeastern locations usually work well because they normally offer protection from our hot afternoon sun. Locations under the light shade canopy of larger trees are also desirable. You will find some great plantings in the various Texas botanical gardens. One example is inside the Japanese Garden section of the Ft. Worth Botanical Garden. Another example is in the Tyler Rose Garden. Some very interesting varieties include 'Bloodgood', 'Ever Red', 'Red Select', 'Viridis', 'Oshio-beni', 'Garnet', and 'Sango-kaku'. Japanese maple is hardy statewide.

Bloom Period and Seasonal Color
Fall foliage in red, and red-orange.

Mature Height × Spread
2 to 20 ft. × 3 to 20 ft.

Lacebark Elm

Ulmus parvifolia

Do not get lacebark elm confused with Siberian elm, U. pumila, which is a "trash tree." Siberian elm is one of those types "I wouldn't plant even if it were given to me." The desirable lacebark elm is a very tough, durable, and drought-resistant tree appropriate for many Texas landscapes. Where wind-resistant plants are important, lacebark elm does the job. Lacebark elms are great specimen yard trees to keep the afternoon sun off your house and are also wonderful avenue or park trees. 'Sempervirens', 'True Green', and 'Prairie Shade' are good cultivars. U. crassifolia, or cedar elm, is a native Texan. It is usually taller and wider than lacebark elm. For more information on cedar elm, see page 97. Lacebark elm is hardy statewide.

Other Common Name
Chinese Elm

Bloom Period and Seasonal Color
Nonshowy early spring bloom. Fall foliage in pale yellow.

Mature Height × Spread
40 to 60 ft. × 30 to 50 ft.

When, Where, and How to Plant

Plant in fall, winter, or early spring. Lacebark elm tolerates poor soils, including deep sand or heavy clay. It does best in deep, moist soil. These trees need room to grow, so don't crowd them. Place them 20 to 30 ft. from the structure(s) to be shaded. Loosen the soil in the planting area several times wider than soilball width. Dig the planting hole as deep as the soilball. Remove tree from the container and place in the planting hole. Backfill with loosened soil, water thoroughly, and apply root stimulator. Mulch bare soil with 3 to 4 in. of bark (I usually use pine bark). The tree may need temporary staking.

Growing Tips

Water if needed to maintain vigor. The young trees may need water in July and August. I fertilize my lacebark elms three times a year with a premium-quality, long-lasting, slow-release 3:1:2 ratio lawn fertilizer (such as 18-6-12 or 15-5-10). Apply first at new spring growth, again approximately ten weeks later, and once in the fall. Water thoroughly after each application.

Care

Prune if needed to remove dead twigs any time of the year. This tree may be visited by aphids on new growth.

Companion Planting and Design

When planting, make sure you have spaced trees far enough from landscape beds. I suggest 30 ft. Shallow fibrous root systems are often invasive in neighboring garden beds. Lacebark elms will grow almost anywhere, including parking areas, street plantings, and confined locations. They work well in a Xeriscape planting.

I Suggest

Our lacebark elm is the 'Drake' cultivar, which is usually in the 30 to 35 ft. tall × 40 to 45 ft. wide range, with a dense canopy for wonderful summertime shade. As a "fast-growing" shade tree in Texas, lacebark elm is tops. If you wish to plant in containers larger than 20 gallons, I suggest you call a landscape contractor to do the job. This is a tree your young gardener can plant and be assured that it will grow for several decades.

Leyland Cypress
× *Cupressocyparis leylandii*

When, Where, and How to Plant

Plant leyland cypress any time of the year, but fall, winter and spring are best. Don't plant in heavy-shade locations. It will grow in heavy clay to light sandy soils, but not in poorly drained or wet locations. Leyland cypress prefers well-drained, relatively loose, fertile, moist soils. Dig the planting hole the same depth as the rootball but two to three times wider. Set the tree in its new home and backfill with the loosened soil. Water thoroughly and mulch the entire planting area with 3 to 4 in. of bark mulch.

Growing Tips

These plants are drought tolerant once established, but they prefer a moist soil. In our typical July and August conditions, leyland cypress will enjoy a deep, slow, thorough drink. A good fertilizing program would include four applications a year of a premium-quality, long-lasting, slow-release 3:1:2 ratio lawn fertilizer (such as 15-5-10 or 21-7-14). Apply just as new growth begins, reapply ten weeks later, again in ten weeks, and once during the fall. Water thoroughly after each fertilizer application.

Care

Prune as needed in spring to maintain desired shape. Bagworms may visit, but leyland cypress is not very susceptible to them. Handpick them and discard in your trash inside sealed bags. (Don't just pick them off and drop on the ground because they can crawl back up your tree). Visit your local retailers for additional options.

Companion Planting and Design

Don't attempt to use as foundation plants, but do use as specimens. Because of their natural shape, color, and ability to shear, they are tops for use as a single specimen or accent. Leyland cypress is excellent as a wind, privacy, or noise screen. Because of its soft foliage, it may be used in areas near pedestrian traffic. In very wide "beds" groundcovers may be utilized if shade is too heavy for grass to grow under the tree's foliage.

I Suggest

When looking for a relatively tall and full evergreen that is cedar tree-shaped yet is not "prickly" like cedars often are, this is the tree to plant.

I was introduced to leyland cypress by our son Aaron. One year we decided to pick a living Christmas tree to use through the season and then plant outside. Aaron selected a leyland. The tree worked great indoors and later as an outdoor specimen lighted during additional holiday seasons. It worked well because of its very soft foliage. Today we have a row of six on the southeastern corner of our landscaped yard area. They are being grown as a screen in this location. This hybrid between a cypress and a cedar is the most welcomed conifer in our landscape. In addition to the original cross, there are some cultivars you can try: 'Castlewellan', 'Moncal', 'Naylor's Blue', 'Green Spire', and 'Silver Dust'. Leyland cypress is hardy statewide.

Other Common Name
Cypress Leylandi

Bloom Period and Seasonal Color
Evergreen foliage

Mature Height × Spread
20 to 40 ft. × 15 to 20 ft.

Mimosa
Albizia julibrissin

Mimosa is one of the longest-flowering and most-frequently-used summer-blooming trees in Texas landscapes. It is a longtime favorite of many older Texas gardeners due to its fast growth and quick shade. Mimosa is one of the last trees to leaf out in the spring. It will grow in loam, clay, or deep, loose, sandy soils. Mimosa is one of the few ornamental blooming shade trees whose leaves fold up each evening. It is short-lived with a life span of approximately twenty-five years. Despite their untidiness (due to flowers, seedpods, twigs, and leafdrop), mimosas are spectacular in full bloom when in sunny locations at their maximum size. Some cultivars and varieties are 'Charlotte' and 'Rosea'. Mimosa is hardy statewide.

Other Common Name
Silk Tree

Bloom Period and Seasonal Color
Summer blooms in pink, rose-red.

Mature Height × Spread
30 to 40 ft. × 30 to 40 ft.

When, Where, and How to Plant
The best planting times are early fall and early spring. Avoid planting in poorly drained locations, under the canopies of larger shade trees, or in soil that is "wet" or "dry." Allow room for full crown development. The best soil is well-drained, fertile, and moist. No special soil preparation is needed. Loosen the native soil wider than the width of the soilball. Dig the planting hole no deeper than the soilball. Remove tree from the container and place in the hole. Backfill with the loosened soil, water thoroughly, and apply root stimulator. Mulch planting area with 3 to 4 in. of bark mulch after planting is finished. If necessary, stake for initial establishment.

Growing Tips
Supplemental watering is usually needed only during establishment. Fertilize thirty days after the last killing frost in your area or just as new spring growth begins, again ten weeks later, and once in the fall. Use a long-lasting, slow-release 3:1:2 ratio lawn fertilizer (such as 15-5-10, 19-5-9, or 21-7-14). Water thoroughly after each application.

Care
Prune young trees to encourage strong branching. Don't perform radical pruning of limbs on a yearly basis—this is harmful to the tree's long-term health and life span. Aphids and their secretions can be a problem. Mimosa webworms may visit. There are several controls available at your local retailer.

Companion Planting and Design
Don't plant mimosas near landscape beds because of large crops of mimosa seedlings. The seeds will germinate and grow. Provide space between a pool and a mimosa to avoid fallen blooms. Planted next to decks, gazebos, or similar structures, they can become "messy." Mimosa should not be used as a companion with other trees or landscape plantings. I have seen them used successfully to line both sides of driveways and around yard structures.

I Suggest
Plant mimosa if you enjoy a long bloom period. If mimosa wilt is a problem, ask for the cultivar 'Union', which is resistant. Mimosa is not as plentiful at nurseries as it once was, so you may need to "hunt" to find one.

Oak

Quercus spp.

When, Where, and How to Plant

Plant any time of the year. Oaks prefer full sun locations with deep, fertile, well-drained soil. Trees in containers larger than twenty gallons should be planted by a landscape contractor. Dig the planting hole wider than the soilball, but only soilball deep. Remove the tree from the container and place in the hole. Backfill with the loosened native soil, water thoroughly, and apply root stimulator. Mulch the entire planting area with 3 to 4 in. of bark mulch. I recommend using pine bark mulch. Stake if necessary during initial establishment.

Growing Tips

Supplemental watering may be necessary during initial establishment, and oaks usually appreciate a deep, long, slow drink in July or August. Oaks will respond with vigor to fertilizing. This is especially true during the first five years of their "new home" in your landscape. To obtain maximum healthy growth, fertilize in early spring just as new growth begins. Apply again ten weeks later, again in another ten weeks, and once during the fall season. Use a premium-quality, long-lasting, slow-release 3:1:2 ratio lawn fertilizer (such as 21-7-14, 18-6-12, or 15-5-10). Water thoroughly after each fertilizer application.

Care

Prune to train, thin, or correct, and remove dead limbs as needed. Pests rarely visit healthy oaks. Some people mistakenly call oaks "slow-growing." If they are cared for properly, it isn't uncommon for them to grow 3 ft. or more each year. Oaks may have leaf galls and aphids. Some varieties such as pin or water oak are vulnerable to Mistletoe.

Companion Planting and Design

Oaks are great as specimens, yard trees, or shade trees. Allow sufficient space from structures, drives, and walks, based on their normal spread.

I Suggest

Decide which oak(s) you wish to plant and determine their normal ultimate height and width in your area. You may contact me or your local retailer for this information.

Oaks are the most popular trees in the Texas landscape. Oak selections may be evergreen or deciduous, upright or rounded in form. Some have good fall color, while others hold their dead leaves well into winter. Q. palustris (pin oak), grows very well in the East Texas sandy acid soils but does very poorly in heavy alkaline clay soil. Q. shumardii, or shumard red oak, grows statewide in deep clay or sandy soils. My wife and I are currently growing shumard red oak, Q. virginiana, or live oak, Q. macrocarpa, or bur oak, and Q. texana, or Texas red oak. Visit your area nurseries to see which one(s) are best for your applications.

Bloom Period and Seasonal Color

Nonshowy spring blooms with acorns in the fall. Foliage ranging from yellow to red, reddish orange, or tan-brown.

Mature Height × Spread

20 to 100+ ft. × 15 to 80 ft.

Palm
Washingtonia filifera

Many people enjoy palm trees, but gardeners sometimes try to plant them in areas for which they are not suited. It is important to consider the hardiness zone of your area. Washington palm is considered hardy in Zones 8 and 9, and in temperatures as low as 12 degrees Fahrenheit, but can be damaged by prolonged temperatures below 25 degrees Fahrenheit. Zone 8 has winter temperatures of 10 to 20 degrees Fahrenheit. If the temperature remains there twenty-four or more hours, however, the Washington palm can have trouble. If you live in either Zone 7b, 8a, or 8b, decide how much of a gamble you are willing to take. Planting palms in Texas is "gardening on the edge." See page 246 for more information on palms.

Other Common Names
Washington Palm, Desert Fan Palm, and California Fan Palm

Bloom Period and Seasonal Color
Evergreen fan-shaped fronds in grayish green.

Mature Height × Spread
30 to 45 ft. × 5 to 15 ft.

When, Where, and How to Plant
Plant in early spring—after any possible frost date has passed—or early summer. For planting in Zone 8, select protected sunny areas. Washington palm requires a well-drained soil. It will adapt to a rather wide range of soil types, but do not plant in poorly drained spots. Washington palm may have a larger-than-normal rootball for its height. If your selection is in a container larger than 20 gallons—or if it is box-balled—have it planted by a landscape contractor. Plant the larger sizes in Zone 8. To plant smaller container sizes, select a sunny, well-drained location, and loosen the soil in an area wider than the soilball. Dig the planting hole only soilball deep, remove the plant from the container, and install it. Backfill with loosened soil, water thoroughly, and apply root stimulator. After planting is completed, mulch with 3 to 4 in. of bark mulch. Stake temporarily if necessary.

Growing Tips
Water as needed to prevent total soil dryness, but don't overwater. Fertilize twice a year, once in early spring as new growth emerges, and once in the fall. Apply a premium-quality, long-lasting, slow-release 3:1:2 ratio lawn fertilizer (such as 15-5-10 or 21-7-14). Water thoroughly after each application.

Care
Prune to remove dead leaves. This plant has no serious pests. To prevent root rot and suffocation, make sure your selected planting location drains well.

Companion Planting and Design
Palm trees are large dominant landscape plants, so place them carefully in the landscape or they may overpower the garden. In suitable locations, Washington palm can be used as avenue plantings, for lining drives, for framing structures, as specimens, or in groups. Palms do well in containers or planters or serve well as accents in swimming pool areas or entry courts.

I Suggest
Look at palms while visiting our Gulf Coast, then look for plantings away from the coast and decide if their "look" is desirable in your location and application. Plant palms only after you become familiar with their characteristics and hardiness.

Purple Leaf Plum

Prunus cerasifera

When, Where, and How to Plant

Plant container-grown trees successfully year-round. The best planting times are fall, winter, and early spring. While purple leaf plum will tolerate a wide range of growing conditions, it prefers moist, well-drained, fertile soil. Plant in full sun with well-drained soil. Don't plant in shady spots, or in locations that are damp-to-wet or dry. Loosen existing soil wider than rootball width, but dig the planting hole rootball deep and no deeper. Remove tree from the container and place in the hole. Backfill with the loose soil, water thoroughly, and apply a root stimulator. Mulch bare soil with 3 to 4 in. of bark after planting is completed. Temporarily stake if needed.

Growing Tips

Water if necessary to prevent soil dryness. Fertilize purple leaf plums four times a year—once as new growth begins, ten weeks later, again in the following ten weeks, and once during the fall. Apply a premium-quality, long-lasting, slow-release 3:1:2 ratio lawn fertilizer (such as 15-5-10, 18-6-12, and 21-7-14) according to label directions. Water after each fertilizer application.

Care

Prune to remove dead branches and twigs, or shape in very early spring. Fireblight may occur. Peach tree borers may pay an unwelcome visit to unhealthy trees. To prevent this problem, keep trees in a healthy condition.

Companion Planting and Design

Purple leaf plum adds great color to patios, decks, and gazebos. It may also be grown in large containers or planters. If you plant it in groups, be sure to space adequately to allow each plant to reach its maximum spread for your area. Due to their small size, these trees may be located rather close to structures, walks, and drives without damage. Be sure not to place so close to a structure as to deform the tree.

I Suggest

Visit areas during spring flower trails and note the bloom of purple leaf plums. Observe their colorful foliage through the growing season, and then decide if the bloom color, size, and shape (plus the purple leaves) are desirable in your landscape. Make notes to help you decide which variety you prefer for your personal landscape.

Purple leaf plums may be used in almost any application where you want a small to medium ornamental tree in a sunny location. By properly selecting, locating, planting, and maintaining purple leaf plum, you and your family can enjoy its beauty for several years. The neighbors, visitors, and people passing by may also enjoy these trees because they put on a rather striking show all summer long with their leaf color displayed most intensely in full sun. If you are seeking spring-to-fall color for your landscape, take a look at purple leaf plum. When visiting gardens, look for name tags or ask which variety of purple leaf plum is being grown. Look for these at gardens and/or nurseries: 'Atropurpurea', 'Newport', 'Thundercloud', and 'Krauter Vesuvius'. Purple leaf plum is hardy statewide.

Other Common Names

Flowering Plum, Ornamental Plum

Bloom Period and Seasonal Color

Spring blooms in white and purple; purple foliage season long.

Mature Height × Spread

15 to 25 ft. × 10 to 20 ft.

Sweet Bay Magnolia
Magnolia virginiana

Nothing beats the smell of magnolias blooming during late spring and summer. Gardeners have enjoyed sweet bay magnolia—along with its much larger cousin, M. grandiflora, or Southern magnolia—for decades. Unlike Southern magnolia, which often dominates the home landscape, sweet bay blends into the landscape. It works well in limited spaces where an ornamental tree is desired. One question some callers to my radio shows ask is, "How do I grow grass under my Southern magnolia?" The answer is, "You don't." With sweet bay magnolia, the answer is: "No problem—if it's St. Augustinegrass." Sweet bay is native to fertile, deep, moist soils along creeks and streams and in swamps and low woodlands. It usually does best in the eastern half of Texas. Sweet bay magnolia is hardy statewide.

Other Common Names
Swamp Bay Magnolia, Swamp Magnolia

Bloom Period and Seasonal Color
Spring to summer fragrant blooms in creamy white. Cherry red seeds in fall. Semi-evergreen to evergreen foliage.

Mature Height × Spread
20 to 40 ft. × 15 to 25 ft.

When, Where, and How to Plant
Plant container-grown selections anytime, but I wouldn't plant during our summers or midwinter. Early fall or spring are great planting times. If you are using them as specimens, plant these beauties in moist-to-damp but not wet areas. They tend to do better when protected from our hot afternoon sun and southwesterly summer winds. If you have a poorly-drained spot, or one that tends to stay damp, try sweet bay. When planted as a specimen, place in a location that is easy to water. Loosen the soil wider than the soilball and dig the planting hole soilball deep. Remove the plant from the container and place in the hole. Backfill with loose soil, water thoroughly, and apply a root stimulator. Mulch with 4 in. of pine bark mulch. Plant in beds the same way, but in improved soil. Stake if necessary.

Growing Tips
A moist soil is very important to successful long-term growth of sweet bay. These trees are not drought tolerant. Maintain a moist soil—do not let the soil become dry. Fertilize three times a year with a premium-quality, long-lasting, granular azalea fertilizer according to label directions. Make the first application as new leaves emerge. Reapply in ten weeks and once again during early fall. Water thoroughly after each fertilizer application.

Care
Prune only if necessary to shape or remove dead or damaged branches. There are no pests.

Companion Planting and Design
This is definitely not an ornamental tree for hot, dry locations. It works well in large beds of groundcover or low-growing shrubs. Cultural requirements are similar to azaleas, and sweet bay will do well planted among them.

I Suggest
The best use of sweet bay in Texas is usually east of I-45 because the soils tend to be acidic and the area receives more rain than other areas. There are exceptions, so check with your local retailer to help determine if sweet bay magnolia is a candidate for your landscape.

Weeping Willow
Salix babylonica

When, Where, and How to Plant

The best planting times are fall and early spring. I wouldn't plant in midsummer. Babylon, as well as other species/varieties of weeping willow, does best in moist to damp soil. Do not plant in heavily shaded locations, in spots that tend to dry out, or in those that are difficult to water. Select a full sun location with consistently adequate moisture (including during July, August, and September). Loosen a planting area wider than the soilball. Dig the planting hole no deeper than the soilball. Remove the tree from the container and place in the hole. Backfill with loosened soil, water thoroughly, and apply a root stimulator. Mulch bare soil with 4 in. of bark mulch.

Growing Tips

Keep moist at all times during the active growing season; maintaining a thick mulch layer will greatly aid in soil moisture retention. Weeping willow responds with vigor to fertilization. Apply a premium-quality, long-lasting, slow-release 3:1:2 ratio lawn fertilizer (such as 21-7-14, 19-5-9, or 18-6-12) according to label directions. Begin your fertilizing program as soon as new growth begins in the spring. Reapply ten weeks later, again in ten weeks, and once during the fall season. Water thoroughly after each fertilizer application.

Care

Prune during establishment and in the early years to produce a straight trunk. Little pruning is needed thereafter. The fast-growing weeping willow often has die back or dead branches. Remove dead wood as it presents itself. Aphids and thrips may occasionally visit, but they usually aren't a concern. Borers may hit unhealthy trees. Tree health is the best control.

Companion Planting and Design

Use this striking tree very sparingly in the landscape. Pick planting spots carefully, and don't locate near known sewage lines, homes, walks, or drives. Willows have fibrous roots that may invade neighboring garden beds. They are best used as accents.

I Suggest

It's important to know the ultimate heights and widths of the various varieties available before you purchase them. Varieties include 'Wisconsin', 'Pendula', 'Golden', 'Snake', 'Corkscrew' and 'Globe'. Some varieties tend to be weak growers exhibiting weak wood and die back.

The original home of weeping willow is northern China. It's a striking tree that dominates both the spot it's growing in and the eye of those viewing. Weeping willow will grow in areas of poorly drained or damp soils where almost no other tree—with the exception of bald cypress—will grow. It isn't picky about soil types, as long as there is adequate moisture. This is a water-loving tree. Do not use it in a Xeriscape landscape application. Its root system is relatively shallow and voracious. Weeping willow should not be located in areas where plants compete for moisture or space. It is a relatively short-lived tree, in the fifteen to twenty-five year range, and some as short as ten years. Weeping willow is hardy statewide.

Other Common Name
Babylon Weeping Willow

Bloom Period and Seasonal Color
Fall foliage in yellow.

Mature Height × Spread
40 to 60 ft. × 30 to 40 ft.

Vines *for Texas*

Many Texas gardeners do not give a second thought to vines. Well, fellow Texans, think again. When properly selected and placed, vines will provide amazing accents to any location or structure in our landscapes. There is hardly anything more appealing than vines growing over pergolas, gazebos, arbors, or fences. Certain vines provide springtime flushes of colors. Others offer season-long bloom. Still others, such as Virginia creeper, *Parthenocissus quinquefolia*, and Boston ivy, *Parthenocissus tricuspidata*, provide outstanding fall foliage color. Not only beautiful, but also functional, vines make excellent groundcovers that help hold the soil together and look great while cascading over embankments and walls.

English Ivy

Far-Reaching Benefits

Most vines are low maintenance, provided the gardener has made the right choice for the given garden location and the landscape need. Deciduous, fast-growing vines provide a quick shade for summer, yet drop their foliage to make way for the desired winter sun. Evergreen vines are selected for screening. Fast growing vines often demand constant pruning for control, yet the more one prunes, the more they grow!

Vines have energy conservation possibilities as well. If you have a very narrow lot and no shade tree, vines placed on growing structures (such as trellises), can greatly reduce the heat in your home. You will be more comfortable during the summer and save money.

Vines have interesting climbing mechanisms, including twining structures, holdfast structures, and tendrils. If you are a town house/apartment/condo dweller or live in a location that has limited growing space, try vines. Grow lots of them in small vertical spaces. Experiment with growing colorful, fragrant plantings of vines on ornamental iron, cast aluminum, or wooden structures. Use vines as screens for privacy, ornamentation, traffic direction, or noise reduction.

Vines grown on rough-cut timber arbors create a lovely, secluded, summertime spot. Visit an example of this at the Stephen F. Austin State University campus, behind the agricultural building in the Mast Arboretum. Rough-cut heavy lumber has been used to create an interesting structure covered with vines.

Wisteria

This pleasant combination works well in home landscapes, offering a naturalistic character. Vines offer a green lushness in a small space because they grow vertically and do not require very much "ground room."

Most vines perform nicely when planted in well-drained soils. If the soil is poorly drained, take the time to improve it before planting. Organic matter—compost (purchased or home-made), brown sphagnum peat moss, and various aged wood by-products—is the best material to improve any soil. A combination of these three components works best.

Over-Achievers

Most vines are fast growing and require little or no fertilization. Most vine selections have few insects and diseases, and these can be easily eliminated. Leaf eaters such as grasshoppers and caterpillars are usually easily controlled and normally cycle out quickly. Sucking insects on new growth, such as aphids, are managed with insecticides for sucking insects. Spider mites, which may appear with summer heat, may be prevented or corrected with a miticide.

Most likely the biggest challenge in growing vines will be over-achievement, and the need to keep their growth in desired bounds. Make sure you understand a vine's growth habit, including how aggressive and invasive it may become, before inviting it into your landscape. For example, *Wisteria sinensis* is great when used by itself on a strong structure away from the house, but I wouldn't want it growing on my house or in my trees. It can overpower some locations, and the next thing you know, it's chainsaw time!

I have included six families of vines or vining plants in my selections for this chapter. If your main interest is bloom, you will find some good recommendations on my list. Have a good time with vines in your landscape.

Boston Ivy
Parthenocissus tricuspidata

Find yourself admiring the ivy-clad halls of Harvard and Yale? Boston ivy gets all the credit, as it is the ivy of choice at Ivy League schools. With bright-green, maple leaf shaped foliage throughout the growing season, it's most spectacular in the fall when it takes on vivid shades of orange and red. It's an outstanding fall color plant. A cousin of Boston ivy is Virginia creeper or P. quinquefolia. The standard Virginia creeper gives outstanding rich red fall color and clings to walls or trellises. The variety 'Engelmannii' has smaller leaves than the native Virginia creeper and is also less vigorous. It clings well to masonry walls with a fall color that is deep burgundy red and with small fruits that birds love. Boston ivy is hardy statewide.

Bloom Period and Seasonal Color
Fall foliage in orange and red.

Mature Length
Vining to 40 ft.

When, Where, and How to Plant
Extremely hardy in Texas, Boston ivy may be planted year-round, though the best times are early spring and early fall. It tends to perform best with morning sun and some shade from the hot, west afternoon sun—though I have seen some plantings that worked successfully in full sun, planted right on brick walls facing directly west. Boston ivy can be grown in woodland locations as well as in prepared beds. If training it on structures, prepare your soil well, blending approximately 3 in. of organic matter into the top 3 in. of the existing soil. Plant one gallon containers of ivy in the prepared bed no deeper than in the container. Firm the mixed soil thoroughly around the new plants, water, and apply root stimulator. Cover with approximately 3 in. of bark mulch.

Growing Tips
Water as necessary to prevent soil dryness. Maintaining a 3- to 4-in. layer of mulch will help hold moisture. Fertilize in early spring as new growth begins. Try a 3:1:2 ratio lawn fertilizer (such as 15-5-10, 19-5-9, or 21-7-14). Remember to use premium-quality, long-lasting, slow-release lawn fertilizer, follow directions, and water thoroughly after each application. Most vines such as Boston ivy are fast growing, so do not overfertilize.

Care
Prune as necessary, training the ivy to the shape or form you desire. If you plant Boston ivy on walls, yearly pruning will be necessary to prevent it from growing into the wooden part of your home. In late summer, spider mites may visit Boston ivy in hot, full-sun locations. Consult your local garden center for controls.

Companion Planting and Design
Overpowering if put in small locations, Boston ivy needs adequate room to grow. It may be used as a groundcover, is excellent on trellises, and may also be grown directly on brick walls.

I Suggest
Because of its shading ability, try Boston ivy on any structure you wish to cool in the summer yet warm in the winter.

Confederate Star Jasmine

Trachelospermum jasminoides

When, Where, and How to Plant

The best time to plant confederate star jasmine is in the early spring in locations that have moist, well-drained soils. Choose full sun to partial shade spots that receive a minimum of six hours of full sun. Do not plant in full shade locations or difficult-to-water spots. Plant in well-prepared beds enriched with organic matter. Incorporate approximately 4 in. of organic matter into the top 4 in. of the existing soil. Install in the prepared bed no deeper than the plant was grown in the container. Firm the mix, water thoroughly, and apply root stimulator. After planting is complete, mulch bare soil with approximately 3 in. of bark mulch.

Growing Tips

Water as necessary to prevent soil dryness. Mulching 3 to 4 in. deep will help conserve soil moisture, and drip irrigation is beneficial. Fertilize as new growth begins in the spring with a long-lasting, slow-release rose fertilizer.

Care

Prune and train as required to obtain desired effect. No pests or insects normally bother confederate star jasmine.

Companion Planting and Design

This beauty may be used in any landscape location. I enjoy it as a backdrop on growing structures or with perennials such as lantana and ruellia planted below it. It's a good accent in a large container with a frame on decks, poolside, and on patios. Good choice for framing and accenting gates and entrances. Handsome dark green foliage, fast growing, with outstanding fragrance.

I Suggest

If you live in Zone 8 or 9, I recommend trying a trellis or small 4 × 6 ft. ground planting of star jasmine for both color and fragrance.

Confederate star jasmine is worth seeking out, especially in Zone 8 or 9. In Zone 7b, try planting in a protected location. I have grown and enjoyed it in Zone 7b for several years. For an excellent spring show that is quite fragrant, grow confederate star jasmine on trellises. I have fashioned mine with treated yellow pine and galvanized poultry netting. Confederate star jasmine may also be grown as a groundcover, and I especially like it on various garden structures. Try one or more plants in large containers planted at the base of a structure on a deck, balcony, patio, or other sunny location.

Other Common Names
Star Jasmine, Confederate Jasmine

Bloom Period and Seasonal Color
Spring star-shaped blooms in white.

Mature Length
60 to 80 ft.

English Ivy
Hedera helix

Probably the most recognizable and commonly used vine in our home landscapes is the English ivy. With over sixty varieties, it is grown in all areas of Texas. English ivy typically performs best in a shady to semi-shady location. It will also grow in full-sun eastern spots where there is no reflected heat, the soil is well prepared, and adequate moisture is maintained. A word of caution: though beautiful in the landscape, English ivy can be an enemy of your trees. A tree can be crippled if English ivy covers its canopy, blocking out sunlight and adding weight to branches that could result in damage during wind storms or ice storms. Grow and train English ivy on specialized structures as a groundcover. It is hardy statewide.

Other Common Name
Ivy

Bloom Period and Seasonal Color
Evergreen foliage year-round.

Mature Length
Vining to 60 ft.

When, Where, and How to Plant
Plant in early spring or early fall. For best results, plant English ivy in well-prepared beds where it will receive morning sun and afternoon shade or dappled sun throughout the day. Incorporate approximately 3 in. of high-quality organic matter (including brown sphagnum peat moss) into the top 3 in. of the existing soil. After bed preparation, plant in a bed no deeper than they were grown in the containers. Firm the soil well, water thoroughly, apply root stimulator, and mulch 3 in. deep.

Growing Tips
Water as necessary to maintain a moist growing condition. Fertilize as new growth begins in the spring with a long-lasting, slow-release lawn fertilizer. The 3:1:2 ratio fertilizers (such as 21-7-14, 18-6-12, or 15-5-10) work well. Remember to water thoroughly after each application. Maintain approximately 2 to 3 in. of bark mulch.

Care
Prune as necessary to maintain and train English ivy. Pests can be avoided by properly choosing your planting location. Bacterial leaf spot may visit ivy in high humidity spots where there is little air movement. Spider mites may visit in hot, dry locations. Visit your local garden center for control possibilities.

Companion Planting and Design
Ivy may be grown as an espalier—trained by routine pruning in desired patterns and designs against a flat, vertical surface. English ivy makes pleasing evergreen forms on many different types of growing structures, including trellises, arbors, fences, and archways. Its lush, evergreen foliage often serves as an underplanting groundcover for larger shrubs and to fill in void bed areas. Ivy is very adaptable to shaded planters and containers. English ivy is welcomed in cottage type gardens.

I Suggest
English ivy is a good soil retention plant in heavily shaded areas. Visit local retailers in the spring and become familiar with the different varieties of English ivy and its cousins before deciding which ones to plant. English ivy offers many varying characteristics such as small leaf, large leaf, curly leaf, needle-point leaf, and variegated leaves.

When, Where, and How to Plant

Fig ivy does best planted in early spring, especially in locations where its hardiness is marginal. Do not plant in total shade. To achieve best results, start your fig ivy in well-prepared beds. Incorporate approximately 3 in. of organic matter into the top 3 in. of the native soil. After bed preparation is complete, remove your selection of fig ivy from its container and plant in the improved bed no deeper than originally grown. Firm the soil well around your new transplants, water thoroughly, and apply root stimulator. Mulch finished plantings with 2 in. of bark mulch.

Growing Tips

Water as necessary to maintain a moist soil. Maintain soil moisture year-round with 2 in. or more of mulch. Do not allow fig ivy to get totally dry, but do not keep it wet. Fertilize in the spring when new growth begins. 3:1:2 ratio long-lasting lawn fertilizers (such as 21-7-14, 19-5-9, or 15-5-10) work well when applied according to label directions.

Care

Prune to improve appearance, to encourage new growth, and to maintain desired direction of growth. There are no serious pest or disease problems.

Companion Planting and Design

Creeping fig is quite attractive in our landscapes, as it clings neatly to its support, offering a green, vertical mat of fine-textured foliage. It is outstanding on native stone walls, forming a wall covering. A fig vine can be grown on a wire frame shaped to a desired form and filled with sphagnum moss, with the vine growing out of the moss. Perennials such as lantana may be planted in areas where this small textured vine grows. Fig ivy is tolerant of a wide range of growing conditions, being drought and heat tolerant.

I Suggest

A topiary is a plant clipped and trained into an ornamental shape. Use fig ivy to create a topiary on a preformed structure in the landscape—especially in Zones 8b and 9.

Fig ivy makes a very interesting pattern if grown on structures like rock and brick. I've seen it grown successfully on a stone wall around an older home. On some occasions there was winter damage, but the plant always recovered rapidly. Try fig ivy if you are looking for a covering vine that does not require much room. It should grow relatively well in protected areas of Zone 7b. Try F. pumila varieties: 'Minima', 'Quercifolia', and 'Variegata'. Fig ivy is hardy in Zones 8a to 9b.

Other Common Names
Creeping Fig, Fig Vine

Bloom Period and Seasonal Color
Evergreen foliage.

Mature Length
Vining to 40 ft.

Japanese Honeysuckle

Lonicera japonica

When I was growing up in Brownwood, Texas, my mother always had some honeysuckle growing on a trellis outside the bedroom windows. My sisters and I always enjoyed the sweet fragrance. Keep in mind that Japanese honeysuckle is an aggressive vining plant. It has, in some areas, escaped cultivation—almost becoming an invasive pest. When grown on structures, it does well. Often seen growing on fences, it lends itself well to breaking up harsh structures. Japanese honeysuckle will also work on steep slopes where erosion control is necessary. Japanese honeysuckle is hardy statewide.

Other Common Names
Hall's Honeysuckle, Green Honeysuckle, Purple Leaf Honeysuckle

Bloom Period and Seasonal Color
Spring to fall blooms in white, yellow, or purple.

Mature Length
Twining to 20 ft.

When, Where, and How to Plant
Extremely winter hardy in Texas, Japanese honeysuckle may be planted twelve months out of the year—though the best time is early spring. While Japanese honeysuckle will grow in almost any type of soil and soil condition, to achieve good results, plant in prepared beds. For Japanese honeysuckle, the best way to improve your bed is to incorporate 3 in. of organic matter into the top 3 in. of the existing soil. After bed improvement is complete, remove your selection from its container. Install it in the bed no deeper than it was grown in the container and firm the soil well. Water thoroughly, apply root stimulator, and cover the bare ground with 3 in. of bark mulch.

Growing Tips
For best results, water as necessary to maintain a moist growing condition. Fertilize as new growth begins in the spring with a long-lasting, slow-release 3:1:2 ratio lawn fertilizer (such as 15-5-10 or 18-6-12) and water thoroughly. Due to its fast rate of growth, Japanese honeysuckle may not require fertilizer. Maintain soil moisture with a 3 in. layer of bark mulch year-round.

Care
Prune and train as necessary to achieve the form that you desire. Normally no insects or diseases are a problem when growing Japanese honeysuckle.

Companion Planting and Design
Remember that Japanese honeysuckle is aggressive. Plant Japanese honeysuckle where it will have room to grow, be easy to maintain, yet not overgrow its location. It is outstanding in open, full-sun locations, planted by itself or on large structures. It thrives on large arbors, providing wonderful shade, fragrance, and blooms. It makes an excellent evergreen, vertical screen. Do not plant on your home or trees.

I Suggest
The native coral honeysuckle is one of my favorite members of this family. (For more information on coral honeysuckle, see page 98.)

When, Where, and How to Plant

Wisteria may be planted twelve months out of the year, though the best time to plant is early fall. It will grow well in full sun or in dappled sun/shade. Wisteria will grow in almost any soil, but to achieve best results, plant in well-prepared beds on strong structures. Caution: do not plant wisteria on your home or trees. The best way to prepare your bed is to incorporate 3 in. of organic matter into the top 3 in. of the existing soil. After bed improvement is complete, remove your selection of wisteria from its container and install in the new bed no deeper than it was growing in the container. Firm the soil well, water thoroughly, apply root stimulator, and cover bare soil with 3 in. of bark mulch.

Growing Tips

Water as necessary to prevent soil dryness. No fertilization is usually required. Growing wisteria in alkaline soils may result in yellowing or chlorotic (lacking iron) leaves; apply iron and sulphur as necessary to correct this situation. Maintain 3 to 4 in. of bark mulch year-round.

Care

Prune wisteria to prevent it from taking over other plants in confined locations. To achieve the "tree" form wisteria, prune severely for several years. Such forms will revert rather quickly to a vine if not maintained. Wisteria normally has no serious pest or disease problems in Texas. When properly trained, wisteria adds outstanding early-spring fragrance and a color blast to the home landscape. Because wisteria has been known to literally take over other plantings, plant it on structures that are separate from other landscape locations. Consider constructing a freestanding arbor and covering it with one or more wisteria plants. I do not recommend any companion plantings with wisteria. Wisteria is elegant planted in large planters and lends itself to a naturalistic arbor—providing summer shade and interesting bare winter vines overhead.

I Suggest

'Purpurea' is great for fragrance and color, and has interesting grape cluster shaped blooms in early spring. It's hard to beat.

Wisteria is an important part of Texas' spring flowers—along with azaleas, dogwoods, redbuds, and spring-blooming bulbs—and is a vining plant that has been long used in Texas landscapes. It is often found growing in abandoned home sites, as well as in some of our most current gardens. In our environment, it will grow in all locations, including soils that are heavy clay as well as those that are extremely light and sandy. After establishment, it will grow with very little overall maintenance. Choose wisteria in spring when it is in bloom at your area retailers. Varieties include 'Alba', 'Caroline', 'Purpurea', and 'Rosea'. Wisteria is hardy statewide.

Other Common Name
Chinese Wisteria

Bloom Period and Seasonal Color
Spring blooms in blue, purple, white, and rose.

Mature Length
Vining to 35 ft.

Dale Groom's Principles of Xeriscaping

As sure as the sun rises and sets, we Texans know that July and August will be hot and dry. It's not only hot and dry during these months, but the hot weather often begins in June and may continue on through September.

By employing a method of landscaping known as Xeriscape, Texans may enjoy interesting landscapes and reduce water usage. The term Xeriscape originated in Denver, Colorado, where the landscape, while attractive, is considered relatively dry. The prefix "xeri" means dry. Combined with "scape," Xeriscape means dry landscape. Xeriscaping involves landscaping with low water usage once plants are established—but Xeriscaping does not mean using only cactus, yucca, agave or all native plants.

The Basics

- Have a plan before shopping. This plan or design should include selecting plants that, after initial establishment, are well-adapted for local use with a relatively low water usage. These plants should also be known to have minimal, if any, pest and disease problems. If you are not aware of this detailed information, be sure to ask your local nursery before choosing the plants in your design.

- Perform thorough soil preparation prior to planting. If you cannot provide what a plant needs in the way of soil preparation—don't plant it! This book provides detailed information on the soil needs for over 170 plants for Texas landscapes.

- Install your plants properly and at the recommended time for relatively quick establishment. Fall is the best time for initial planting of all winter-hardy woody landscape plants in Texas. The statement, "Fall is for planting," is very true.

- Mulch, mulch, and mulch! Mulch after initial planting and continue doing it on a year-round basis. Most of the soil around my plants is covered with a 3 to 4 in. layer of bark mulch. Mulch is a layer or a blanket of material on top of the ground. I am frequently asked, "What is the best mulch?" My answer always is, "The one you use." No mulch is good if you are not using it. I prefer bark mulches and other organic mulches over materials such as pea gravel, lava rock, or other crushed stone products.

- Properly maintain your plants. This includes fertilizing, pruning, controlling pests (including weeds, insects, and diseases), maintaining your selected mulch layer, and watering wisely. Drip irrigation systems are more efficient than standard systems for landscape plantings. However, standard sprinkler irrigation systems may also be used, especially in lawn areas. Water only when plants need irrigating, then do so thoroughly. Don't water on a preset schedule, but do water when plants need a drink.

It's always important to remember two words: "once established." When you read or hear about plants that are drought tolerant or that will fit into a Xeriscape, remember that most plants need, require, and benefit from a little help during initial establishment.

Just because a plant is drought tolerant and will work in a Xeriscape, that doesn't automatically mean it is winter hardy in your zone or would do well in your type of native soil. It's always wise to ask your local nursery if a plant is winter hardy and does well in our native soils before purchasing and planting.

The following is a list of plants I recommend for Texas Xeriscapes. Remember, Texas is diverse, so check with your local nursery or contact me if you have a question about specific plants for Xeriscapes.

Annuals

Bachelor Buttons

Black-Eyed Susan

Bluebonnet

Coneflower (Clasping-leaf)

Copper Plant

Coreopsis (Plains)

Indian Blanket

Phlox (*Phlox drummondii*)

Texas Bluebells

Bulbs

Canna

Crinum

Daylily

Iris (Bearded and Louisiana)

Grasses

Bermuda (Common, Tex turf 10™ and Coastal)

Buffalo

Fountain Grass

Maidengrass

Pampas Grass

Groundcovers

Artemisia

Jasmine (Asian and Confederate Star)

Liriope

Ophiopogon

Prostrate Rosemary

Santolina

Sedum

Wintercreeper

Vinca Major

Perennials

Artemisia

Bouncing Bet

Butterfly Weed

Coneflower (Purple)

Coreopsis (Lanceleaf and Sunray)

Evening Primrose (Buttercup)

Four-O'-Clock

Gaillardia

Gayfeather

Lantana

Mexican Firebush

Mexican Hat

Phlox (*Phlox pilosa*, Fragrant or Prairie)

Plumbago (White and Blue)

Prairie Verbena

Purple Coneflower

Ruellia (Mexican or Summer Petunia)

Salvia/Sage (Scarlet *coccinea*, Mealy Blue *farinacea*, Mexican bush *leucantha*, Autumn *greggii*)

Skullcap

Roses

Species Roses

Shrubs

Abelia

Agarito

Althea or Rose-of-Sharon

American Beautyberry

Arborvitae

Barberry

Boxwood (Winter Gem and Japanese)

Butterfly Bush

Cacti

Cenizo or Texas Sage

Cherry Laurel

Crape Myrtle

Elaeagnus

Evergreen Sumac

Flowering Quince

Forsythia

Gray Cotoneaster

Holly (Burford, Dwarf Burford, Chinese Horned, Dwarf Chinese Horned, Willowleaf, Nellie R. Stevens, Carissa, Yaupon, Dwarf Yaupon, Possomhaw, and American)

Indian Hawthorne

Nandina (Domestica, Compacta, Harbor Dwarf, Gulf Stream, and Firepower)

Oleander

Palmetto

Pittosporum

Rosemary

Spirea

Texas Mountain Laurel

Vitex

Wax Myrtle

Wooly Butterfly Bush

Yucca

Trees

Ash (Texas and Green)

Bald Cypress

Bois 'd Arc/Osage Orange

Deodar Cedar

Desert Willow

Elm (Cedar and Lacebark)

Flowering Pear

Ginkgo

Golden Rain Tree

Juniper (Alligator, Ashe, Eastern Red, and Weeping)

Mesquite

Mexican Buckeye

Oak (Blackjack, Bur, Chinquapin, Chisos Red, Escarpment Live, Lacey, Live, Texas Red, and Vasey)

Parkinsonia/Paloverde

Pecan

Persimmon

Pine (Aleppo, Eldarica, Loblolly, Mexican Pinyon Slash)

Pistachio, Chinese and Texas

Poinciana

Redbud (*Cercis canadensis*, Texas and Oklahoma)

Vines

Boston Ivy

Carolina Jessamine/Jasmine

Honeysuckle (Coral, Flame, Hall's, and Purpurea)

English Ivy

Fig Ivy/Creeping Fig

Silverlace Vine

Trumpet Vine

Virginia Creeper

Wisteria (Chinese and Texas)

Deer Resistant Landscapes and Gardens

When I make personal appearances at various home and garden shows in Texas, I always have several questions regarding keeping Texas deer out of landscapes and specialty gardens.

Something to keep in mind on this topic is the fact that deer will eat almost anything if they are hungry enough. Wouldn't you? Most of the deer are whitetail that are doing the damage in Texas. The key words here, folks, are . . . "deer resistant" not "deer proof."

If you want to help keep them out of your area(s) of concern, do not feed them. This actually increases the damage to landscapes and gardens. Feeding them increases their numbers in your area, and the deer will prune your plants in addition to taking the food offered. Bottom line, don't feed the deer in your neighborhood because it also effects your neighbor's property.

Various types of fences may be used to prevent deer from visiting your gardens and landscape. Specific plans for them are available from local sources including the Extension Service, the Texas Parks and Wildlife Department, and retailers specializing in "game proof" fences. Certainly, it's up to you to fence or not. Done correctly, fences nearly always provide the desired results.

Judy and I live in rural South Van Zandt County and have whitetail deer in our woods. However, we have never experienced damage to our landscape and gardens from deer in the twenty-three years we have lived here. We have a sizeable outside dog that believes our property is his, too. He's a male Australian Shepard that even asks the birds to leave when they land on our property. I therefore contribute at least part of our success to our canine partner. Remember, dogs can be trained to provide all types of services for us.

Some Extra Help

In addition to plants, fences, and trained dogs, there are commercial aids available also. Following are some that are available. I'm neutral on their uses because I have not used them and can't testify to their effectiveness. Should you decide to try one, always read and follow label directions.

1. Plantskydd® Animal Repellent
2. Deer Off® Deer, Rabbit & Squirrel Repellent, Liquid
3. Plant Pro-Tec®, Garlic Oil Dispensers
4. Garlic Barrier® AG+
5. Repellx™ Deer Repellant, Systemic Tablets and Liquid

When using deer repellant products, it is best to utilize them before feeding habits are established.

The following is a list of deer "resistant" and not "deer proof" plants for Texas landscapes and gardens. Some are more resistant than others. Deer can't read nor do they respect your landscape and garden efforts. It is up to you to fence and plant less desirable plants to prevent the damage. This list should be an aid.

Deer Resistant Plants

Annuals and Perennials

Ageratum *Ageratum* spp.

Angel Trumpet, *Datura* spp.

Annual Sunflower *Helianthus annuus*

Artemisia *A. ludoviciana*

Autum Sage *Salvia greggii*

Beargrass *Nolina* spp.

Begonia *Begonia* spp.

Black-Eyed Susan *Rudbeckia hirta*

Blackfoot Daisy *Melampodium leucanthum*

Bluebonnet *Lupinus texensis*

Candytuft *Iberis sempervirens*

Cardinal Flower *Lobelia cardinalis*

Cedar Sage *Salvia roemeriana*

Chrysanthemum *Dendranthema* spp.

Columbine *Aquilegia* spp.

Copper Canyon Daisy *Tagetes lemonii*

Coreopsis *Coreopsis* spp.

Drummond's Skullcap *Scutellaria drummondii*

Cosmos *Cosmos bipinnatus*

Dusty Miller *Centaurea cineraria*

Flame Acanthus *Anisacanthus wrightii*

Four-O'-Clock *Mirabilis* spp.

Foxglove *Digitalis* spp.

Gayfether *Liatris* spp.

Hardy or Mallow Hibiscus *Hibiscus moscheutos*

Hummingbird Bush *Anisacanthus wrightii*

Indian Blanket *Gaillardia pulchella*

Indigo Spires *Salvia* spp.

Iris *Iris spp.*

Jerusalem sage *Phlomis fruticosa*

Lantana *Lantana horrida*

Larkspurs *Delphinium carolinianum*

Marigolds *Tagetes* spp.

Maximilian Sunflower *Helianthus maximiliani*

Mealy Blue Sage *Salvia farinacea*

Mexican Bush Sage *Salvia leucanthia*

Mexican Hat *Ratibida columnaris*

Mexican Mint Marigold *Tagetes*

Mountain Pink *Centaurium beyrichii*

Milkweeds *Asclepias* spp.

Nightshades *Solanum* spp.

Oxeye Daisy *Luecanthemum*

Penstemons *Penstemon* spp.

Periwinkle *Vinca rosea*

Pink Wood Sorrel *Oxalis drummondii*

Plumbago *Plumbago auriculata*

Prickly Pear Cactus *Opuntia lindheimeri*

Purple Cone Flower *Echinacea angustifolia*

Red Salvia *Salvia vanhouttei*

Rock Rose *Pavonia lasiopetala*

Rosemary *Rosemarinus officinalis*

Savory *Satureia* spp.

Snow-on-the-Mountain *Euphorbia marginata*

Snow-on-the-Prairie *Euphorbia bicolor*

Sedum *Sedum acre*

Texas Sage *Salvia texana*

Texas Betony *Stachys coccinea*

Wedelia *Wedelia triobata*

Verbena *Verbena* spp.

Yarrow *Achillea filipendulina*

Yellow Wood Sorrel *Oxalis dillenii*

Zexmenia *Wedelia hispida*

Zexmenia *Zexmenia hispida*

Zinnia *Zinnia* spp.

Bulbs

Hardy Red Amaryllis
   Hippeastrum × Johnsonii

Lily of the Nile *Agapanthus* spp.

Grasses

Gulf Muhley *Muhlenbergia capillaris*

Inland Sea Oats *Chasmanthium latifolium*

Lindhreimer's Muhley
   Muhlenbergia lindheimeri

Maidengrass *Miscanthus sinensis*

Pampas Grass *Cortaderia selloana*

Purple Fountain Grass *Pennisetum setaceum*

Groundcovers, Herbs and Ferns

Aaron's Beard *Hypericum calycinum*

Asian Jasmine *Trachelospermum asiaticum*

Carpet Bugle *Ajuga reptans*

Germander *Teucrium chamaedrys*

Gray Santolina *Santolina chamaecyparissus*

Green Santolina *S. virens*

Holly Fern *Cyrtomium falicatum*

Lemon Mint *Monarda citriodora*

Lavender *Lavandula* spp.

Maidenhair fern
   Adinatum capillus-verneris

Mexican Oregano *Poliomintha longifolia*

Mondo Grass *Ophiopogon japonica*

Sword Fern *Nephrolepis* spp.

Spearmint *Menta spicata*

Thyme *Thymus* spp.

Vinca *Vinca major*

Wood's Fern *Dryopteris* spp.

Shrubs

Abelia *Abelia* spp.

Acuba *Acuba japonica*

Autumn Sage *Salvia greggii*

Barberry *Berberis thunbergii*

Boxleaf Euonymus
   Euonymus japonica 'Microphylla'

Boxwood *Buxus microphylla*

Ceniza/Texas Sage *Leucopyllum* spp.

Cherry Laurel *Prunus caroliniana*

Cotoneaster *Cotoneaster* spp.

Damianita *Chrysactinia mexicana*

Deciduous or Possomhaw Holly
   Ilex decidua

Dwarf Chinese Holly *Ilex cornuta*

Eleagnus *Eleagnus* spp.

Evergreen Sumac *Rhus virens*

Fragrant Mimosa *Mimosa borealis*

Germander *Teucrium* spp.

Goldcup *Hypericum* spp.

Japanese Aralia *Arelia sieboldii*

Japanese Boxwood *Buxus microphylla*

Japanese Yew *Podocarpus macrophyllus*

Jerusalem Cherry
   Solanum pseudocapsicum

Juniper *Juniperus* spp.

Lavender *Lavandula* spp.

Mexican Buckeye *Ungnadia speciosa*

Mexican Silktassle *Garrya lindheimeri*

Nandina *Nandina* spp.

Oleander *Nerium* oleander

Pineapple Guava *Fijoa sellowiana*

Pomegranate *Punica granatum*

Pyracantha *Pyracantha coccinea*

Red-leaf or Japanese Barberry
   Berberis thunbergii

Reeve's Spirea *Spiraea reevesiana*

Rosemary *Rosmarinus officinalis*

Scotch Broom *Cytisus scoparius*

Texas Mountain Laurel *Sophora secundiflora*

Turks Cap
   Malvaviscus arboreus and *drummondii*

Wax Myrtle *Myrica cerifera*

Yaupon *Ilex vomitoria*

Yucca *Yucca* spp.

Large Shrubs, Small Trees

Desert Willow *Cilopsis linearis*

Eastern Redbud *Cercis canadensis*

Figs *Ficus* spp.

Flame Sumac *Rhus lanceolata*

Golden Leadball Tree *Leucana retusa*

Kidneywood *Eysenhardtia texana*

Roughleaf Dogwood *Cornus drummondii*

Texas Buckeye *Aesculus arguta*

Texas Persimmon *Diospyros texana*

Trees

Note: None are truly resistant when the unwanted visitors decide to rub on them for whatever purposes, including shaping up their antlers. It is usually best to construct individual protective barriers around any desired tree not protected inside your yard. These structures may include steel posts on three or four corners with panels or wire installed on them to prevent deer from reaching the protected tree(s). This is especially important for newly planted and young trees.

Vines

Carolina Jessamine *Gelsemium sempervirens*

Clematis *Clematis* spp.

Cross-vine *Bignonia capreolata*

Confederate Star Jasmine *Trachelospermum jasminoides*

Grasshopper Resistant Plants

On my radio show, through my garden columns, and during public appearances in Texas, people ask me for assistance in controlling grasshoppers in their lawns, gardens, and landscapes. Yes, there are plenty of products to "kill" these plant eating pests but I have not achieved control nor have fellow gardeners. True, there are wizards who claim to have . . . the answer.

There are many varieties of grasshoppers so they don't all have the same eating habits, rates of growing, or reproducing. One shoe does not fit all in controlling grasshoppers. For example, some bait products are attached to bran, and all grasshoppers do not eat bran. Because of this, products attached to bran are not effective on these specific grasshoppers.

With the assistance of horticulturists and master gardeners, I have compiled a list of plants that have proven (by experience) to be grasshopper resistant.

Keep in mind that this list of grasshopper resistant plants is based on subjective observations, and not scientific studies. Depending on grasshopper populations and available "food" for the pests, plants that normally have light damage may be consumed more heavily.

Normally Not Preferred

American Beautyberry

Artemisia

Bouncing Bet

Bridal Wreath Spirea

Bur Oak

Camellia

Carolina Jessamine(Jasmine)

Chaltapa

Chinese Pistachio

Confederate Star Jasmine

Coralberry

Crossvine

Crape Myrtle

Dwarf Burning Bush

Euonymus (Evergreen varieties)

Evergreen Sumac

Fig Ivy

Flame Acanthus

Elderica or Afghan Pine

Fall Aster

Forsythia

Gaura (Whirling Butterfly)

Goldenrod

Gregg Dahlia

Indian Hawthorne

Junipers

Lacebark Elm

Lantana

Lemon Mint

Leyland Cypress

'Lady In Red' Salvia

Live Oak

Loblolly Pine

Maximillian Sunflower

Mealy Blue Sage

Mexican Mint Marigold

Mexican Oregano

Obedient Plant

Oleander

Passion Vine

Pavonia (Rock Rose)

Perennial Verbena

Portulaca (Moss Rose)

Privet

Purslane

Pygmy Barberry

Rosemary

Rue

Sage (Autumn)

Scott's Pine

Shumard Red Oak

St John's Wort (Hypericum)

Texas Bluebell (Lisianthus)

Texas Red Oak

Turk's Cap

Vitex

Wax Myrtle

Wegelia

'Winter Gem' Boxwood

Wisteria

Yaupon Holly (Standard and Dwarf)

Consumed

Althea (Rose-of-Sharon)

Amaryllis

Bachelor Buttons

Bush Honeysuckle

Butterfly Bush (*Buddleia*)

Canna

Carissa Holly

Cherry Laurel

Daylily

Dianthus (Pinks)

Dwarf Burford Holly

Elaeagnus

Flowering Quince

Hardy Hibiscus

Iris

Liriope

Mondo Grass

Moss Rose

Mums

Needlepoint Holly

Nellie R. Stevens Holly

Passion Vine

Peach

Privet

Purslane

Roses

Russian Sage

Tradescantia

Wegelia

Wisteria

Texas Climatic Conditions

Climatic Conditions

The climate of Texas is relatively mild. The United States Department of Agriculture divides the state into four hardiness zones based on the average minimum temperatures experienced during the winter. One-half of our state is in Zones 8 and 9, with average winter lows of 10 to 20 degrees Fahrenheit in Zone 8. Coastal areas around Houston, Corpus Christi, and Padre Island are in Zone 9 and experience average winter lows of 20 to 30 degrees. Our relatively mild climate allows a year-round growing season for flower and vegetable gardens, particularly in the southern two-thirds of the state. Zone 7 may reach lows of 10 to 0 degrees and Zone 6 in our Panhandle may reach 0 to -10 degrees. Texas is, overall, considered to have a relatively mild winter climate.

Average Freeze Dates

Last freeze dates and first freeze dates are of great importance to many garden activities, but it is important to understand that no one knows when the last or first freeze will actually occur during a particular year. Average dates can be helpful, but freezes can and do occur before the average first freeze date and after the average last freeze date. You must use experience and information from knowledgeable local individuals (friends, professional horticulturists, local nurseries, and your County Agent with the Texas Agricultural Extension Service) when making planting decisions.

The first frosts usually occur in northwest Texas in early November, in areas around Dallas/Fort Worth in mid- to late November, and along the Gulf Coast in early to mid-December. Experience shows that first freezes are more likely to occur later rather than earlier than these average dates.

Average last freeze dates are particularly important to gardeners who want to set out tender vegetables and bedding plants in the spring. North Texas freezes generally end in late March, freezes in areas south of Austin usually end in early to mid-March, and freezes along the Gulf Coast generally end in mid- to late February. Late freezes will occasionally occur after these dates. The conservative gardener should consider the frost-free date—when the chance of freezing temperatures is very unlikely—to be about four weeks after the average-last-freeze date.

Average Annual Rainfall Amounts

Average annual rainfall is abundant in some areas. Amounts range from fifty-six inches in southeast Texas to nine inches in El Paso. Unfortunately, the rain does not appear regularly. Some areas of the state may receive five to ten inches of rain or more in a single rainfall and then go for weeks or months without significant precipitation. Well-drained beds are needed to handle periods of high rainfall, and proper irrigation is important during dry periods, especially during hot weather.

Gardening Seasons Explained

According to the calendar, spring, summer, fall, and winter begin and end at the same time everywhere in the United States. Common sense tells us, though, that the dates for spring gardening activities must be very different between Maine and Texas.

Spring begins in early February in south Texas when deciduous trees like magnolias and redbuds begin to bloom and grow. When the calendar tells us that spring has officially begun, we in Texas can say, "It's passed in south Texas and arriving in north Texas," while at the same time in Maine it could be snowing. All Texas gardeners need to divide the year in a way that makes sense for us.

The terms spring, summer, fall, and winter carry strong associations with certain types of weather, and that can be a problem for Texas gardeners. Winter, for instance, brings to mind a picture of snow-covered dormant gardens with little or no activity. What we actually experience in our state is episodes of cold weather interspersed with periods of mild temperatures. Planting and harvesting vegetables, planting hardy annuals, perennials, trees, and shrubs, and controlling weeds and insects may continue throughout the season in some areas of Texas.

To get around those preconceived notions, we can divide the gardening year into seasons that more accurately reflect the weather we have at that time. We can divide the gardening year into a first warm season (spring), a hot season (summer), a second warm/cool season (fall), and a cool/cold season (winter), depending on the zone you live in. There are no sharp boundaries between these seasons, and gardeners should always be aware that unusually high or low temperatures may occur at any time, especially during season transitions.

The first warm season of the year runs from late March through mid-May. This warm season is characterized by mild to warm daytime highs generally in the 70s and 80s Fahrenheit, cool nights in the 50s and 60s, and limited danger of nighttime freezes. It is a lovely time of the year that is appreciated by gardeners and non-gardeners alike.

The Warm Season

The first warm season is an excellent time to plant tender annuals and perennials in the landscape. Trees, shrubs, and groundcovers, as well as lawns, can be fertilized to encourage the vigorous growth that takes place in this season. Tender vegetables such as tomatoes, peppers, squash, and snap beans can be planted now after all danger of frost/freeze has passed. New plantings of trees and shrubs in the landscape should be completed as soon as possible since hot weather is right around the corner. The first warm season also includes the peak blooming of the spring bulbs and cool-season bedding plants that were planted several months before, such as pansies, dianthus, petunias, snapdragons, and sweet peas. For new bed planting, focus on warm-season plants such as marigolds, periwinkles, lantanas, and zinnias that will bloom for a long time, rather than cool-season plants that will play out as temperatures heat up in May.

The Hot Season

May offers a transition into the hot season, which is characterized by brutally hot days in the upper 80s and 90s and warm nights in the mid- to upper 70s. The hot season is our longest season, and it can last through September. High humidity, rainy periods, drought conditions, insects, and diseases combine with heat to make this a stressful time of year for many plants. Numerous trees, shrubs, and perennials that are grown successfully up North cannot be grown here because they will not tolerate the hot season. Tropical perennials such as hibiscus, gingers, blue daze, banana, and pentas really shine during the hot season, and many gardeners plant them every year even though they are prone to freeze injury or death. If there is a down time in our gardens, the hot season is it. In July and August, and often September, it is so hot that many gardeners retreat to the air-conditioned indoors and spend less time in the garden than at any other season. But in spite of the heat, the hot season is a time of lush growth and abundant flowers from those plants that can deal with it.

There are a variety of things to do during the hot season. Controlling pests such as weeds, diseases, and insects is an important part of gardening at this time of year. Trees and shrubs grown in containers can be planted in the landscape but will require more care, and their survival is often not as sure as those planted during the cool season. Pruning is important to control the growth of a variety of plants, but avoid heavy pruning on spring-flowering trees and shrubs after June. Provide irrigation to the landscape during hot, dry periods.

The Warm/Cool Season

Late September and early October offer a transition into the second warm season, which may last until late November. The weather at this time of year is similar to that of the first warm season, generally mild and pleasant. This is not the end of the gardening year as it is in the colder climates that have cold, harsh winters. For us, this time of year celebrates the flowers that are still lingering and looks toward a mild cool season. As the heat diminishes, garden activities become more pleasurable . . . and there is lots to do. Many cool-season vegetables like broccoli, lettuce, cabbage, and turnips may be planted now. Flower gardeners can usually plant cool-season bedding plants like pansies, snapdragons, and dianthus. Deciduous trees, shrubs, and perennials begin to lose their leaves in November and finally enter dormancy, but we use so many broadleaf evergreen plants in our landscapes that they rarely look barren.

The Cool/Cold Season

Late November to early December sees the arrival of the cool/cold season and the possibility of freezing temperatures. Although snow and severe freezes in the teens can occur, harsh weather rarely lasts long. Much of the time, the weather is mild with lows above freezing and highs in the 50s, 60s, and even 70s, particularly in the southern half of the state. Tropical plants can be covered or brought in for protection on those occasional freezing nights. Along the Coast, the planting of cool-season vegetables and bedding plants can continue. This season is by far the best time to plant hardy trees, shrubs, ground covers, and herbaceous perennials. In March and April, the cool season makes a transition into the first warm season, bringing us full circle.

Soil Moisture Determination

Determination of Soil Moisture Content

HOW SOIL FEELS AND LOOKS

SOIL MOISTURE LEVEL	Coarse (sand)	Light (loamy sand, sandy loam)	Medium (fine sandy loam, silt loam)	Heavy (clay loam, clay)
No available soil moisture. Plants wilt. Irrigation required. (First Range)	Dry, loose, single grained, flows through fingers. No stain or smear on fingers.	Dry, loose, clods easily crushed and flows through fingers. No stain or smear on fingers.	Crumbly, dry, powdery, barely maintain shape. Clods break down easily. May leave slight smear or stain when worked with hand or fingers.	Hard, firm baked, cracked. Usually too stiff or tough to work or ribbon* by squeezing between thumb or forefinger. May leave slight smear or stain.
Moisture is available, but level is low. Irrigation needed. (Second Range)	Appears dry; will not retain shape when squeezed in hand.	Appears dry; may make a cast when squeezed in hand but seldom holds together.	May form a week ball** under pressure but is still crumbly. Color is pale with no obvious moisture.	Pliable, forms a ball; ribbons but usually breaks or is crumbly. May leave slight stain or smear.
Moisture is available. Level is high. Irrigation not yet needed. (Third Range)	Color is dark with obvious moisture. Soil may stick together in very weak cast or ball.	Color is dark with obvious moisture. Soil forms weak ball or cast under pressure. Slight finger stain but no ribbon when squeezed between thumb and forefinger.	Color is dark from obvious moisture. Forms a ball. Works easily, clods are soft with mellow feel. Stains finger and has slick feel when squeezed.	Color is dark with obvious moisture. Forms good ball. Ribbons easily, has slick feel. Leaves stain on fingers.
Soil moisture level following an irrigation. (Fourth Range)	Appears and feels moist. Color is dark. May form weak cast or ball. Leaves wet outline or slight smear on hand.	Appears and feels moist. Color is dark. Forms cast or ball. Will not ribbon but shows smear or stain and leaves wet outline on hand.	Appears and feels moist. Color is dark. Has smooth mellow feel. Forms a ball and ribbons when squeezed. Stains and smears. Leaves wet outline on hand.	Color is dark. Appears moist; may feel sticky. Ribbons out easily; smears and stains hands; leaves wet outline. Forms good ball.

* Ribbon is formed by squeezing and working soil between thumb and forefinger.. ** Cast or ball is formed by squeezing soil in hand.

Reprinted from: The Texas Agriculture Extension Service publication #B-1496

Planning and Caring for Trees

Planning and Caring for Trees

Trees are a vital part of most landscapes. They provide shade, privacy, windbreaks, fruit or nuts, and flowers, and can increase real-estate value as well. Select them carefully. They will be around for a long time. Proper placement is very important, as mistakes are not easily corrected later on when trees are large.

Planning

There is no one perfect tree for all of Texas. Trees have advantages and disadvantages, depending on their planting locations and desired characteristics. Here are some points you need to consider:

1. Select a tree that will mature at a size right for its site. This cannot be stressed too much. Planting trees that will grow too large for their locations is one of the most common mistakes people make (along with planting too many trees). Generally, small trees are those that grow from 15 to 25 feet tall, medium-sized trees grow from 30 to 55 feet tall, and large trees are those that grow 60 feet or taller.

2. Think about the purpose of the tree and why you feel it is needed. This will help you determine what characteristics the tree should have, such as its shape, size, and rate of growth. Ornamental features such as flowers, attractive berries, brightly colored fall foliage, or unusual bark should also be considered.

3. Decide if you want a tree that retains its foliage year-round (evergreen) or loses its leaves in the winter (deciduous). Deciduous trees are particularly useful where you want shade in the summer and sun in the winter.

4. Choose trees that are well adapted to our growing conditions. They must be able to tolerate long, hot summers and mild/cold winters. A number of northern species of beech, maple, conifers, and others you might see in catalogs are often unsuitable for our state. Trees that are not completely winter hardy are not good choices either.

5. Check the location of overhead power lines, and if you must plant under them, use small, low-growing trees. Consider underground water lines and septic tanks as well as walks, drives, and paved surfaces that may be damaged by the roots of large trees. Locate large trees at least 15 to 25 feet away from your house.

Care for Your Trees

Keep the area one to two feet out from the trunk of a newly planted tree mulched and free from weeds and grass. This will encourage the tree to establish faster by eliminating competition from grass roots. It also prevents lawn mowers and string trimmers from damaging the bark at the base of the tree, which can cause stunting or death. The mulch should be about four inches deep.

People tend to think of established trees as almost indestructible. Trees do not need a great deal of care compared to other plants in the landscape, but they do occasionally need water, fertilizer, and pest control.

Perhaps the greatest threat to trees is people. A common misconception is that tree roots are located deep in the soil and so are well protected from damage. Actually, tree roots are remarkably shallow. The majority of the root system responsible for absorbing water and minerals is located in the upper 18 inches of soil, and it spreads out at least twice as far as the branches. As a result, many people damage or kill their trees in a variety of ways. Tree roots are vulnerable to damage from soil compaction caused by excessive foot traffic or vehicular traffic. Whether building a new home on a lot with existing trees, an addition to an existing home, or a new patio, construction work kills lots of trees. Even repairing driveways, sidewalks, and streets may cause extensive damage to tree roots. If filling is needed, no more than 2 inches of fill per year should be spread over a tree's root system.

Watering

Water a newly planted or transplanted tree whenever the soil is dry. This is the single most important thing you can do to ensure its survival, especially during the first summer after planting. To properly water a tree its first year, turn a hose on trickle and lay the end on top of the ground within 6 inches of the trunk. Let the water trickle for about 30 to 45 minutes or as long as needed to thoroughly water the tree being irrigated. This should be done as needed during hot, dry weather.

Older, established trees rarely have to be watered, but exceptionally dry weather during the months of July, August, and September may place enough stress on trees to make watering necessary. Lawn sprinklers are good devices for watering the expansive root systems of established trees. Set the sprinkler to apply about an inch of water, and water about once a week until sufficient rain occurs. Apply water in the tree's dripline—the area where the branches reach their maximum length.

Fertilizing

In the first five to ten years after planting, young trees can be encouraged to grow significantly faster if fertilized annually. Older trees can be fertilized less often. In fact, for older trees with good vigor, color, and rate of growth, fertilization is optional. Trees are generally fertilized in late February in south Texas in anticipation of growth beginning in February or March. In north Texas, fertilize two to four weeks later.

Pest Control

Although they require less pest control than other plants in the landscape, trees do occasionally have pest problems that need to be controlled. The best trees are relatively free from pest problems or will not be badly damaged or killed by pests that do attack them. This is fortunate, as the average gardener does not have the proper equipment to spray a large tree. When selecting a tree for your landscape and before purchasing, be sure you are familiar with its potential pest problems, how serious they tend to be, and how often they are likely to occur. Properly selected, planted, and maintained trees usually have few or no pest problems.

Pruning

For a variety of reasons, virtually all trees are pruned at some time. Lower branches are gradually removed from a young, growing tree to lift its canopy to an appropriate height. Dead or diseased branches should occasionally be removed. Fruit trees are pruned in a variety of specialized forms. Problems with poorly placed branches or an unattractive shape may need to be corrected. Pruning needs to be done correctly. Except for certain types of fruit trees, pruning is generally kept to a minimum but should certainly not be avoided when necessary.

Thinning Before

Thinning After

Planting Overview

Woody plant materials such as trees and shrubs are sold in one of three forms: bare root, balled and burlapped, or container grown. Trees are generally planted into individual planting holes, while shrubs are usually planted in well-prepared beds.

Bare root: Because bare-root plants are perishable, shipping and selling bare root is the least common method. You should purchase and plant bare-root plants only when they are dormant, generally from December through February. Roses are still sold bare root, and mail-ordered plants are also sometimes shipped bare root. Never allow the roots to dry out. Plant bare-root plants immediately or as soon as possible after you get them, and be sure they are planted at the same level they were growing previously. This can sometimes be difficult to determine, but look at the stem carefully and you can often detect the original soil line. Stem tissue is usually a lighter color below the ground.

It is better to plant a little too shallow than too deep. Make a mound of soil in the bottom of the hole where the plant will be planted, spread the roots over the mound, and fill in with more soil, covering the roots. Water thoroughly to settle them in.

Note: It is nearly always better to purchase bare-root plants locally than by mail order because you can actually see "in person" what you are buying.

Balled and burlapped: A balled-and-burlapped plant is grown in a field. When it reaches its desired size, it is dug up with a soilball that will be tightly wrapped with burlap and fastened with nails, wrapped with twine, or placed in a wire basket. When it is dug out of the ground, such a plant loses much or most of its root system and is susceptible to transplant shock. For this reason, balled-and-burlapped plants are best planted during the cooler months of October through March.

Depth of Hole

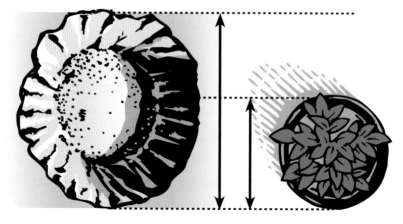

Width of Hole

Many larger trees and shrubs are sold in this form, although today large trees grown in containers are also available.

Container grown: Container-grown plants are the most common plants for sale. They have well-developed root systems and suffer less transplant shock when planted. For this reason, you may plant them virtually year-round, even though it is better to plant them during the milder weather that occurs from October to March.

Avoid planting in the stressful months of June, July, and August whenever possible. Remember, fall is for planting, including trees and shrubs.

Planting in Individual Holes

Planting trees properly in individual holes is not difficult, but it can make the difference between success and failure.

1. Whether the tree is balled and burlapped or container grown, dig the hole at least twice the diameter of the rootball and no deeper than the rootball's height.

Balled-and-Burlapped Tree   Removing Container

2. Remove a container-grown tree from its container, and place it gently onto the firm, undisturbed soil in the bottom of the hole. A rootball that is tightly packed with thick encircling roots indicates a rootbound condition. Try to unwrap or open up the rootball to encourage the roots to spread into the surrounding soil. Do not remove the burlap from balled-and-burlapped trees unless it is synthetic burlap (check with the nursery staff when you purchase the tree). Once the tree is in the hole, try to remove any nylon twine or wire basket that may have been used, and fold down the burlap from the top of the rootball. Whether the tree is container grown or balled and burlapped, the top of its rootball should be level with or slightly above the surrounding soil. It is crucial that you do not plant the tree too deep. If planted too deeply, trees, shrubs, and other plants may terminate.

3. Pulverize the soil dug out from the hole thoroughly; use this soil, without any additions, to backfill around the tree. Research shows that blending amendments such as peat moss or compost into the fill soil slows establishment; it encourages the roots to grow primarily in the planting hole and delays their spread into the soil beyond. As a tree grows, its roots will grow out well beyond the reach of its branches. Since the roots will spend most of the tree's life growing in native soil outside of the planting hole, they might as well get used to it from the beginning.

4. Add soil around the tree until the hole is half full, then firm the soil to eliminate air pockets—but do not pack it tight. Finish filling the hole, firm again, and then water the tree thoroughly to settle it in. We do not generally add fertilizer to the planting hole, although it is all right to use some premium-quality, long-lasting, slow-release fertilizer in the upper few inches if you like. We apply a root stimulator after planting trees and shrubs.

5. Stake the tree only if it is tall enough to be unstable—otherwise, staking is not necessary. Do not drive the stakes into place directly against the trunk. Two or three stakes should be firmly driven into the ground just beyond the rootball and planting hole. Tie cloth strips, old nylon stockings, or wire (covered with a piece of garden hose where it touches the trunk) to the stakes and

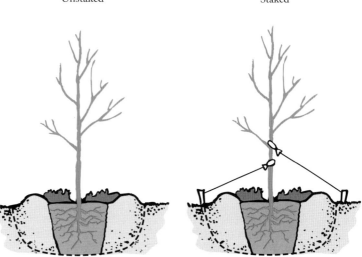

Unstaked   Staked

then to the trunk of the tree. Leave the support in place for no longer than nine to twelve months. Always place one stake on the side of prevailing wind. In Texas this is usually a southwest direction.

6. It is beneficial to keep the area one to two feet out from the trunk mulched and free of weeds and grass. This encourages the tree to establish faster by eliminating competition from grass roots. It also prevents lawn mowers and string trimmers from damaging the bark at the base of the tree, which can cause stunting or death. The mulch should be about four inches deep.

7. Water your tree when the weather is dry. This is the single most important thing you can do to ensure its survival, especially during its first summer. To properly water a tree the first year, turn a hose on to a trickle and lay the end on top of the ground within 6 inches of the trunk. Let the water trickle for about 30 to 45 minutes, or longer if necessary to water the tree thoroughly. This should be done once or twice a week during hot, dry weather. Apply a root stimulator monthly during its first year of growth.

Bed Preparation

Shrubs, ground covers, annuals, and perennials are almost always planted in well-prepared beds. Since their roots are less extensive than trees, amendments are generally added during bed preparation. Soil amendments are materials that are blended with the soil to improve it and can be organic matter (compost, aged manure, finely ground pine bark, peat moss), and sand (for heavy clay soils). Here are the basic steps for preparing the bed:

1. First, do a thorough job of removing unwanted vegetation in the bed. Weeds or turfgrass may be removed physically or eliminated with a weed-control aid (always read and follow label directions).

2. Next, turn over the soil to a depth of 8 to 10 inches. Spread any desired soil amendment over the turned soil. Add 6 inches of organic matter and tilling into the top 6 inches of native soil. (Have a soil test done to find out the specific needs of your soil.)

3. Blend the amendments thoroughly into the soil of the bed. A rear-tined tiller works well for heavy soil and organic matter.

4. Rake and you're ready to plant.

5. Apply soil amendments and fertilizer according to label directions when planting each plant. Use premium-quality slow-release granular fertilizers for great results.

Winter Protection

Covering Your Plants

Covering plants works particularly well when temperatures dip into the mid-20s overnight and rise again the following day. Providing a heat source under the cover improves protection when there are more severe freezes or prolonged temperatures below freezing. One of the safest and easiest methods is to wrap or drape the plant with miniature Christmas lights. Not enough heat is generated to damage the plant, but the heat that is given off by the small bulbs can make a big difference in the plant's survival. If you want to use lights, remember a cover is still necessary to trap and hold in the heat. Be sure to use outdoor extension cords. To avoid covering your plants or using lights, always plant selections that are winter hardy in your area.

Bringing Plants Indoors

You must also decide what to do with tender plants growing in containers outside. You have three choices. One, leave them outside and let them take their chances (at least gather them together under some protection such as a carport or patio cover). This could be an option with low-value, easily replaced plants. Two, bring them inside and keep them in through the winter. Make sure you put them in a good location that receives plenty of light. Or three, move them inside on those nights when a freeze is predicted and back out again when the freezing episode is over.

Good: Sheets or Quilts

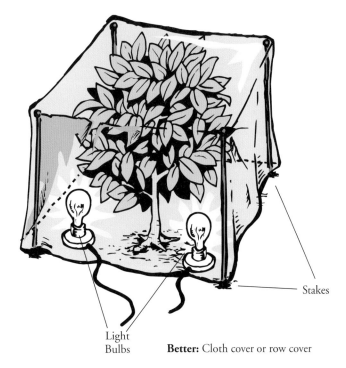

Stakes

Light Bulbs

Better: Cloth cover or row cover

Identifying Turfgrass Pests

Damage Symptoms of Common Turfgrass Pest Problems and Possible Causes

Symptom(s):   Possible causal agent(s):

A. Disruption of soil:

  1. Hills, piles or structures of loose dirt on turf . . . . *ants*

    a. Mounds up to 18 inches tall with no visible entrance(s), or mound with ants emerging in mass when disturbed . . . .*red imported fire ant*

Controlling Fire Ants

    b. Small mounds with rims around single central entrance holes and presence of small (³/16 in.) grayish-black ants . . . .*pyramid ants*

    c. Many hills of coarse soil with central exit holes and presence of large (³/8 in.) red-brown ant with spines on the thorax . . . .*Texas leafcutting ant*

    d. Flat cleared areas up to 3 ft. in diameter made of coarse soil particles with a single central exit hole and with the presence of large (³/8 in.) reddish-brown ants with square heads
. . . .*red harvester ant*

  2. Trails of raised, loose dirt roughly ¹/2 inch wide in an "S" shaped pattern through turf . .*mole crickets*

  3. Small piles of dirt "pellets" (³/16 in.) scattered through thatch . . . .*earth worms*

  4. Earthen "chimneys" with central holes (about ¹/2 inch diameter) . . . .*crawfish*

5. Small piles of loose dirt associated with exit holes . . . . *green June beetle larvae*

6. Round holes (up to ½ inch diameter) in soil . . . . *digger wasp nests or cicada exit holes*

B. Direct damage to grass causing yellowing or plant death:

1. Grass blades chewed or missing . . . . *caterpillars*

   a. Presence of gray-brown caterpillars up to 1 in. long with an inverted cream-colored "Y" on the fronts of the head capsules . . . . *armyworms*

   b. Presence of gray-brown caterpillars up to 1 in. long that curl into a tight "C" position when disturbed . . . . *cutworms*

   c. Presence of translucent greenish caterpillars up to ¾ in. long with black raised spots on each body segment . . . . *tropical sod webworm*

2. Yellow or dead grass:

   a. Roots missing and presence of cream-colored "C" shaped grubs with three legs on body segments behind brown head capsule . . . . *white grubs*

   b. No tissue removed, with presence of pinkish-orange, white and black nymph and adult stages of bugs up to ³/₁₆ in. . . . . *long chinch bugs*

   c. No tissue removed, but "galls" or globular objects (scales) in the root zone . . . . *Rhodesgrass scale or ground pearls*

   d. No tissue removed, but with shortened internodes producing a typical rosetting and tufted growth, or "witch broom" effect; grass may be very yellow or whitish in appearance with no insects visible to the naked eye . . . . *Bermudagrass (stunt) mites or buffalograss (stunt) mites*

White Grub

Sod Webworm

Reprinted from:
The Texas Agriculture Extension Service publication B#-5083

Texas Palms

After visiting our Gulf Coast or the Rio Grande Valley, you may be one of the visitors wishing for palm trees in your own backyard. While this is not possible in all areas of Texas, it is possible in approximately 40 percent of the state. This is especially true if you take the time to select winter hardy palms for your particular area. By making this extra effort, you too may enjoy a backyard tropical (or at least semi-tropical) planting of palms.

The following is a list of palms, including common and scientific names, suggested USDA plant hardiness zones, and suggested cold tolerances. Know this about palms—cold hardiness is often a combination of lowest temperatures and how long sustained. If temperatures drop low and rise quickly little damage may occur, but if the lower temperatures remain for several hours, or on into days, freeze damage is more likely.

For the most part, growing palms in Texas landscapes is part of what I call . . . "gardening on the edge!" Should you decide to go for it, be aware of my cautions listed in the above paragraph.

Palm Name		Hardiness Zones	Suggested Cold Tolerances
Spiny Fiber Palm	*Trithrinax acanthocoma*	8-9	10F
South American Needle Palm	*Trithrinax campestris*	8-9	20F
Takil Palm	*Trachycarpus takil*	8-9	10F
Dwarf Windmill Palm		8-9	10F
Sikkim or Windamere Palm	*Trachycarpus latisectus*	8-9	10F
Windmill or Chusan Palm		8-9	10F
Mexican Blue Palm	*Brahea armata*	8-9	15F
Guadalupe Palm	*Brahea edulis*	8-9	15F
Chilean Wine Palm	*Jubaea chilensis*	8-9	15F
Mazari Palm	*Nannorrhops ritchieana*	7b-9	20F
Needle Palm	*Raphidophyllum hystrix*	7b-9	10F
Bermuda Palmetto	*Sabal bermudana*	8-9	15F
Florida Scrub Palmetto	*Sabal etonia*	8-9	15F
Mayan Palm	*Sabal guatemalensis*	8-9	15F
Texas or Mexican Palmetto	*Sabal mexicana*	8-9	15F
Dwarf Palmetto	*Sabal minor*	7b-9	15F
Cabbage or Florida Sabal Palm	*Sabal palmetto*	8-9	15F
Sonoran Blue Palmetto	*Sabal uresana*	8-9	15F
Brazoria Palm	*Sabal × texensis*	8-9	15F
Yatay Palm	*Butia yatay*	8-9	15F
Wooly Butina Palm	*Butia eriospatha*	8-9	15F
Pindo or Jelly Palm	*Butia capita*	8-9	15F
Canary Island date Palm	*Phoenix canariensis*	8b-9	25F

Remember, the low temperatures listed here are for short durations only, and there is no guarantee damage won't occur.

Glossary

Alkaline soil: soil with a pH greater than 7.0. It lacks acidity, often because it has limestone in it.

All-purpose balanced fertilizer: powdered, liquid, or granular fertilizer with a balanced proportion of the three key nutrients—nitrogen (N), phosphorus (P), and potassium (K). It is suitable for maintenance nutrition for most plants.

Annual: a plant that lives its entire life in one season. It is genetically determined to germinate, grow, flower, set seed, and die the same year.

Balled and burlapped: describes a tree or shrub grown in the field whose soilball was wrapped with protective burlap and twine when the plant was dug up to be sold or transplanted.

Bare root: describes plants that have been packaged without any soil around their roots. (Often young shrubs and trees purchased through the mail arrive with their exposed roots covered with moist peat or sphagnum moss, sawdust, or similar material, and wrapped in plastic.) They may also be packaged in plastic sleeves with moist sawdust or wood shavings and available at local retailers.

Barrier plant: a plant that has intimidating thorns or spines and is sited purposely to block foot traffic or other access to the home or yard.

Beneficial insects: insects or their larvae that prey on pest organisms and their eggs. They may be flying insects, such as ladybugs, parasitic wasps, praying mantis, and soldier bugs, or soil dwellers, such as predatory nematodes, spiders, and ants.

Berm: a narrow raised ring of soil around a tree, used to hold water so it will be directed to the root zone. A raised mound of soil used as a sound barrier, privacy screen, and/or location for landscape beds.

Bract: a modified leaf structure on a plant stem near its flower that resembles a petal. Often it is more colorful and visible than the actual flower, as in dogwood.

Bud union: the place where the top of a plant was grafted to the rootstock. Example: most rose plants are bud grafted.

Canopy: the overhead branching area of a tree, usually referring to its spread including foliage.

Cold hardiness: the ability of any plant to survive the winter cold in a particular area.

Composite: a flower that is actually composed of many tiny flowers. Typically, they are flat clusters of tiny, tight florets, sometimes surrounded by wider-petaled florets. Composite flowers are highly attractive to bees and beneficial insects.

Compost: organic matter that has undergone progressive decomposition by microbial and macrobial activity until it is reduced to a spongy, fluffy texture. Added to soil of any type, it improves the soil's ability to hold air, nutrients, and water and to drain well.

Corm: the swollen energy-storing structure, analogous to a bulb, under the soil at the base of the stem of plants such as crocus and gladiolus.

Crown: the base of a plant at, or just beneath, the surface of the soil where the roots meet the stems.

Cultivar: a CULTIvated VARiety. It is a naturally occurring form of a plant that has been identified as special or superior and is purposely selected for propagation and production.

Deadhead: a pruning technique that removes faded flower heads from plants to improve their appearance, abort seed production, and stimulate further flowering. Often done when growing roses.

Deciduous plants: unlike evergreens, these plants including trees, vines, and shrubs lose their leaves in the fall.

Desiccation: drying out of foliage tissues, usually due to drought or wind.

Deer-resistant plants: plants that our whitetail deer usually do not prefer for their food.

Division: the practice of splitting apart plants to create several smaller-rooted segments. The practice is useful for controlling the plant's size and for acquiring more plants; it is also essential to the health and continued flowering of certain ones.

Dormancy: the period, usually the winter, when plants temporarily cease active growth and rest. Dormant is the verb form, as used in this sentence: Some plants, such as spring-blooming bulbs, go dormant in the summer.

Dwarf or dwarf type: this term indicates types of plants known to grow shorter in height than other members of the same family. For example Dwarf Yaupon Holly as opposed to the standard type of Yapon Holly. Dwarf plant types also include annuals, perennials, and other plants used in our gardens and landscapes. It is a relative term and not specific.

Established: the point at which a newly planted tree, shrub, or flower begins to produce new growth, either foliage or stems. This is an indication that the roots have recovered from transplant shock and have begun to grow and spread.

Evergreen: woody plants that do not lose their foliage annually with the onset of winter. Needled or broadleaf foliage will persist and continues to function on a plant through one or more winters, aging and dropping unobtrusively in cycles of three or four years or more.

Foliar: of or about foliage—usually refers to the practice of spraying foliage, as in fertilizing or treating with insecticide; leaf tissues absorb liquid directly for fast results, and the soil is not affected.

Floret: a tiny flower, usually one of many forming a cluster that comprises a single blossom.

Germinate: to sprout. Germination is a fertile seed's first stage of development.

Graft (union): the point on the stem of a woody plant with sturdier roots where a stem from a highly ornamental plant is inserted so it will join with the sturdier-rooted stem. Roses are commonly grafted.

Grasshopper-resistant plants: plants that grasshopper pests usually or may not prefer for their food.

Hands: the female flowers on a banana tree; they turn into bananas.

Hardscape: the permanent, structural, nonplant part of a landscape, such as walls, sheds, pools, patios, arbors, and walkways.

Herbaceous: plants having fleshy or soft stems that die back with frost, the opposite of "woody."

Hybrid: a plant that is the result of intentional or natural cross-pollination between two or more plants of the same species or genus.

Low water demand: describes plants that tolerate dry soil for varying periods of time. Typically, they have succulent, hairy, or silvery-gray foliage and tuberous roots or taproots. Also known as "thrifty" plants because they go a long way with little water. Often used in Xeriscape activities.

Mulch: a layer of material over bare soil to protect it from erosion and compaction by rain, and to discourage weeds. It may be inorganic (gravel, fabric) or organic (wood chips, bark, pine needles, chopped leaves). Think of it as a "blanket" of material on top of bare soil.

Naturalize: (a) to plant seeds, bulbs, or plants in a random, informal pattern as they would appear in their natural habitat; (b) to adapt to and spread throughout adopted habitats (a tendency of some non-native plants).

Nectar: the sweet fluid produced by glands on flowers that attract pollinators such as hummingbirds and honeybees for which it is a source of energy.

Organic material, organic matter: any material or debris that is derived from plants. It is carbon-based material capable of undergoing decomposition and decay.

Peat moss: organic matter from peat sedges (United States) or sphagnum mosses (Canada) often used to improve soil texture. The acidity of sphagnum peat moss makes it ideal for boosting or maintaining soil acidity while also improving drainage. The most commonly used type in Texas is brown Canadian sphagnum peat moss.

Perennial: a flowering plant that lives over two or more seasons. Many die back with frost, but their roots survive the winter and generate new shoots during the next growing season.

pH: a measurement of the relative acidity (low pH) or alkalinity (high pH) of soil or water based on a scale of 1 to 14, 7 being neutral. Individual plants require soil to be within a certain range so that nutrients can dissolve in moisture and be available to them. Soil pH above 7 is alkaline while pH below 7 is acidic.

Pinch: to remove tender stems and/or leaves by pressing them between thumb and forefinger. This pruning technique encourages branching, compactness, and flowering in plants, or it removes aphids clustered at growing tips.

Pollen: the yellow, powdery grains in the center of a flower. A plant's male sex cells, they are transferred to the female plant parts by means of wind or animal pollinators to fertilize them and create seeds.

Raceme: an arrangement of single stalked flowers along an elongated, unbranched axis.

Rhizome: a swollen, energy-storing creeping stem structure, similar to a bulb, that lies horizontally in the soil, with roots emerging from its lower surface and growth shoots from a growing point at or near its tip, as in bearded iris or Bermuda grass.

Rootbound (or potbound): the condition of a plant that has been confined in a container too long, its roots having been forced to wrap around themselves and even swell out of the container. Successful transplanting or repotting may require untangling and trimming away some of the matted roots.

Root flare: the transition at the base of a tree trunk where the bark tissue begins to differentiate and roots begin to form just before entering the soil. This area should not be covered with soil when planting a tree.

Self-seeding: the tendency of some plants to sow their seeds freely around the yard. It creates many seedlings the following season that may or may not be welcome. This causes some annuals to act almost like perennials.

Semi-evergreen: tending to be evergreen in a mild climate but deciduous in colder zones.

Shearing: the pruning technique whereby plant stems and branches are cut uniformly with long-bladed pruning shears (hedge shears) or powered hedge trimmers. This technique is used when creating and maintaining hedges and topiary.

Slow-acting fertilizer: fertilizer that is water soluble and therefore releases its nutrients gradually as a function of soil temperature, moisture, and related microbial activity. Typically granular, it may be organic or synthetic.

Standard or standard type: usually refers to plant sizes. Example: standard Burford Holly as opposed to dwarf Burford Holly, and likewise with perennials, annuals, and other plants used in our landscapes and gardens. May indicate the species. Does not indicate specific sizes.

Succulent growth: the sometimes undesirable production of fleshy, water-storing leaves or stems that may result from over-fertilization. Often occurs with new spring growth.

Sucker: a new growing shoot. Underground plant roots produce suckers to form new stems and spread by means of these suckering roots to form large plantings, or colonies. Some plants produce root suckers or branch suckers as a result of pruning or wounding.

Tuber: a type of underground storage structure in a plant stem, analogous to a bulb. It generates roots below and stems above ground (example: dahlia).

Variegated: having various colors or color patterns. The term usually refers to plant foliage that is streaked, edged, blotched, or mottled with a contrasting color, often green with yellow, cream, or white.

White grubs: fat, off-white, wormlike larvae in Texas that are usually from "June Bugs". They reside in the soil and feed on plant (especially grass) roots until summer when they emerge as adults.

Wings: (a) the corky tissue that forms edges along the twigs of some woody plants such as winged euonymus; (b) the flat, dried extension of tissue on some seeds, such as maple, that catch the wind and help them disseminate.

Xeriscape/Xeriscaping: utilizing locally well adapted plants that survive on minimal water in Texas landscapes and gardens.

Information Sources

American Hemerocallis Society (Daylily), 3803 Graystone Drive, Austin, TX 78731.
American Iris Society, 7414 East 60th St., Tulsa, OK 74145.
American Rose Society, 8877 Jefferson-Paige Road, Shreveport, LA 71130;
mailing address: P.O. Box 30000, Shreveport, LA 71130.
Austin Area Garden Council, 220 Barton Springs Road, Zilker Park, Austin, TX 78746.
Bayou Bend Gardens, 1 Wescott St., Houston, TX 77219.
Botanical Resources Institute of Texas, 509 Pecan St., Ft. Worth, TX 76102.
City of Tyler Municipal Rose Garden, 420 South Rosepark Drive, Tyler, TX 75710.
Corpus Christi Botanical Garden, 8510 South Staples, Corpus Christi, TX 78413.
Corpus Christi Botanical Society, P.O. Box 8113, Corpus Christi, TX 78412.
Dale Groom, The Plant Groom™ contact information: P.O. Box 365, Eustace, TX 75124;
e-mail: dalegroom@tvec.net; appearing at Canton's First Monday Trade Day's, Hwy. 19, west end
and between Original Pavillions 1 and 2 year round. See www.firstmondaycanton.com or call
903-567-6556 for First Monday dates. Read "Ask The Plant Groom™" on www.KTBB.com
Dallas Arboretum and Botanical Garden, 8617 Garland Road, Dallas, TX 75218.
El Paso Native Plant Society, 6804 Tolvea, El Paso, TX 79912.
Fort Worth Botanical Garden, 3220 Botanic Garden Blvd., Ft. Worth, TX 76107.
Friends of the Ft. Worth Nature Center and Refuge, P.O. Box 11694, Ft. Worth, TX 76109.
Heritage Roses Group, 810 East 30th Street, Austin, TX 78705.
Houston Arboretum and Botanical Society, 4501 Woodway Drive, Houston, TX 77024.
Lady Bird Johnson Wildflower Center; 4801 La Crosse Avenue, Austin, TX 78739; 512-292-4200,
Information line: 512-292-4100; www.wildflower.org
McMurray College, Iris Garden, Sayles Blvd. and South 16th St., c/o Abilene Chamber of Commerce,
325 Hickory St., Abilene, TX.
Mercer Arboretum and Botanical Garden, 22306 Adline Westfield, Humble, TX 77338.
Moody Gardens, 1 Hope Blvd., Galveston, TX 78739.
Native Plant Society of Texas (and local chapter information), P.O. Box 891, Georgetown, TX 78627;
www.npsot.org; email: coordinator@nspot.org.
Native Prairies Association of Texas, Texas Woman's University, P.O. Box 22675, Denton, TX 76204.
San Antonio Botanical Garden, 555 Funston Place, San Antonio, TX 78209.
Society for Louisiana Irises, 1216 Cedar Pine Lane, Little Elm, TX 75068.
South Texas Plant Materials Center, Caesar Kleberg Wildlife Research Center, Texas A&I University, P.O.
Box 218, Kingsville, TX 78363.
Stephen F. Austin State University Mast Arboretum, P.O. Box 13000, Nacogdoches, TX 75962.
Texas Nursery and Landscape Association, Inc., 512 East Riverside Drive, Suite 207, Austin, TX 78704.
Texas Botanical Garden Society, P.O Box 5642, Austin, TX 78763.
Texas Department of Agriculture, P.O. Box 12847, Austin, TX 78711.
Texas Department of Highways, Landscape Division, 11th at Brazos, Austin, TX 78701.
Texas Garden Clubs, Inc., 3111 Botanic Garden Road, Ft. Worth, TX 76107.
The Plant Groom™ half-hour TV series on RFD-TV, Dish Network 9409 and Direct TV 379.
"The Plant Groom™" lawn/garden/landscape newspaper column, syndicated throughout Texas.

Another great source of information is the local representative of the Texas Agricultural Extension Service
in your county. We typically call these folks the "County Agent." Their offices are usually located in
the county courthouse, annex buildings, or other county properties. Look for their numbers in the
phone directory under listings for your county's offices. Their numbers are also listed in the back of
Month-By-Month-Gardening-In-Texas by Dale Groom and Dan Gill (Cool Springs Press, July 2001).

Additional References

All-America Rose Selections (AARS):
    "Discover the Pleasure of Roses," Chicago, Illinois.
    "Wonderful World of Roses," Chicago Illinois.
American Rose Society (ARS):
    "Classification of Roses Information Sheet," Shreveport, Louisiana.
Blankenship, Allen G:
    Personal tips on roses.
Dallas, Mid-Cities, and Fort Worth Rose Societies:
    "Everything's Coming Up Roses," Mary Carle, ed., 1986.
Greenleaf Nursery Company:
    Wholesale Catalog, Parkhill, Oklahoma, 1996.
Groom, Dale, The Plant Groom™:
    "Color For Sun and Fall," 1990.
    "List of Powdery Mildew Resistant Crape Myrtles," 1992.
    "Plants For Shady Areas," 1987.
    "The Plant Groom's Lawn Fertilizing Time Table," 1993.
    "The Plant Groom's Trees for Texas," 1995.
Hines Nurseries:
    Wholesale Catalog, Hines Nurseries, Houston, Texas, 1995.
Monrovia Nursery Company:
    1996 Wholesale Catalog, Asuza, California, 1997.
National Wildflower Research Center Clearing House:
    "Recommended Species of Wildflowers, Shrubs, Trees, Grasses and Vines for All Areas of Texas,"
    Patricia Alholm, Austin, Texas.
Texas Agricultural Extension Service:
    "Deer in the Urban Landscape: Coping with the Deer," Forest W. Appleton, Bexar County, Texas.
    "Efficient Use of Water in the Garden and Landscape," Revised 1990.
    "Fact Sheet: Annual Flowers in the Home Landscape #L-1848," Everette Janne, 1981.
    "Fact Sheet: Lawn Establishment #L-188," Richard L. Duble, 1982.
    "Fact Sheet: Turfgrasses for Texas Lawns #L-1865," Richard L. Duble, and A.C. Novosad, 1981.
    "Home Lawns #M P-1180," Richard L. Duble, and A.C. Novosad, 1978.
    "Integrated Pest Management of Texas Turfgrass," 1993.
    "Ornamental Plants for North and East Texas #LH4," Dwight S. Hall, Overton, Texas.
    "Recommended Landscape Plant Materials for North Texas," Stephen George, Ph.D., Dallas, Texas.
    Texas Master Gardener's Training Manual, Vascular Plants of Texas, 1990.
    "Trees, Shrubs, Vines, and Groundcovers for North Central Texas," M. L. Baker, 1987.
    "Up With Trees!" Dwight S. Hall, Overton, Texas.
Thompson & Morgan:
    Thompson & Morgan Seed Catalog, 1997.
Turfgrass Producers International (TPI):
    Tipsheets: "Bermudagrass," "Centipedegrass," "St. Augustinegrass," "Tall Fescue," "Rye," "Zoysia."
Wildseed Inc.:
    "A Grower's Guide to Wildflowers," John R. Thomas, 1988.

Bibliography

Adams, William D. *Shrubs and Vines for Southern Landscapes*. Houston, Texas: Gulf Publishing Co., 1979.
——. *Southern Flower Gardening*. Houston, Texas: Gulf Publishing Co., 1980.
——. *Trees for Southern Landscapes*. Houston, Texas: Gulf Publishing Co., 1976.
Ajilvsgi, Geyata. *Wild Flowers of Texas*. Fredericksburg, Texas: Shearer Publishing, 1991.
——. *Wild Flowers of the Big Thicket*. College Station, Texas: Texas A&M University Press, 1979.
Burke, Ken, ed. *All about Roses*. San Ramon, California: Chevron Chemical Co., 1983.
Clements, John K. Mac, ed. *Garden Color, Annuals and Perennials*. Menlo Park, California: Lane Publishing Co., 1981.
Cox, Jeff and Marilyn Cox. *The Perennial Garden*. Emmaus, Pennsylvania: Rodale Press, 1985.
Damude, Noreen, Kelly Conrad Bender et al. *Texas Wildscapes Gardening for Wildlife* Austin, Texas: Texas Parks and Wildlife Press, 1999
Ellefson, Connie Lockhart, Thomas L. Stephens and Doug Welsh, Ph.D. *Xeriscape Gardening: Water Conservation for the American Landscape*. New York, New York: MacMillan Publishing Company, 1992.
Engelke, M.C., Ph.D. *Research Reports on Crowne, Cavalier and Palisade Zoysia Grasses*. Dallas, Texas: Texas A&M University and Research Center, 1996.
Erwin, Howard S. *Roadside Flowers of Texas*. Austin, Texas: University of Texas Press, 1961.
Ferguson, Barbara, ed. *Color With Annuals*. San Francisco, California: Chevron Chemical Co., 1987.
Harris, N.J. ed. *Dallas Planting Manual*. Dallas, Texas: Dallas Garden Club of the Dallas Women's Club, 1981.
Horton, Alvin and James McNair. *All About Bulbs*. San Francisco, California: Chevron Chemical Co., 1986.
Johnson, Eric A. and Scott Millard. *The Low-Water Flower Gardener*. Tucson, Arizona: Millard Publishing Services, 1993.
Laughmiller, Campbell, Lynn Laughmiller, and Lynn Sherwood. *Texas Wildflowers: A Field Guide*. Austin, Texas: University of Texas Press, 1984.
Loewer, Peter. *The Annual Garden*. Emmaus, Pennsylvania: Rodale Press, 1988.
Lovelace John, Stan Lovelace, Barbara Diltz. "Grasshopper-Resistant Plants." Denton County, Texas Agricultural Extension Service, 1998
Miller, George O. *Landscaping With Native Plants of Texas and the Southwest*. Stillwater, Minnesota: Voyageur Press, 1991.
Monrovia Nursery Company Wholesale Catalog. Azusa, California: Monrovia Nursery, 1996.
Nokes, Jill. *How to Grow Native Plants of Texas and the Southwest*. Austin, Texas: Texas Monthly Press, 1986.
Ogden, Scott. *Garden Bulbs for the South*. Dallas, Texas: Taylor Publishing Co., 1994.
Scheider, Alfred F. *Park's Success with Bulbs*. Greenwood, South Carolina: Geo. W. Park Seed Co., 1981.
Scott, George Harmon. *Bulbs: How to Select, Grow and Enjoy*. Tucson, Arizona: H.P. Books, 1982.
Simpson, Benny J. *A Field Guide to Texas Trees*. Houston, Texas: Gulf Publishing Co., 1988.
Sinnes, A. Cort. *All About Perennials*. San Francisco, California: Chevron Chemical Co., 1981.
Van der Voort, Henk. *Dutch Gardens 1992 Fall Planting Catalog* Adelphia, New Jersey: Dutch Gardens, 1992.
Wasowski, Sally, with Andy Wasowski. *Native Texas Plants, Landscaping Region by Region*. Austin, Texas: Texas Monthly Press, 1988.
Welch, William C., Ph.D. *Perennial Garden Color for Texas and the South*. Dallas, Texas: Taylor Publishing Co., 1989.
Whitcomb, Carl E., Ph.D. *Know It and Grow It II*. Stillwater, Oklahoma: Lacebark Publications, 1983.
White Flower Farm, The Garden Book, Southern Edition. Litchfield, Connecticut: White Farms, 1997.

Photography Credits

Thomas Eltzroth: pages 15, 16, 20, 30, 31, 32, 33, 34, 35, 36, 37, 38, 39, 40, 41, 42, 45, 47, 48, 53, 56, 59, 61, 63, 64, 66, 67, 69, 71, 72, 74, 76, 77, 78, 80, 81, 83, 86, 88, 89, 95, 100, 107, 112, 113, 114, 116, 117, 118, 121, 124, 125, 127, 135 (bottom), 137, 138, 139, 140, 142, 143, 146, 147, 148, 149, 150, 151, 152, 153, 154, 155, 158, 159, 162, 163, 166, 168, 172, 173, 174, 175, 180, 182, 183, 184, 185, 186, 188, 189, 190, 194, 199, 200, 203, 208, 209, 210, 211, 213, 214, 216, 217, 218, back cover (first and second photos)

Liz Ball and Rick Ray: pages 25, 29, 43, 46, 49, 52, 57, 58, 65, 84, 99, 136, 144, 160, 161, 165, 169, 170, 171, 181, 191, 197, 198, 201, 202, 205, 221

Jerry Pavia: pages 19, 44, 50, 51, 55, 70, 82, 91, 104, 120, 122, 128, 130, 132, 141, 145, 156, 157, 167, 176, 177, 187, 192, 219

William Adams: pages 14, 18, 54, 68, 73, 75, 79, 87, 92, 97, 109, 111, 119, 131, back cover (third photo)

Pamela Harper: pages 85, 93, 98, 129, 193, 195, 206, 207, 212, back cover (fourth photo)

Andre Viette: pages 21, 22, 24, 28, 62, 134, 135 (top), 215

Michael Dirr: pages 60, 96, 110, 123, 196, 204

Lorenzo Gunn: pages 90, 102, 106, 164, 179

Charles Mann: pages 105, 108, 126, 220

Karen Bussolini: pages 12 (design by Big Red Sun, Austin, TX), 17 (design by John and Jan Trimble)

Roger Hammer: page 133

Dency Kane: page 101

Judy Mielke: page 94

Scott Millard: page 115

Ralph Snodsmith: page 178

Mark Turner: page 103

Plant Index

Featured plant selections are indicated in **boldface**. See Introductions for additional plants.

Garden Notes

Garden Notes

Garden Notes

Meet Dale Groom

Dale Groom

Texas native, horticulturist, author, and columnist Dale Groom is nationally recognized as The Plant Groom™. Through his extensive work on television, radio, newspapers and "The Plant Groom™"television series, Dale helps viewers, young and old, become gardeners. A father of three, Groom launched the national campaign, "How to Grow . . . a Gardener" to encourage America's families to garden together.

Groom's radio programs have been aired coast-to-coast on the USA Radio Network, American Forum Radio Network, and Salem Radio Network. His newspaper column, "The Plant Groom™," is syndicated throughout Texas.

A thirty-two year veteran of the gardening industry, Groom is co-author of *Month-By-Month Gardening in Texas* (Cool Springs Press, 2000). This informative publication covers Texas gardening on a month-by-month, subject-by-subject timetable.

Groom, a respected speaker and consultant of all things green is a native of Brownwood in Brown County where he comes from a long line of farmers and gardeners. The author received his Bachelor of Science degree in horticulture from Stephen F. Austin State University and a Master of Science in horticulture from East Texas State University. Groom established the Ornamental Horticultural program at Tyler Junior College.

As a member of the Texas Association of Nurserymen, Groom served as the group's regional director and reporter for its trade publication. He is a certified professional nurseryman and plant/flower show judge. Groom is also a veteran of the U.S. Navy.

The author and his wife, Judy, live with their youngest child, Ashley, on their farm in northeast Texas. Dale enjoys receiving questions and comments via e-mail at dalegroom@tvec.net.